The Ultimate

Tower Air Fryer

Cookbook

500 Savory and Foolproof

Tower Air Fryer Recipes with 5 Ingredients

for Healthy Eating Every Day

Reece Ball

Notice Of Disclaimer.

Please note that the information in this document is intended for educational and entertainment purposes only. Every effort has been made to provide accurate, up-to-date, reliable and complete information. No warranty of any kind is declared or implied. The reader acknowledges that the author does not engage in the provision of legal, financial, medical or professional advice. The content in this book has been obtained from a variety of sources. Please consult a licensed professional before attempting any of the techniques described in this book. By reading this document, the reader agrees that in no event shall the author be liable for any direct or indirect damages, including but not limited to errors, omissions or inaccuracies, resulting from the use of the information in this document.

CONTENTS

Chapter 3. Appetizers And Snacks..28

Chapter 4. Beef,pork & Lamb Recipes..42

Chapter 5. Poultry Recipes......................................55

Chapter 6. Fish And Seafood Recipes..........................67

Chapter 7. Vegetable Side Dishes Recipes...80

Chapter 8. Vegetarians Recipes...92

Chapter 9. Desserts And Sweets..............................104

Introduction

Frying is a common cooking method; it is quick easy, and tasty. Many restaurants and fast-food chains use deep-frying as an economical and quick way to prepare foods. Honestly, everybody likes the taste of popular deep-fried foods such as fish sticks, French fries, chicken nuggets, doughnuts, and so on. Mmm, that is oh so delicious! Fatty foods taste so good! Unfortunately, deep-fried food is not good for your health. Deep fried foods tend to be high in calories and trans- fats, which can have negative effects on your weight and overall health.

However, you don't have to sacrifice flavor when trying to eat healthier and shed a few pounds. You should find another solution. An Air Fryer is a unique kitchen device designed to fry food in a healthy way. The Air Fryer cooks food with super-heated air that is circulated by high-powered fans, delivering that crispy, golden-brown exterior and a moist and tender interior. In other words, hot air is a new oil! With the Tower Air Fryer, you can cook ingredients with a tablespoon or two of healthy olive oil, and get a crispy, delicious food. Best of all – fried food does not taste like the fat. The Air Fryer cuts calories, not flavor! It makes cooking at home easy, quick, and most importantly – healthy!

This Tower Air Fryer cookbook is suitable for both beginner and experienced users of the Air Fryer and has a wide variety of recipes for any taste. The recipes included are also easy to follow with only 5 ingredients. This cookbook not only introduces what a Tower Air Fryer is but also the answers to some frequently asked questions.

Now get cooking up your very own amazing storm and knock the socks of your friends and family with this fantastic collection of recipes!

Chapter 1. Preparing for Your Tower Air Fryer Journey

What a Tower Air Fryer is

An Air Fryer is a kitchen appliance that utilizes super-heated air to cook food in a special chamber using the convection mechanism. Technically speaking, a mechanical fan blows heat around the space so the hot air circulates around your food at high speed, cooking evenly from all sides, producing crispy browning results. This is called the Maillard effect. According to Wikipedia "The Maillard reaction is a chemical reaction between amino acids and reducing sugars that gives browned food its distinctive flavor. Seared steaks, pan-fried dumplings, cookies and other kinds of biscuits, bread, toasted marshmallows, and many other foods undergo this reaction. It is named after French chemist Louis-Camille Maillard, who first described it in 1912 while attempting to reproduce biological protein synthesis."

This simple but intelligent machine radiates heat from heating elements and uses rapid air technology to fry roast, and bake your food with less oil. The Air Fryer can also warm your food. You don't have slave over a hot stove since the Air Fryer features an automatic temperature control. Thanks to its convection settings, it produces crispier and more flavorful food than conventional cooking methods.

If you are thinking of cutting down on fat consumption, here is a great solution. Studies have shown that air fried veggies contain up to 80% less fat in comparison to veggies that are deep fried. Just to give you an idea of the calorie content – deep-fried onion rings contain about 411 Calories vs air fried that contain about 176 Calories. Deep-fried Chicken Nuggets = 305 calories vs air fried = 180 Calories.

In order to understand how to use an Air Fryer, it would be good to find out more about the anatomy of this magical device. There is the inside i.e. electric-coil heating elements. A specially designed fan distributes the hot air evenly throughout the cooking basket. Then, the Air Fryer has a removable cooking basket with a mesh bottom that is coated with a non-stick material. It is placed in a frying basket drawer, cooking your food in the sealed environment. Air Fryers come with accessories, such as baking dishes, pans, trays, grill pans, skewer racks, and so forth; it will vary from model to model. However, make sure to use pans and racks that are designed to fit into the Air Fryer.

Advantages of the Tower Air Fryers

Still wondering if you made the right decision when you purchased an air fryer? Wonder no more.

1. **Air frying is better for your health.**

In fact, most recipes cook without any added fat. The recipes that do use oil use only a very small amount for flavor, usually just a few teaspoons. If there is too much oil on the food, it will melt off, and the appliance may emit smoke.

2. **It's very safe, even for beginning cooks.**

The system is completely closed, unlike deep-frying in a pan on the stovetop. There's no danger of a pan full of hot oil falling off the stove. Because the machine is closed while it's cooking, you won't burn your fingers or be splattered with hot liquid as the food cooks.

3. **Most air fryers have automatic cooking functions, so there's no guesswork.**

Depending on the model you choose, you can cook French fries, chicken fingers, tater tots, and other foods with just a press of a button. The machine controls the cooking times and cooking temperatures of these foods for you.

4. **Cleanup is a breeze.**

Air fryers are made with nonstick material, so, to clean, you simply wash the basket and pan in the sink with soap and water, using a sponge that won't scratch. If any food is burned onto the basket, a quick soak will loosen it. The appliance itself can be cleaned with a damp paper towel or sponge. You don't have to worry about safely disposing of cups of oil.

5. **Using only one appliance to prepare your food is extremely convenient.**

The cooking method is hands-free, so you can prepare a salad while your food cooks. If you have a small kitchen, this may be the only appliance you need.

Some Common Questions about the Tower Air Fryers

1. **Can you cook battered food in an air fryer oven?**

Crispy food needs enough oil to bind batters and coatings, but not too much or you'll end up with soggy results. If the food has a crumbly or floury outside texture, try spraying it with a little bit more oil.

If you're making air fried food from scratch, spray your homemade items with a light coating of oil (too much and the food won't get crispy) and arrange foods so the hot air circulates around each piece as much as possible.

2. **Can you use olive oil while air frying?**

Using cooking oils that can stand up to high temperatures is key while air frying, so avocado, grapeseed, and peanut oil are great for achieving crispy goodness. For best results, brush on lightly or spray an even coat of cooking spray made from these oils. Extra virgin olive oil is not an air fry-friendly oil due to its low smoke point, but extra light olive oil can be used for air frying because of its high smoke point. Other types of olive oil and some vegetable oils smoke at lower temperatures, meaning they will cause food to dry up quickly and prevent them from getting crispy.

3. Can you use aluminum foil in an air fryer oven?

Air fry works best on dark pans because they get and stay hot very quickly. Shiny foil reflects heat off the bakeware, which may change your results. When cooking with the Air fry Tray, we suggest putting a baking sheet on a rack a couple of positions below your tray. You can line that sheet with foil or parchment (or both) to catch any drips or crumbs, but you should never put aluminum foil, liners, or bakeware on the oven bottom. Items in this location can cause issues with air circulation and direct heat in any oven. Always keep the bottom of the oven clear so the air can circulate properly.

4. How do I keep my air frying oven clean?

Before using the air fry feature, place a cookie or baking sheet a rack or two under the Air Fry Tray to catch crumbs or drips. This will keep the bottom of the oven clean and free of fallen bits that can burn or cause odors later. Remember, do not place pans directly on the oven bottom to keep heat circulating correctly.

The Air Fry Tray is dishwasher safe, but for optimal cleaning, we recommend washing it by hand. It's designed to hold foods that already have some oil on them, which should keep food from sticking.

5. How do I limit the amount of smoke when using the Air Fry Tray?

Air fry uses really hot air to cook food fast and make it crunchy. Although air fry uses hot air to cook, remember that you are still frying your food so that it gets crispy! When some high-fat or greasy foods (like fresh wings) meet that hot air inside an oven, some smoke is normal. If air fry is making a lot of smoke, try these tips. When using the Air Fry Tray, put a baking sheet on a rack or two below the Air Fry Tray. This keeps drips and crumbs from landing on the oven bottom, where they can burn and create smoke. For additional protection, place some foil-lined parchment paper on the baking sheet. Parchment paper traps oil and keeps it from smoking. Use cooking oils that can stand up to high temperatures like avocado, grapeseed, and peanut oils. Cooking sprays made from these oils are available at the grocery store.

10 Useful Tower Air Fryer Tricks and Tips

Here is an easy-to-follow list to get you fully acquainted with your new purchase and creating some amazing meals in the shortest time.

1. Always make sure you place the fryer on a nice level surface with a good gap behind it when using it. This is because it has vents at the back to release steam so make sure it is pulled safely away from any wall power sockets. And definitely do not put it on top of your stove!

2. Don't put too much food in the basket as it needs air to circulate all surfaces in order to cook it evenly and get it nice and crispy. A single layer of food is best so cook in batches, if necessary.

3. Never spray the food with oil or sprinkle with seasoning once it is in the air fryer. Always do this before placing the food in the basket.

4. It is always best to preheat your air fryer to get optimum results. Just 2-3 minutes is fine and I recommend using the timer and then resetting it with the cooking time once you have put the food inside.

5. Please note that batter doesn't do well in an air fryer as the fan splatters it everywhere, creating smoke and making a mess that can be pretty tough to clean. Breaded foods are far safer and better but need to be prepared properly. So, make sure you coat the food first with flour, then egg and then the breadcrumbs, pressing them firmly with your hand into the surface of the food. Finally, spray the surface with oil to ensure the crumbs don't blow off and to give your food that wonderfully crispy fried coating.

6. Turn the food over halfway through cooking just like you would if regular frying or roasting to ensure even browning and crisping.

7. Check the food regularly when first using your air fryer to check if it's done. This is until you get used to it because you don't want to burn or dry out your food.

8. Make sure you place the basket on a heat proof mat or rack when you remove it as it will be extremely hot and damage your countertop.

9. Use oven mitts and tongs or other suitable utensils to remove any items to avoid seriously burning yourself.

10. After use, don't scrub the racks or basket with metal scourers as you will damage the coating. They can be left in soak in hot soapy water for about 30 mins and then will clean easily with a regular sponge or cloth.

So now it's time for you to dive right into our delectable and diverse super-size collection of 500 fabulous air-fryer recipes and get cooking without the guilt and minus the extra pounds!

Chapter 2. Bread And Breakfast

Chocolate-hazelnut Bear Claws

Servings:4
Cooking Time: 10 Minutes
Ingredients:
- 1 sheet frozen puff pastry dough, thawed
- 1 large egg, beaten
- ½ cup chocolate-hazelnut spread
- 1 tablespoon confectioners' sugar
- 1 tablespoon sliced almonds

Directions:
1. Preheat the air fryer to 320°F.
2. Unfold puff pastry and cut into four equal squares.
3. Brush egg evenly over puff pastry.
4. To make each bear claw, spread 2 tablespoons chocolate-hazelnut spread over a pastry square. Fold square horizontally to form a triangle and cut four evenly spaced slits about halfway through the top of folded square. Repeat with remaining spread and pastry squares.
5. Sprinkle confectioners' sugar and almonds over bear claws and place directly in the air fryer basket. Cook 10 minutes until puffy and golden brown. Serve warm.

Perfect Burgers

Servings: 3
Cooking Time: 13 Minutes
Ingredients:
- 1 pound 2 ounces 90% lean ground beef
- 1½ tablespoons Worcestershire sauce (gluten-free, if a concern)
- ½ teaspoon Ground black pepper
- 3 Hamburger buns (gluten-free if a concern), split open

Directions:
1. Preheat the air fryer to 375°F .
2. Gently mix the ground beef, Worcestershire sauce, and pepper in a bowl until well combined but preserving as much of the meat's fibers as possible. Divide this mixture into two 5-inch patties for the small batch, three 5-inch patties for the medium, or four 5-inch patties for the large. Make a thumbprint indentation in the center of each patty, about halfway through the meat.
3. Set the patties in the basket in one layer with some space between them. Air-fry undisturbed for 10 minutes, or until an instant-read meat thermometer inserted into the center of a burger registers 160°F. You may need to add 2 minutes cooking time if the air fryer is at 360°F.
4. Use a nonstick-safe spatula, and perhaps a flatware fork for balance, to transfer the burgers to a cutting board. Set the buns cut side down in the basket in one layer and air-fry undisturbed for 1 minute, to toast a bit and warm up. Serve the burgers in the warm buns.

Garlic Bread Knots

Servings: 8
Cooking Time: 5 Minutes
Ingredients:
- ¼ cup melted butter
- 2 teaspoons garlic powder
- 1 teaspoon dried parsley
- 1 tube of refrigerated French bread dough

Directions:
1. Mix the melted butter, garlic powder and dried parsley in a small bowl and set it aside.
2. To make smaller knots, cut the long tube of bread dough into 16 slices. If you want to make bigger knots, slice the dough into 8 slices. Shape each slice into a long rope about 6 inches long by rolling it on a flat surface with the palm of your hands. Tie each rope into a knot and place them on a plate.
3. Preheat the air fryer to 350°F.
4. Transfer half of the bread knots into the air fryer basket, leaving space in between each knot. Brush each knot with the butter mixture using a pastry brush.
5. Air-fry for 5 minutes. Remove the baked knots and brush a little more of the garlic butter mixture on each. Repeat with the remaining bread knots and serve warm.

Cheddar Soufflés

Servings:4
Cooking Time: 12 Minutes
Ingredients:
- 3 large eggs, whites and yolks separated
- ¼ teaspoon cream of tartar
- ½ cup shredded sharp Cheddar cheese
- 3 ounces cream cheese, softened

Directions:
1. In a large bowl, beat egg whites together with cream of tartar until soft peaks form, about 2 minutes.
2. In a separate medium bowl, beat egg yolks, Cheddar, and cream cheese together until frothy, about 1 minute. Add egg yolk mixture to whites, gently folding until combined.
3. Pour mixture evenly into four 4" ramekins greased with cooking spray. Place ramekins into air fryer basket. Adjust the temperature to 350°F and set the timer for 12 minutes. Eggs will be browned on the top and firm in the center when done. Serve warm.

Spinach Spread

Servings: 4
Cooking Time: 10 Minutes
Ingredients:
- 2 tablespoons coconut cream
- 3 cups spinach leaves

- 2 tablespoons cilantro
- 2 tablespoons bacon, cooked and crumbled
- Salt and black pepper to the taste

Directions:

1. In a pan that fits the air fryer, combine all the ingredients except the bacon, put the pan in the machine and cook at 360°F for 10 minutes. Transfer to a blender, pulse well, divide into bowls and serve with bacon sprinkled on top.

Country Gravy

Servings: 2
Cooking Time: 7 Minutes

Ingredients:

- ¼ pound pork sausage, casings removed
- 1 tablespoon butter
- 2 tablespoons flour
- 2 cups whole milk
- ½ teaspoon salt
- freshly ground black pepper
- 1 teaspoon fresh thyme leaves

Directions:

1. Preheat a saucepan over medium heat. Add and brown the sausage, crumbling it into small pieces as it cooks. Add the butter and flour, stirring well to combine. Continue to cook for 2 minutes, stirring constantly.

2. Slowly pour in the milk, whisking as you do, and bring the mixture to a boil to thicken. Season with salt and freshly ground black pepper, lower the heat and simmer until the sauce has thickened to your desired consistency – about 5 minutes. Stir in the fresh thyme, season to taste and serve hot.

Maple-bacon Doughnuts

Servings:8
Cooking Time: 5 Minutes

Ingredients:

- 1 can refrigerated biscuit dough, separated
- 1 cup confectioners' sugar
- ¼ cup heavy cream
- 1 teaspoon maple extract
- 6 slices bacon, cooked and crumbled

Directions:

1. Preheat the air fryer to 350°F.
2. Place biscuits in the air fryer basket and cook 5 minutes, turning halfway through cooking time, until golden brown. Let cool 5 minutes.
3. In a medium bowl, whisk together confectioners' sugar, cream, and maple extract until smooth.
4. Dip top of each doughnut into glaze and set aside to set for 5 minutes. Top with crumbled bacon and serve immediately.

Almond Oatmeal

Servings: 4
Cooking Time: 15 Minutes

Ingredients:

- 2 cups almond milk
- 1 cup coconut, shredded
- 2 teaspoons stevia
- 2 teaspoons vanilla extract

Directions:

1. In a pan that fits your air fryer, mix all the ingredients, stir well, introduce the pan in the machine and cook at 360°F for 15 minutes. Divide into bowls and serve for breakfast.

Roasted Golden Mini Potatoes

Servings:4
Cooking Time: 22 Minutes

Ingredients:

- 6 cups water
- 1 pound baby Dutch yellow potatoes, quartered
- 2 tablespoons olive oil
- ½ teaspoon garlic powder
- ¾ teaspoon seasoned salt
- ¼ teaspoon salt
- ½ teaspoon ground black pepper

Directions:

1. In a medium saucepan over medium-high heat bring water to a boil. Add potatoes and boil 10 minutes until fork-tender, then drain and gently pat dry.
2. Preheat the air fryer to 400°F.
3. Drizzle oil over potatoes, then sprinkle with garlic powder, seasoned salt, salt, and pepper.
4. Place potatoes in the air fryer basket and cook 12 minutes, shaking the basket three times during cooking. Potatoes will be done when golden brown and edges are crisp. Serve warm.

Chocolate Almond Crescent Rolls

Servings: 4
Cooking Time: 8 Minutes

Ingredients:

- 1 tube of crescent roll dough
- ⅔ cup semi-sweet or bittersweet chocolate chunks
- 1 egg white, lightly beaten
- ¼ cup sliced almonds
- powdered sugar, for dusting
- butter or oil

Directions:

1. Preheat the air fryer to 350°F.
2. Unwrap the crescent roll dough and separate it into triangles with the points facing away from you. Place a row of chocolate chunks along the bottom edge of the dough. Roll the dough up around the chocolate and then place another row of chunks on the dough. Roll again and finish

with one or two chocolate chunks. Be sure to leave the end free of chocolate so that it can adhere to the rest of the roll.

3. Brush the tops of the crescent rolls with the lightly beaten egg white and sprinkle the almonds on top, pressing them into the crescent dough so they adhere.

4. Brush the bottom of the air fryer basket with butter or oil and transfer the crescent rolls to the basket. Air-fry at 350°F for 8 minutes. Remove and let the crescent rolls cool before dusting with powdered sugar and serving.

Spinach Omelet

Servings:2
Cooking Time: 12 Minutes
Ingredients:
- 4 large eggs
- 1½ cups chopped fresh spinach leaves
- 2 tablespoons peeled and chopped yellow onion
- 2 tablespoons salted butter, melted
- ½ cup shredded mild Cheddar cheese
- ¼ teaspoon salt

Directions:
1. In an ungreased 6" round nonstick baking dish, whisk eggs. Stir in spinach, onion, butter, Cheddar, and salt.
2. Place dish into air fryer basket. Adjust the temperature to 320°F and set the timer for 12 minutes. Omelet will be done when browned on the top and firm in the middle.
3. Slice in half and serve warm on two medium plates.

Cinnamon Rolls

Servings:12
Cooking Time: 20 Minutes
Ingredients:
- 2½ cups shredded mozzarella cheese
- 2 ounces cream cheese, softened
- 1 cup blanched finely ground almond flour
- ½ teaspoon vanilla extract
- ½ cup confectioners' erythritol
- 1 tablespoon ground cinnamon

Directions:
1. In a large microwave-safe bowl, combine mozzarella cheese, cream cheese, and flour. Microwave the mixture on high 90 seconds until cheese is melted.
2. Add vanilla extract and erythritol, and mix 2 minutes until a dough forms.
3. Once the dough is cool enough to work with your hands, about 2 minutes, spread it out into a 12" × 4" rectangle on ungreased parchment paper. Evenly sprinkle dough with cinnamon.
4. Starting at the long side of the dough, roll lengthwise to form a log. Slice the log into twelve even pieces.
5. Divide rolls between two ungreased 6" round nonstick baking dishes. Place one dish into air fryer basket. Adjust the temperature to 375°F and set the timer for 10 minutes.

6. Cinnamon rolls will be done when golden around the edges and mostly firm. Repeat with second dish. Allow rolls to cool in dishes 10 minutes before serving.

Scrambled Eggs

Servings: 2
Cooking Time: 6 Minutes
Ingredients:
- 4 eggs
- 1/4 tsp garlic powder
- 1/4 tsp onion powder
- 1 tbsp parmesan cheese
- Pepper
- Salt

Directions:
1. Whisk eggs with garlic powder, onion powder, parmesan cheese, pepper, and salt.
2. Pour egg mixture into the air fryer baking dish.
3. Place dish in the air fryer and cook at 360°F for 2 minutes. Stir quickly and cook for 3-4 minutes more.
4. Stir well and serve.

Blueberry Scones

Servings:8
Cooking Time:15 Minutes
Ingredients:
- ½ cup cold salted butter, divided
- 2 cups all-purpose flour
- ½ cup granulated sugar
- 1 teaspoon baking powder
- 1 large egg
- ½ cup whole milk
- ½ cup fresh blueberries

Directions:
1. Chill 6 tablespoons butter in the freezer 10 minutes. In a small microwave-safe bowl, microwave remaining 2 tablespoons butter 30 seconds until melted.
2. Preheat the air fryer to 320°F. Cut parchment paper to fit the air fryer basket.
3. In a large bowl, mix flour, sugar, and baking powder.
4. Add egg and milk and stir until a sticky dough forms.
5. Remove butter from freezer and grate into bowl. Fold grated butter into dough until just combined.
6. Fold in blueberries. Turn dough onto a lightly floured surface. Sprinkle dough with flour and fold a couple of times, then gently form into a 6" round. Cut into eight triangles.
7. Place scones on parchment in the air fryer basket, leaving at least 2" of space between each, working in batches as necessary.
8. Brush each scone with melted butter and cook 15 minutes until scones are dark golden brown and crispy on the edges, and a toothpick inserted into the center comes out clean. Serve warm.

Buttery Scallops

Servings: 2
Cooking Time: 8 Minutes
Ingredients:
- 1 lb jumbo scallops
- 1 tbsp fresh lemon juice
- 2 tbsp butter, melted

Directions:
1. Preheat the air fryer to 400°F.
2. In a small bowl, mix together lemon juice and butter.
3. Brush scallops with lemon juice and butter mixture and place into the air fryer basket.
4. Cook scallops for 4 minutes. Turn halfway through.
5. Again brush scallops with lemon butter mixture and cook for 4 minutes more. Turn halfway through.
6. Serve and enjoy.

Mini Pita Breads

Servings: 8
Cooking Time: 6 Minutes
Ingredients:
- 2 teaspoons active dry yeast
- 1 tablespoon sugar
- 1¼ to 1½ cups warm water
- 3¼ cups all-purpose flour
- 2 teaspoons salt
- 1 tablespoon olive oil, plus more for brushing
- kosher salt (optional)

Directions:
1. Dissolve the yeast, sugar and water in the bowl of a stand mixer. Let the mixture sit for 5 minutes to make sure the yeast is active – it should foam a little. Combine the flour and salt in a bowl, and add it to the water, along with the olive oil. Mix with the dough hook until combined. Add a little more flour if needed to get the dough to pull away from the sides of the mixing bowl, or add a little more water if the dough seems too dry.
2. Knead the dough until it is smooth and elastic. Transfer the dough to a lightly oiled bowl, cover and let it rise in a warm place until doubled in bulk. Divide the dough into 8 portions and roll each portion into a circle about 4-inches in diameter. Don't roll the balls too thin, or you won't get the pocket inside the pita.
3. Preheat the air fryer to 400°F.
4. Brush both sides of the dough with olive oil, and sprinkle with kosher salt if desired. Air-fry one at a time at 400°F for 6 minutes, flipping it over when there are two minutes left in the cooking time.

Blueberry Muffins

Servings:12
Cooking Time:15 Minutes
Ingredients:
- 1 cup all-purpose flour
- ½ cup granulated sugar
- 1 teaspoon baking powder
- ¼ cup salted butter, melted
- 1 large egg
- ½ cup whole milk
- 1 cup fresh blueberries

Directions:
1. Preheat the air fryer to 300°F.
2. In a large bowl, whisk together flour, sugar, and baking powder.
3. Add butter, egg, and milk to dry mixture. Stir until well combined.
4. Gently fold in blueberries. Divide batter evenly among twelve silicone or aluminum muffin cups, filling cups about halfway full.
5. Place cups in the air fryer basket, working in batches as necessary. Cook 15 minutes until muffins are brown at the edges and a toothpick inserted in the center comes out clean. Serve warm.

Pancake For Two

Servings:2
Cooking Time: 30 Minutes
Ingredients:
- 1 cup blanched finely ground almond flour
- 2 tablespoons granular erythritol
- 1 tablespoon salted butter, melted
- 1 large egg
- ⅓ cup unsweetened almond milk
- ½ teaspoon vanilla extract

Directions:
1. In a large bowl, mix all ingredients together, then pour half the batter into an ungreased 6" round nonstick baking dish.
2. Place dish into air fryer basket. Adjust the temperature to 320°F and set the timer for 15 minutes. The pancake will be golden brown on top and firm, and a toothpick inserted in the center will come out clean when done. Repeat with remaining batter.
3. Slice in half in dish and serve warm.

Baked Eggs

Servings: 4
Cooking Time: 6 Minutes
Ingredients:
- 4 large eggs
- ⅛ teaspoon black pepper
- ⅛ teaspoon salt

Directions:
1. Preheat the air fryer to 330°F. Place 4 silicone muffin liners into the air fryer basket.
2. Crack 1 egg at a time into each silicone muffin liner. Sprinkle with black pepper and salt.

3. Bake for 6 minutes. Remove and let cool 2 minutes prior to serving.

Scones

Servings: 9
Cooking Time: 8 Minutes Per Batch
Ingredients:
- 2 cups self-rising flour, plus ¼ cup for kneading
- ⅓ cup granulated sugar
- ¼ cup butter, cold
- 1 cup milk

Directions:
1. Preheat air fryer at 360°F.
2. In large bowl, stir together flour and sugar.
3. Cut cold butter into tiny cubes, and stir into flour mixture with fork.
4. Stir in milk until soft dough forms.
5. Sprinkle ¼ cup of flour onto wax paper and place dough on top. Knead lightly by folding and turning the dough about 6 to 8 times.
6. Pat dough into a 6 x 6-inch square.
7. Cut into 9 equal squares.
8. Place all squares in air fryer basket or as many as will fit in a single layer, close together but not touching.
9. Cook at 360°F for 8minutes. When done, scones will be lightly browned on top and will spring back when pressed gently with a dull knife.
10. Repeat steps 8 and 9 to cook remaining scones.

Smoked Fried Tofu

Servings: 2
Cooking Time:22 Minutes
Ingredients:
- 1 tofu block; pressed and cubed
- 1 tbsp. smoked paprika
- 1/4 cup cornstarch
- Salt and black pepper to the taste
- Cooking spray

Directions:
1. Grease your air fryer's basket with cooking spray and heat the fryer at 370°F.
2. In a bowl; mix tofu with salt, pepper, smoked paprika and cornstarch and toss well.
3. Add tofu to you air fryer's basket and cook for 12 minutes shaking the fryer every 4 minutes. Divide into bowls and serve for breakfast.

Egg In A Hole

Servings: 4
Cooking Time: 10 Minutes
Ingredients:
- 4 slices white sandwich bread
- 4 large eggs
- ½ teaspoon salt
- ¼ teaspoon ground black pepper

Directions:
1. Preheat the air fryer to 350°F. Spray a 6" round cake pan with cooking spray.
2. Place as many pieces of bread as will fit in one layer in prepared pan, working in batches as necessary.
3. Using a small cup or cookie cutter, cut a circle out of the center of each bread slice. Crack an egg directly into each cutout and sprinkle eggs with salt and pepper.
4. Cook 5 minutes, then carefully turn and cook an additional 5 minutes or less, depending on your preference. Serve warm.

Greek-style Frittata

Servings:2
Cooking Time: 10 Minutes
Ingredients:
- 2 tbsp heavy cream
- 2 cups spinach, chopped
- 1 cup chopped mushrooms
- 3 oz feta cheese, crumbled
- A handful of fresh parsley, chopped
- Salt and black pepper

Directions:
1. Spray your air fryer basket with cooking spray. In a bowl, whisk eggs and until combined. Stir in spinach, mushrooms, feta, parsley, salt, and black pepper.
2. Pour into the basket and cook for 6 minutes at 350°F. Serve immediately with a touch of tomato relish.

Mini Bacon Egg Quiches

Servings:6
Cooking Time: 30 Minutes
Ingredients:
- 3 eggs
- 2 tbsp heavy cream
- ¼ tsp Dijon mustard
- Salt and pepper to taste
- 3 oz cooked bacon, crumbled
- ¼ cup grated cheddar

Directions:
1. Preheat air fryer to 350°F. Beat the eggs with salt and pepper in a bowl until fluffy. Stir in heavy cream, mustard, cooked bacon, and cheese. Divide the mixture between 6 greased muffin cups and place them in the frying basket. Bake for 8-10 minutes. Let cool slightly before serving.

Bacon Puff Pastry Pinwheels

Servings: 8
Cooking Time: 10 Minutes
Ingredients:
- 1 sheet of puff pastry
- 2 tablespoons maple syrup
- ¼ cup brown sugar
- 8 slices bacon (not thick cut)

- coarsely cracked black pepper
- vegetable oil

Directions:

1. On a lightly floured surface, roll the puff pastry out into a square that measures roughly 10 inches wide by however long your bacon strips are. Cut the pastry into eight even strips.

2. Brush the strips of pastry with the maple syrup and sprinkle the brown sugar on top, leaving 1 inch of dough exposed at the far end of each strip. Place a slice of bacon on each strip of puff pastry, letting 1/8-inch of the length of bacon hang over the edge of the pastry. Season generously with coarsely ground black pepper.

3. With the exposed end of the pastry strips away from you, roll the bacon and pastry strips up into pinwheels. Dab a little water on the exposed end of the pastry and pinch it to the pinwheel to seal the pastry shut.

4. Preheat the air fryer to 360°F.

5. Brush or spray the air fryer basket with a little vegetable oil. Place the pinwheels into the basket and air-fry at 360°F for 8 minutes. Turn the pinwheels over and air-fry for another 2 minutes to brown the bottom. Serve warm.

Garlic-cheese Biscuits

Servings: 8
Cooking Time: 8 Minutes
Ingredients:

- 1 cup self-rising flour
- 1 teaspoon garlic powder
- 2 tablespoons butter, diced
- 2 ounces sharp Cheddar cheese, grated
- ½ cup milk
- cooking spray

Directions:

1. Preheat air fryer to 330°F.

2. Combine flour and garlic in a medium bowl and stir together.

3. Using a pastry blender or knives, cut butter into dry ingredients.

4. Stir in cheese.

5. Add milk and stir until stiff dough forms.

6. If dough is too sticky to handle, stir in 1 or 2 more tablespoons of self-rising flour before shaping. Biscuits should be firm enough to hold their shape. Otherwise, they'll stick to the air fryer basket.

7. Divide dough into 8 portions and shape into 2-inch biscuits about ¾-inch thick.

8. Spray air fryer basket with nonstick cooking spray.

9. Place all 8 biscuits in basket and cook at 330°F for 8 minutes.

Crunchy Falafel Balls

Servings: 8
Cooking Time: 16 Minutes
Ingredients:

- 2½ cups Drained and rinsed canned chickpeas
- ¼ cup Olive oil
- 3 tablespoons All-purpose flour
- 1½ teaspoons Dried oregano
- 1½ teaspoons Dried sage leaves
- 1½ teaspoons Dried thyme
- ¾ teaspoon Table salt
- Olive oil spray

Directions:

1. Preheat the air fryer to 400°F.

2. Place the chickpeas, olive oil, flour, oregano, sage, thyme, and salt in a food processor. Cover and process into a paste, stopping the machine at least once to scrape down the inside of the canister.

3. Scrape down and remove the blade. Using clean, wet hands, form 2 tablespoons of the paste into a ball, then continue making 9 more balls for a small batch, 15 more for a medium one, and 19 more for a large batch. Generously coat the balls in olive oil spray.

4. Set the balls in the basket in one layer with a little space between them and air-fry undisturbed for 16 minutes, or until well browned and crisp.

5. Dump the contents of the basket onto a wire rack. Cool for 5 minutes before serving.

Oregano And Coconut Scramble

Servings: 4
Cooking Time: 20 Minutes
Ingredients:

- 8 eggs, whisked
- 2 tablespoons oregano, chopped
- Salt and black pepper to the taste
- 2 tablespoons parmesan, grated
- ¼ cup coconut cream

Directions:

1. In a bowl, mix the eggs with all the ingredients and whisk. Pour this into a pan that fits your air fryer, introduce it in the preheated fryer and cook at 350°F for 20 minutes, stirring often. Divide the scramble between plates and serve for breakfast.

Strawberry Bread

Servings: 6
Cooking Time: 28 Minutes
Ingredients:

- ½ cup frozen strawberries in juice, completely thawed (do not drain)
- 1 cup flour
- ½ cup sugar
- 1 teaspoon cinnamon
- ½ teaspoon baking soda
- ⅛ teaspoon salt
- 1 egg, beaten
- ⅓ cup oil

- cooking spray

Directions:

1. Cut any large berries into smaller pieces no larger than ½ inch.
2. Preheat air fryer to 330°F.
3. In a large bowl, stir together the flour, sugar, cinnamon, soda, and salt.
4. In a small bowl, mix together the egg, oil, and strawberries. Add to dry ingredients and stir together gently.
5. Spray 6 x 6-inch baking pan with cooking spray.
6. Pour batter into prepared pan and cook at 330°F for 28 minutes.
7. When bread is done, let cool for 10minutes before removing from pan.

Whole-grain Cornbread

Servings: 6
Cooking Time: 25 Minutes

Ingredients:

- 1 cup stoneground cornmeal
- ½ cup brown rice flour
- 1 teaspoon sugar
- 2 teaspoons baking powder
- ¼ teaspoon salt
- 1 cup milk
- 2 tablespoons oil
- 2 eggs
- cooking spray

Directions:

1. Preheat the air fryer to 360°F.
2. In a medium mixing bowl, mix cornmeal, brown rice flour, sugar, baking powder, and salt together.
3. Add the remaining ingredients and beat with a spoon until batter is smooth.
4. Spray air fryer baking pan with nonstick cooking spray and add the cornbread batter.
5. Bake at 360°F for 25 minutes, until center is done.

Medium Rare Simple Salt And Pepper Steak

Servings:3
Cooking Time: 30 Minutes

Ingredients:

- 1 ½ pounds skirt steak
- Salt and pepper to taste

Directions:

1. Preheat the air fryer at 390°F.
2. Place the grill pan accessory in the air fryer.
3. Season the skirt steak with salt and pepper.
4. Place on the grill pan and cook for 15 minutes per batch.
5. Flip the meat halfway through the cooking time.

Avocado Tempura

Servings: 4

Cooking Time: 20 Minutes

Ingredients:

- ½ cup breadcrumbs
- ½ tsp. salt
- 1 Haas avocado, pitted, peeled and sliced
- Liquid from 1 can white beans or aquafaba

Directions:

1. Set your Air Fryer to 350°F and allow to warm.
2. Mix the breadcrumbs and salt in a shallow bowl until well-incorporated.
3. Dip the avocado slices in the bean/aquafaba juice, then into the breadcrumbs. Put the avocados in the fryer, taking care not to overlap any slices, and fry for 10 minutes, giving the basket a good shake at the halfway point.

Green Scramble

Servings: 4
Cooking Time: 20 Minutes

Ingredients:

- 1 tablespoon olive oil
- ½ teaspoon smoked paprika
- 12 eggs, whisked
- 3 cups baby spinach
- Salt and black pepper to the taste

Directions:

1. In a bowl, mix all the ingredients except the oil and whisk them well. Heat up your air fryer at 360°F, add the oil, heat it up, add the eggs and spinach mix, cover, cook for 20 minutes, divide between plates and serve.

Chocolate Chip Muffins

Servings:6
Cooking Time: 15 Minutes

Ingredients:

- 1½ cups blanched finely ground almond flour
- ⅓ cup granular brown erythritol
- 4 tablespoons salted butter, melted
- 2 large eggs, whisked
- 1 tablespoon baking powder
- ½ cup low-carb chocolate chips

Directions:

1. In a large bowl, combine all ingredients. Evenly pour batter into six silicone muffin cups greased with cooking spray.
2. Place muffin cups into air fryer basket. Adjust the temperature to 320°F and set the timer for 15 minutes. Muffins will be golden brown when done.
3. Let muffins cool in cups 15 minutes to avoid crumbling. Serve warm.

Hash Browns

Servings:2
Cooking Time: 30 Minutes
Ingredients:
- 2 large russet potatoes, peeled
- 2 cups cold water
- 1 tablespoon olive oil
- ½ teaspoon salt

Directions:
1. Grate potatoes into a bowl filled with cold water. Let soak 10 minutes. Drain into a colander, then press into paper towels to remove excess moisture.
2. Dry the bowl and return potatoes to it. Toss with oil and salt.
3. Preheat the air fryer to 375°F. Spray a 6" round cake pan with cooking spray.
4. Pour potatoes into prepared pan, pressing them down.
5. Cook 20 minutes until brown and crispy. Serve warm.

Cinnamon Granola

Servings:4
Cooking Time: 7 Minutes
Ingredients:
- 2 cups shelled pecans, chopped
- 1 cup unsweetened coconut flakes
- 1 cup slivered almonds
- 2 tablespoons granular erythritol
- 1 teaspoon ground cinnamon

Directions:
1. In a large bowl, mix all ingredients. Place mixture into an ungreased 6" round nonstick baking dish.
2. Place dish into air fryer basket. Adjust the temperature to 320°F and set the timer for 7 minutes, stirring halfway through cooking.
3. Let cool in dish 10 minutes before serving. Store in airtight container at room temperature up to 5 days.

Green Onion Pancakes

Servings: 4
Cooking Time: 8 Minutes
Ingredients:
- 2 cup all-purpose flour
- ½ teaspoon salt
- ¾ cup hot water
- 1 tablespoon vegetable oil
- 1 tablespoon butter, melted
- 2 cups finely chopped green onions
- 1 tablespoon black sesame seeds, for garnish

Directions:
1. In a large bowl, whisk together the flour and salt. Make a well in the center and pour in the hot water. Quickly stir the flour mixture together until a dough forms. Knead the dough for 5 minutes; then cover with a warm, wet towel and set aside for 30 minutes to rest.

2. In a small bowl, mix together the vegetable oil and melted butter.
3. On a floured surface, place the dough and cut it into 8 pieces. Working with 1 piece of dough at a time, use a rolling pin to roll out the dough until it's ¼ inch thick; then brush the surface with the oil and butter mixture and sprinkle with green onions. Next, fold the dough in half and then in half again. Roll out the dough again until it's ¼ inch thick and brush with the oil and butter mixture and green onions. Fold the dough in half and then in half again and roll out one last time until it's ¼ inch thick. Repeat this technique with all 8 pieces.
4. Meanwhile, preheat the air fryer to 400°F.
5. Place 1 or 2 pancakes into the air fryer basket, and cook for 2 minutes or until crispy and golden brown. Repeat until all the pancakes are cooked. Top with black sesame seeds for garnish, if desired.

Seasoned Herbed Sourdough Croutons

Servings: 4
Cooking Time: 7 Minutes
Ingredients:
- 4 cups cubed sourdough bread, 1-inch cubes
- 1 tablespoon olive oil
- 1 teaspoon fresh thyme leaves
- ¼ – ½ teaspoon salt
- freshly ground black pepper

Directions:
1. Combine all ingredients in a bowl and taste to make sure it is seasoned to your liking.
2. Preheat the air fryer to 400°F.
3. Toss the bread cubes into the air fryer and air-fry for 7 minutes, shaking the basket once or twice while they cook.
4. Serve warm or store in an airtight container.

Parmesan Garlic Naan

Servings: 6
Cooking Time: 4 Minutes
Ingredients:
- 1 cup bread flour
- 1 teaspoon baking powder
- ⅛ teaspoon salt
- 1 teaspoon garlic powder
- 2 tablespoon shredded parmesan cheese
- 1 cup plain 2% fat Greek yogurt
- 1 tablespoon extra-virgin olive oil

Directions:
1. Preheat the air fryer to 400°F.
2. In a medium bowl, mix the flour, baking powder, salt, garlic powder, and cheese. Mix the yogurt into the flour, using your hands to combine if necessary.

3. On a flat surface covered with flour, divide the dough into 6 equal balls and roll each out into a 4-inch-diameter circle.

4. Lightly brush both sides of each naan with olive oil and place one naan at a time into the basket. Cook for 3 to 4 minutes. Remove and repeat for the remaining breads.

5. Serve warm.

Strawberry Pastry

Servings:8
Cooking Time: 15 Minutes Per Batch
Ingredients:
- 1 package refrigerated piecrust
- 1 cup strawberry jam
- 1 large egg, whisked
- ½ cup confectioners' sugar
- 2 tablespoons whole milk
- ½ teaspoon vanilla extract

Directions:

1. Preheat the air fryer to 320°F. Cut parchment paper to fit the air fryer basket.

2. On a lightly floured surface, lay piecrusts out flat. Cut each piecrust round into six 4" × 3" rectangles, reserving excess dough.

3. Form remaining dough into a ball, then roll out and cut four additional 4" × 3" rectangles, bringing the total to sixteen.

4. For each pastry, spread 2 tablespoons jam on a pastry rectangle, leaving a 1" border around the edges. Top with a second pastry rectangle and use a fork to gently press all four edges together. Repeat with remaining jam and pastry.

5. Brush tops of each pastry with egg and cut an X in the center of each to prevent excess steam from building up.

6. Place pastries on parchment in the air fryer basket, working in batches as necessary. Cook 12 minutes, then carefully flip and cook an additional 3 minutes until each side is golden brown. Let cool 10 minutes.

7. In a small bowl, whisk confectioners' sugar, milk, and vanilla. Brush each pastry with glaze, then place in the refrigerator 5 minutes to set before serving.

Tuscan Toast

Servings: 4
Cooking Time: 5 Minutes
Ingredients:
- ¼ cup butter
- ½ teaspoon lemon juice
- ½ clove garlic
- ½ teaspoon dried parsley flakes
- 4 slices Italian bread, 1-inch thick

Directions:

1. Place butter, lemon juice, garlic, and parsley in a food processor. Process about 1 minute, or until garlic is pulverized and ingredients are well blended.

2. Spread garlic butter on both sides of bread slices.

3. Place bread slices upright in air fryer basket.

4. Cook at 390°F for 5minutes or until toasty brown.

All-in-one Breakfast Toast

Servings: 1
Cooking Time: 10 Minutes
Ingredients:
- 1 strip of bacon, diced
- 1 slice of 1-inch thick bread (such as Texas Toast or hand-sliced bread)
- 1 tablespoon softened butter (optional)
- 1 egg
- salt and freshly ground black pepper
- ¼ cup grated Colby or Jack cheese

Directions:

1. Preheat the air fryer to 400°F.

2. Air-fry the bacon for 3 minutes, shaking the basket once or twice while it cooks. Remove the bacon to a paper towel lined plate and set aside.

3. Use a sharp paring knife to score a large circle in the middle of the slice of bread, cutting halfway through, but not all the way through to the cutting board. Press down on the circle in the center of the bread slice to create an indentation. If using, spread the softened butter on the edges and in the hole of the bread.

4. Transfer the slice of bread, hole side up, to the air fryer basket. Crack the egg into the center of the bread, and season with salt and pepper.

5. Air-fry at 380°F for 5 minutes. Sprinkle the grated cheese around the edges of the bread leaving the center of the yolk uncovered, and top with the cooked bacon. Press the cheese and bacon into the bread lightly to help anchor it to the bread and prevent it from blowing around in the air fryer.

6. Air-fry for one or two more minutes, just to melt the cheese and finish cooking the egg. Serve immediately.

Breakfast Bake

Servings:4
Cooking Time: 15 Minutes
Ingredients:
- 6 large eggs
- 2 tablespoons heavy cream
- ½ teaspoon salt
- ¼ teaspoon ground black pepper
- ⅓ pound ground pork breakfast sausage, cooked and drained
- ½ cup shredded Cheddar cheese

Directions:

1. Preheat the air fryer to 320°F. Spray a 6" round cake pan with cooking spray.

2. In a large bowl, whisk eggs, cream, salt, and pepper until fully combined.

3. Arrange cooked sausage in the bottom of prepared pan. Pour egg mixture into pan on top of sausage. Sprinkle Cheddar on top.

4. Place in the air fryer basket and cook 15 minutes until the top begins to brown and the center is set. Let cool 5 minutes before serving. Serve warm.

Bagels

Servings:4
Cooking Time: 10 Minutes
Ingredients:
- 1 cup self-rising flour
- 1 cup plain full-fat Greek yogurt
- 2 tablespoons granulated sugar
- 1 large egg, whisked

Directions:
1. Preheat the air fryer to 320°F.
2. In a large bowl, mix flour, yogurt, and sugar together until a ball of dough forms.
3. Turn dough out onto a lightly floured surface. Knead dough for 3 minutes, then form into a smooth ball. Cut dough into four sections. Roll each piece into an 8" rope, then shape into a circular bagel shape. Brush top and bottom of each bagel with egg.
4. Place in the air fryer basket and cook 10 minutes, turning halfway through cooking time to ensure even browning. Let cool 5 minutes before serving.

Banana-nut Muffins

Servings:12
Cooking Time: 15 Minutes
Ingredients:
- 1 ½ cups all-purpose flour
- ½ cup granulated sugar
- 1 teaspoon baking powder
- ½ cup salted butter, melted
- 1 large egg
- 2 medium bananas, peeled and mashed
- ½ cup chopped pecans

Directions:
1. Preheat the air fryer to 300°F.
2. In a large bowl, whisk together flour, sugar, and baking powder.
3. Add butter, egg, and bananas to dry mixture. Stir until well combined. Batter will be thick.
4. Gently fold in pecans. Divide batter evenly among twelve silicone or aluminum muffin cups, filling cups about halfway full.
5. Place cups in the air fryer basket, working in batches as necessary. Cook 15 minutes until muffin edges are brown and a toothpick inserted into the center comes out clean. Let cool 5 minutes before serving.

Breakfast Chimichangas

Servings: 4

Cooking Time: 8 Minutes
Ingredients:
- Four 8-inch flour tortillas
- ½ cup canned refried beans
- 1 cup scrambled eggs
- ½ cup grated cheddar or Monterey jack cheese
- 1 tablespoon vegetable oil
- 1 cup salsa

Directions:
1. Lay the flour tortillas out flat on a cutting board. In the center of each tortilla, spread 2 tablespoons refried beans. Next, add ¼ cup eggs and 2 tablespoons cheese to each tortilla.
2. To fold the tortillas, begin on the left side and fold to the center. Then fold the right side into the center. Next fold the bottom and top down and roll over to completely seal the chimichanga. Using a pastry brush or oil mister, brush the tops of the tortilla packages with oil.
3. Preheat the air fryer to 400°F for 4 minutes. Place the chimichangas into the air fryer basket, seam side down, and air fry for 4 minutes. Using tongs, turn over the chimichangas and cook for an additional 2 to 3 minutes or until light golden brown.

Banana Baked Oatmeal

Servings:2
Cooking Time:10 Minutes
Ingredients:
- 1 cup quick-cooking oats
- 1 cup whole milk
- 2 tablespoons unsalted butter, melted
- 1 medium banana, peeled and mashed
- 2 tablespoons brown sugar
- ½ teaspoon vanilla extract
- ½ teaspoon salt

Directions:
1. Preheat the air fryer to 360°F.
2. In a 6" round pan, add oats. Pour in milk and butter.
3. In a medium bowl, mix banana, brown sugar, vanilla, and salt until combined. Add to pan and mix until well combined.
4. Place in the air fryer and cook 10 minutes until the top is brown and oats feel firm to the touch. Serve warm.

Coconut Pudding

Servings: 4
Cooking Time: 20 Minutes
Ingredients:
- 1 cup cauliflower rice
- ½ cup coconut, shredded
- 3 cups coconut milk
- 2 tablespoons stevia

Directions:

1. In a pan that fits the air fryer, combine all the ingredients and whisk well. Introduce the in your air fryer and cook at 360°F for 20 minutes. Divide into bowls and serve for breakfast.

Sausage Solo

Servings:4
Cooking Time:22 Minutes
Ingredients:
- 6 eggs
- 4 cooked sausages, sliced
- 2 bread slices, cut into sticks
- ½ cup mozzarella cheese, grated
- ½ cup cream

Directions:
1. Preheat the Air fryer to 355°F and grease 4 ramekins lightly.
2. Whisk together eggs and cream in a bowl and beat well.
3. Transfer the egg mixture into ramekins and arrange the bread sticks and sausage slices around the edges.
4. Top with mozzarella cheese evenly and place the ramekins in Air fryer basket.
5. Cook for about 22 minutes and dish out to serve warm.

Bacon Cups

Servings: 2
Cooking Time: 40 Minutes
Ingredients:
- 2 eggs
- 1 slice tomato
- 3 slices bacon
- 2 slices ham
- 2 tsp grated parmesan cheese

Directions:
1. Preheat your fryer to 375°F
2. Cook the bacon for half of the directed time.
3. Slice the bacon strips in half and line 2 greased muffin tins with 3 half-strips of bacon
4. Put one slice of ham and half slice of tomato in each muffin tin on top of the bacon
5. Crack one egg on top of the tomato in each muffin tin and sprinkle each with half a teaspoon of grated parmesan cheese.
6. Bake for 20 minutes.
7. Remove and let cool.
8. Serve!

Parsley Omelet

Servings: 4
Cooking Time: 15 Minutes
Ingredients:
- 4 eggs, whisked
- 1 tablespoon parsley, chopped
- ½ teaspoons cheddar cheese, shredded
- 1 avocado, peeled, pitted and cubed

- Cooking spray

Directions:
1. In a bowl, mix all the ingredients except the cooking spray and whisk well. Grease a baking pan that fits the Air Fryer with the cooking spray, pour the omelet mix, spread, introduce the pan in the machine and cook at 370°F for 15 minutes. Serve for breakfast.

Pigs In A Blanket

Servings: 10
Cooking Time: 8 Minutes
Ingredients:
- 1 cup all-purpose flour, plus more for rolling
- 1 teaspoon baking powder
- ¼ cup salted butter, cut into small pieces
- ½ cup buttermilk
- 10 fully cooked breakfast sausage links

Directions:
1. In a large mixing bowl, whisk together the flour and baking powder. Using your fingers or a pastry blender, cut in the butter until you have small pea-size crumbles.
2. Using a rubber spatula, make a well in the center of the flour mixture. Pour the buttermilk into the well, and fold the mixture together until you form a dough ball.
3. Place the sticky dough onto a floured surface and, using a floured rolling pin, roll out until ½-inch thick. Using a round biscuit cutter, cut out 10 rounds, reshaping the dough and rolling out, as needed.
4. Place 1 fully cooked breakfast sausage link on the left edge of each biscuit and roll up, leaving the ends slightly exposed.
5. Using a pastry brush, brush the biscuits with the whisked eggs, and spray them with cooking spray.
6. Place the pigs in a blanket into the air fryer basket with at least 1 inch between each biscuit. Set the air fryer to 340°F and cook for 8 minutes.

Sweet And Spicy Breakfast Sausage

Servings:6
Cooking Time: 10 Minutes
Ingredients:
- 1 pound 84% lean ground pork
- 2 tablespoons brown sugar
- 1 teaspoon salt
- ½ teaspoon ground black pepper
- ½ teaspoon garlic powder
- ½ teaspoon dried fennel
- ½ teaspoon crushed red pepper flakes

Directions:
1. Preheat the air fryer to 400°F.
2. In a large bowl, mix all ingredients until well combined. Divide mixture into eight portions and form into patties.
3. Spritz patties with cooking spray and place in the air fryer basket. Cook 10 minutes until patties are brown and internal temperature reaches at least 145°F. Serve warm.

Cream Cheese Danish

Servings:4
Cooking Time: 10 Minutes
Ingredients:
- 1 sheet frozen puff pastry dough, thawed
- 1 large egg, beaten
- 4 ounces full-fat cream cheese, softened
- ¼ cup confectioners' sugar
- 1 teaspoon vanilla extract
- ½ teaspoon lemon juice

Directions:
1. Preheat the air fryer to 320°F.
2. Unfold puff pastry and cut into four equal squares. For each pastry, fold all four corners partway to the center, leaving a 1" square in the center.
3. Brush egg evenly over folded puff pastry.
4. In a medium bowl, mix cream cheese, confectioners' sugar, vanilla, and lemon juice. Scoop 2 tablespoons of mixture into the center of each pastry square.
5. Place danishes directly in the air fryer basket and cook 10 minutes until puffy and golden brown. Cool 5 minutes before serving.

Scotch Eggs

Servings:6
Cooking Time: 15 Minutes
Ingredients:
- 1 pound ground pork breakfast sausage
- 6 large hard-boiled eggs, peeled
- 1 cup all-purpose flour
- 2 large eggs, beaten
- 2 cups plain bread crumbs

Directions:
1. Preheat the air fryer to 375°F.
2. Separate sausage into six equal amounts and flatten into patties.
3. Form sausage patties around hard-boiled eggs, completely enclosing them.
4. In three separate small bowls, place flour, eggs, and bread crumbs.
5. Roll each sausage-covered egg first in flour, then egg, and finally bread crumbs. Place rolled eggs in the air fryer basket and spritz them with cooking spray.
6. Cook 15 minutes, turning halfway through cooking time and spraying any dry spots with additional cooking spray. Serve warm.

Eggplant Parmesan Subs

Servings: 2
Cooking Time: 13 Minutes
Ingredients:
- 4 Peeled eggplant slices
- Olive oil spray
- 2 tablespoons plus 2 teaspoons Jarred pizza sauce, any variety except creamy
- ¼ cup (about ⅔ ounce) Finely grated Parmesan cheese
- 2 Small, long soft rolls, such as hero, hoagie, or Italian sub rolls (gluten-free, if a concern), split open lengthwise

Directions:
1. Preheat the air fryer to 350°F .
2. When the machine is at temperature, coat both sides of the eggplant slices with olive oil spray. Set them in the basket in one layer and air-fry undisturbed for 10 minutes, until lightly browned and softened.
3. Increase the machine's temperature to 375°F. Top each eggplant slice with 2 teaspoons pizza sauce, then 1 tablespoon cheese. Air-fry undisturbed for 2 minutes, or until the cheese has melted.
4. Use a nonstick-safe spatula, and perhaps a flatware fork for balance, to transfer the eggplant slices cheese side up to a cutting board. Set the roll(s) cut side down in the basket in one layer and air-fry undisturbed for 1 minute, to toast the rolls a bit and warm them up. Set 2 eggplant slices in each warm roll.

Easy Egg Bites

Servings:2
Cooking Time: 9 Minutes
Ingredients:
- 2 large eggs
- ¼ cup full-fat cottage cheese
- ¼ cup shredded sharp Cheddar cheese
- ¼ teaspoon salt
- ⅛ teaspoon ground black pepper
- 6 tablespoons diced cooked ham

Directions:
1. Preheat the air fryer to 300°F. Spray six silicone muffin cups with cooking spray.
2. In a blender, place eggs, cottage cheese, Cheddar, salt, and pepper. Pulse five times until smooth and frothy.
3. Place 1 tablespoon ham in the bottom of each prepared baking cup, then divide egg mixture among cups.
4. Place in the air fryer basket and cook 9 minutes until egg bites are firm in the center. Carefully remove cups from air fryer basket and cool 3 minutes before serving. Serve warm.

Parsley Egg Scramble With Cottage Cheese

Servings:2
Cooking Time: 15 Minutes
Ingredients:
- 1 tbsp cottage cheese, crumbled
- 4 eggs
- Salt and pepper to taste
- 2 tsp heavy cream
- 1 tbsp chopped parsley

Directions:

1. Preheat air fryer to 400ºF. Grease a baking pan with olive oil. Beat the eggs, salt, and pepper in a bowl. Pour it into the pan, place the pan in the frying basket, and Air Fry for 5 minutes. Using a silicone spatula, stir in heavy cream, cottage cheese, and half of parsley and Air Fry for another 2 minutes. Scatter with parsley to serve.

Pizza Eggs

Servings:2
Cooking Time: 10 Minutes
Ingredients:

- 1 cup shredded mozzarella cheese
- 7 slices pepperoni, chopped
- 1 large egg, whisked
- ¼ teaspoon dried oregano
- ¼ teaspoon dried parsley
- ¼ teaspoon garlic powder
- ¼ teaspoon salt

Directions:

1. Place mozzarella in a single layer on the bottom of an ungreased 6" round nonstick baking dish. Scatter pepperoni over cheese, then pour egg evenly around baking dish.
2. Sprinkle with remaining ingredients and place into air fryer basket. Adjust the temperature to 330°F and set the timer for 10 minutes. When cheese is brown and egg is set, dish will be done.
3. Let cool in dish 5 minutes before serving.

Flaky Cinnamon Rolls

Servings:8
Cooking Time: 12 Minutes Per Batch
Ingredients:

- 1 sheet frozen puff pastry, thawed
- 6 tablespoons unsalted butter, melted
- ¾ cup granulated sugar
- 2 tablespoons ground cinnamon
- ½ cup confectioners' sugar
- 2 tablespoons heavy cream

Directions:

1. Preheat the air fryer to 320°F. Cut parchment paper to fit the air fryer basket.
2. Unroll puff pastry into a large rectangle. Brush with butter, then evenly sprinkle sugar and cinnamon around dough, coating as evenly as possible.
3. Starting at one of the long sides, roll dough into a log, then use a little water on your fingers to seal the edge.
4. Slice dough into eight rounds. Place on parchment in the air fryer basket, working in batches as necessary, and cook 12 minutes until golden brown and flaky. Let cool 5 minutes.
5. In a small bowl, whisk confectioners' sugar and cream together until smooth. Drizzle over cinnamon rolls and serve.

Denver Eggs

Servings:2

Cooking Time: 15 Minutes
Ingredients:

- 3 large eggs
- 1 tablespoon salted butter, melted
- ¼ cup seeded and chopped green bell pepper
- 2 tablespoons peeled and chopped yellow onion
- ¼ cup chopped cooked no-sugar-added ham
- ¼ teaspoon salt
- ¼ teaspoon ground black pepper

Directions:

1. Crack eggs into an ungreased 6" round nonstick baking dish. Mix in butter, bell pepper, onion, ham, salt, and black pepper.
2. Place dish into air fryer basket. Adjust the temperature to 320°F and set the timer for 15 minutes. The eggs will be fully cooked and firm in the middle when done.
3. Slice in half and serve warm on two medium plates.

Sweet Potato-cinnamon Toast

Servings: 6
Cooking Time: 8 Minutes
Ingredients:

- 1 small sweet potato, cut into ⅜-inch slices
- oil for misting
- ground cinnamon

Directions:

1. Preheat air fryer to 390°F.
2. Spray both sides of sweet potato slices with oil. Sprinkle both sides with cinnamon to taste.
3. Place potato slices in air fryer basket in a single layer.
4. Cook for 4minutes, turn, and cook for 4 more minutes or until potato slices are barely fork tender.

Egg Muffins

Servings: 4
Cooking Time: 11 Minutes
Ingredients:

- 4 eggs
- salt and pepper
- olive oil
- 4 English muffins, split
- 1 cup shredded Colby Jack cheese
- 4 slices ham or Canadian bacon

Directions:

1. Preheat air fryer to 390°F.
2. Beat together eggs and add salt and pepper to taste. Spray air fryer baking pan lightly with oil and add eggs. Cook for 2minutes, stir, and continue cooking for 4minutes, stirring every minute, until eggs are scrambled to your preference. Remove pan from air fryer.
3. Place bottom halves of English muffins in air fryer basket. Take half of the shredded cheese and divide it among the muffins. Top each with a slice of ham and one-quarter of the eggs. Sprinkle remaining cheese on top of the eggs. Use

a fork to press the cheese into the egg a little so it doesn't slip off before it melts.

4. Cook at 360°F for 1 minute. Add English muffin tops and cook for 4minutes to heat through and toast the muffins.

Cheesy Mustard Toasts

Servings:4

Cooking Time: 15 Minutes

Ingredients:
- 4 bread slices
- 2 tablespoons cheddar cheese, shredded
- 2 eggs, whites and yolks, separated
- 1 tablespoon mustard
- 1 tablespoon paprika

Directions:
1. Set the temperature of Air Fryer to 355°F.
2. Place the bread slices in an Air fryer basket.
3. Air Fry for about 5 minutes or until toasted.
4. Add the egg whites in a clean glass bowl and beat until they form soft peaks.
5. In another bowl, mix together the cheese, egg yolks, mustard, and paprika.
6. Gently, fold in the egg whites.
7. Spread the mustard mixture over the toasted bread slices.
8. Air Fry for about 10 minutes.
9. Serve warm!

Thai Turkey Sausage Patties

Servings:4

Cooking Time: 30 Minutes

Ingredients:
- 12 oz turkey sausage
- 1 tsp onion powder
- 1 tsp dried coriander
- ¼ tsp Thai curry paste
- ¼ tsp red pepper flakes
- Salt and pepper to taste

Directions:
1. Preheat air fryer to 350°F. Place the sausage, onion, coriander, curry paste, red flakes, salt, and black pepper in a large bowl and mix well. Form into eight patties. Arrange the patties on the greased frying basket and Air Fry for 10 minutes, flipping once halfway through. Once the patties are cooked, transfer to a plate and serve hot.

Zucchini And Spring Onions Cakes

Servings: 4

Cooking Time: 8 Minutes

Ingredients:
- 8 ounces zucchinis, chopped
- 2 spring onions, chopped
- 2 eggs, whisked
- Salt and black pepper to the taste
- ¼ teaspoon sweet paprika, chopped
- Cooking spray

Directions:
1. In a bowl, mix all the ingredients except the cooking spray, stir well and shape medium fritters out of this mix. Put the basket in the Air Fryer, add the fritters inside, grease them with cooking spray and cook at 400°F for 8 minutes. Divide the fritters between plates and serve for breakfast.

Chapter 3. Appetizers And Snacks

Sausage And Cheese Rolls

Servings: 3

Cooking Time: 18 Minutes

Ingredients:
- 3 3- to 3½-ounce sweet or hot Italian sausage links
- 2 1-ounce string cheese stick(s), unwrapped and cut in half lengthwise
- Three quarters from one thawed sheet A 17.25-ounce box frozen puff pastry

Directions:
1. Preheat the air fryer to 400°F.
2. When the machine is at temperature, set the sausage links in the basket and air-fry undisturbed for 12 minutes, or until cooked through.
3. Use kitchen tongs to transfer the links to a wire rack. Cool for 15 minutes.
4. Cut the sausage links in half lengthwise. Sandwich half a string cheese stick between two sausage halves, trimming the ends so the cheese doesn't stick out beyond the meat.
5. Roll each piece of puff pastry into a 6 x 6-inch square on a clean, dry work surface. Set the sausage-cheese sandwich at one edge and roll it up in the dough. The ends will be open like a pig-in-a-blanket. Repeat with the remaining puff pastry, sausage, and cheese.
6. Set the rolls seam side down in the basket. Air-fry undisturbed for 6 minutes, or until puffed and golden brown.
7. Use a nonstick-safe spatula, and perhaps a flatware fork for balance, to transfer the rolls to a wire rack. Cool for at least 5 minutes before serving.

Pita Chips

Servings: 4
Cooking Time: 10 Minutes
Ingredients:

- 2 rounds Pocketless pita bread
- Olive oil spray or any flavor spray you prefer, even coconut oil spray
- Up to 1 teaspoon Fine sea salt, garlic salt, onion salt, or other flavored salt

Directions:

1. Preheat the air fryer to 400°F.
2. Lightly coat the pita round(s) on both sides with olive oil spray, then lightly sprinkle each side with salt.
3. Cut each coated pita round into 8 even wedges. Lay these in the basket in as close to a single even layer as possible. Many will overlap or even be on top of each other, depending on the exact size of your machine.
4. Air-fry for 6 minutes, shaking the basket and rearranging the wedges at the 4-minute marks, until the wedges are crisp and brown. Turn them out onto a wire rack to cool a few minutes or to room temperature before digging in.

Prosciutto Mozzarella Bites

Servings: 8
Cooking Time: 6 Minutes
Ingredients:

- 8 pieces full-fat mozzarella string cheese
- 8 thin slices prosciutto
- 16 basil leaves

Directions:

1. Preheat the air fryer to 360°F.
2. Cut the string cheese in half across the center, not lengthwise. Do the same with the prosciutto.
3. Place a piece of prosciutto onto a clean workspace. Top the prosciutto with a basil leaf and then a piece of string cheese. Roll up the string cheese inside the prosciutto and secure with a wooden toothpick. Repeat with the remaining cheese sticks.
4. Place the prosciutto mozzarella bites into the air fryer basket and cook for 6 minutes, checking for doneness at 4 minutes.

Roasted Red Pepper Dip

Servings: 2
Cooking Time: 15 Minutes
Ingredients:

- 2 Medium-size red bell pepper(s)
- 1¾ cups Canned white beans, drained and rinsed
- 1 tablespoon Fresh oregano leaves, packed
- 3 tablespoons Olive oil
- 1 tablespoon Lemon juice
- ½ teaspoon Table salt
- ½ teaspoon Ground black pepper

Directions:

1. Preheat the air fryer to 400°F.
2. Set the pepper(s) in the basket and air-fry undisturbed for 15 minutes, until blistered and even blackened.
3. Use kitchen tongs to transfer the pepper(s) to a zip-closed plastic bag or small bowl. Seal the bag or cover the bowl with plastic wrap. Set aside for 20 minutes.
4. Peel each pepper, then stem it, cut it in half, and remove all its seeds and their white membranes.
5. Set the pieces of the pepper in a food processor. Add the beans, oregano, olive oil, lemon juice, salt, and pepper. Cover and process until smooth, stopping the machine at least once to scrape down the inside of the canister. Scrape the dip into a bowl and serve warm, or cover and refrigerate for up to 3 days.

Mozzarella Sticks

Servings: 4
Cooking Time: 5 Minutes
Ingredients:

- 1 egg
- 1 tablespoon water
- 8 eggroll wraps
- 8 mozzarella string cheese "sticks"
- sauce for dipping

Directions:

1. Beat together egg and water in a small bowl.
2. Lay out egg roll wraps and moisten edges with egg wash.
3. Place one piece of string cheese on each wrap near one end.
4. Fold in sides of egg roll wrap over ends of cheese, and then roll up.
5. Brush outside of wrap with egg wash and press gently to seal well.
6. Place in air fryer basket in single layer and cook 390°F for 5 minutes. Cook an additional 1 or 2minutes, if necessary, until they are golden brown and crispy.
7. Serve with your favorite dipping sauce.

Croutons

Servings:4
Cooking Time: 5 Minutes
Ingredients:

- 4 slices sourdough bread, diced into small cubes
- 2 tablespoons salted butter, melted
- 1 teaspoon chopped fresh parsley
- 2 tablespoons grated Parmesan cheese

Directions:

1. Preheat the air fryer to 400°F.
2. Place bread cubes in a large bowl.
3. Pour butter over bread cubes. Add parsley and Parmesan. Toss bread cubes until evenly coated.

4. Place bread cubes in the air fryer basket in a single layer. Cook 5 minutes until well toasted. Serve cooled for maximum crunch.

Skinny Fries

Servings: 2
Cooking Time: 15 Minutes
Ingredients:
- 2 to 3 russet potatoes, peeled and cut into ¼-inch sticks
- 2 to 3 teaspoons olive or vegetable oil
- salt

Directions:
1. Cut the potatoes into ¼-inch strips. Rinse the potatoes with cold water several times and let them soak in cold water for at least 10 minutes or as long as overnight.
2. Preheat the air fryer to 380°F.
3. Drain and dry the potato sticks really well, using a clean kitchen towel. Toss the fries with the oil in a bowl and then air-fry the fries in two batches at 380°F for 15 minutes, shaking the basket a couple of times while they cook.
4. Add the first batch of French fries back into the air fryer basket with the finishing batch and let everything warm through for a few minutes. As soon as the fries are done, season them with salt and transfer to a plate or basket. Serve them warm with ketchup or your favorite dip.

Crunchy Spicy Chickpeas

Servings: 6
Cooking Time: 12 Minutes
Ingredients:
- 2½ cups Canned chickpeas, drained and rinsed
- 2½ tablespoons Vegetable or canola oil
- up to 1 tablespoon Cajun or jerk dried seasoning blend (see here for a Cajun blend, here for a jerk blend)
- up to ¾ teaspoon Table salt (optional)

Directions:
1. Preheat the air fryer to 400°F.
2. Toss the chickpeas, oil, seasoning blend, and salt (if using) in a large bowl until the chickpeas are evenly coated.
3. When the machine is at temperature, pour the chickpeas into the basket. Air-fry for 12 minutes, removing the basket at the 4- and 8-minute marks to toss and rearrange the chickpeas, until very aromatic and perhaps sizzling but not burned.
4. Pour the chickpeas into a large serving bowl. Cool for a couple of minutes, gently stirring once, before you dive in.

Parmesan Pizza Nuggets

Servings: 8
Cooking Time: 6 Minutes
Ingredients:
- ¾ cup warm filtered water
- 1 package fast-rising yeast
- ½ teaspoon salt
- 2 cups all-purpose flour

- ¼ cup finely grated Parmesan cheese
- 1 teaspoon Italian seasoning
- 2 tablespoon extra-virgin olive oil
- 1 teaspoon kosher salt

Directions:
1. Preheat the air fryer to 370°F.
2. In a large microwave-safe bowl, add the water. Heat for 40 seconds in the microwave. Remove and mix in the yeast and salt. Let sit 5 minutes.
3. Meanwhile, in a medium bowl, mix the flour with the Parmesan cheese and Italian seasoning. Set aside.
4. Using a stand mixer with a dough hook attachment, add the yeast liquid and then mix in the flour mixture ⅓ cup at a time until all the flour mixture is added and a dough is formed.
5. Remove the bowl from the stand, and then let the dough rise for 1 hour in a warm space, covered with a kitchen towel.
6. After the dough has doubled in size, remove it from the bowl and punch it down a few times on a lightly floured flat surface.
7. Divide the dough into 4 balls, and then roll each ball out into a long, skinny, sticklike shape.
8. Using a sharp knife, cut each dough stick into 6 pieces. Repeat for the remaining dough balls until you have about 24 nuggets formed.
9. Lightly brush the top of each bite with the egg whites and cover with a pinch of sea salt.
10. Spray the air fryer basket with olive oil spray and place the pizza nuggets on top. Cook for 6 minutes, or until lightly browned. Remove and keep warm.
11. Repeat until all the nuggets are cooked.
12. Serve warm.

Crispy Spiced Chickpeas

Servings: 2
Cooking Time: 20 Minutes
Ingredients:
- 1 can chickpeas, drained
- ½ teaspoon salt
- ½ teaspoon chili powder
- ¼ teaspoon ground cinnamon
- ⅛ teaspoon smoked paprika
- pinch ground cayenne pepper
- 1 tablespoon olive oil

Directions:
1. Preheat the air fryer to 400°F.
2. Dry the chickpeas as well as you can with a clean kitchen towel, rubbing off any loose skins as necessary. Combine the spices in a small bowl. Toss the chickpeas with the olive oil and then add the spices and toss again.
3. Air-fry for 15 minutes, shaking the basket a couple of times while they cook.
4. Check the chickpeas to see if they are crispy enough and if necessary, air-fry for another 5 minutes to crisp them

further. Serve warm, or cool to room temperature and store in an airtight container for up to two weeks.

Mustard Greens Chips With Curried Sauce

Servings: 4
Cooking Time: 20 Minutes
Ingredients:
- 1 cup plain yogurt
- 1 tbsp lemon juice
- 1 tbsp curry powder
- 1 bunch of mustard greens
- 2 tsp olive oil
- Sea salt to taste

Directions:
1. Preheat air fryer to 390°F. Using a sharp knife, remove and discard the ribs from the mustard greens. Slice the leaves into 2-3-inch pieces. Transfer them to a large bowl, then pour in olive oil and toss to coat. Air Fry for 5-6 minutes. Shake at least once. The chips should be crispy when finished. Sprinkle with a little bit of sea salt. Mix the yogurt, lemon juice, salt, and curry in a small bowl. Serve the greens with the sauce.

Sweet-and-salty Pretzels

Servings: 4
Cooking Time: 5 Minutes
Ingredients:
- 2 cups Plain pretzel nuggets
- 1 tablespoon Worcestershire sauce
- 2 teaspoons Granulated white sugar
- 1 teaspoon Mild smoked paprika
- ½ teaspoon Garlic or onion powder

Directions:
1. Preheat the air fryer to 350°F .
2. Put the pretzel nuggets, Worcestershire sauce, sugar, smoked paprika, and garlic or onion powder in a large bowl. Toss gently until the nuggets are well coated.
3. When the machine is at temperature, pour the nuggets into the basket, spreading them into as close to a single layer as possible. Air-fry, shaking the basket three or four times to rearrange the nuggets, for 5 minutes, or until the nuggets are toasted and aromatic. Although the coating will darken, don't let it burn, especially if the machine's temperature is 360°F.
4. Pour the nuggets onto a wire rack and gently spread them into one layer. Cool for 5 minutes before serving.

Thick-crust Pepperoni Pizza

Servings: 2
Cooking Time: 10 Minutes
Ingredients:
- 10 ounces Purchased fresh pizza dough (not a prebaked crust)
- Olive oil spray
- ¼ cup Purchased pizza sauce
- 10 slices Sliced pepperoni
- ⅓ cup Purchased shredded Italian 3- or 4-cheese blend

Directions:
1. Preheat the air fryer to 400°F.
2. Generously coat the inside of a 6-inch round cake pan for a small air fryer, a 7-inch round cake pan for a medium air fryer, or an 8-inch round cake pan for a large model with olive oil spray.
3. Set the dough in the pan and press it to fill the bottom in an even, thick layer. Spread the sauce over the dough, then top with the pepperoni and cheese.
4. When the machine is at temperature, set the pan in the basket and air-fry undisturbed for 10 minutes, or until puffed, brown, and bubbling.
5. Use kitchen tongs to transfer the cake pan to a wire rack. Cool for only a minute or so. Use a spatula to loosen the pizza from the pan and lift it out and onto the rack. Continue cooling for a few minutes before cutting into wedges to serve.

Greek Turkey Meatballs

Servings:5
Cooking Time: 15 Minutes Per Batch
Ingredients:
- 1 pound 85/15 ground turkey
- 1 cup chopped fresh spinach
- ½ cup diced red onion
- ½ cup crumbled feta cheese
- ½ cup bread crumbs
- ½ teaspoon salt
- ¼ teaspoon ground black pepper
- Cooking spray

Directions:
1. Preheat the air fryer to 350°F.
2. In a large bowl, mix all ingredients until well combined.
3. Roll mixture into balls, about 1 heaping tablespoon for each, to make twenty meatballs.
4. Spritz with cooking spray and place in the air fryer basket, working in batches as necessary. Cook 15 minutes, shaking the basket three times during cooking time, until golden brown and internal temperature reaches at least 165°F. Serve warm.

Beef Taco–stuffed Meatballs

Servings:6
Cooking Time: 15 Minutes
Ingredients:
- 4 ounces Colby jack cheese cut into ½" cubes
- 1 pound 80/20 ground beef
- 1 packet taco seasoning
- ½ cup bread crumbs

Directions:

1. Preheat the air fryer to 350°F. Chill cheese in the freezer 15 minutes.
2. In a large bowl, mix beef, taco seasoning, and bread crumbs. Roll mixture into balls, about 2" each, to make eighteen meatballs.
3. Remove cheese from freezer. Place one cube into each meatball by pressing gently into the center and shaping meat around cheese. Roll into a ball.
4. Spritz meatballs with cooking spray and place in the air fryer basket. Cook 15 minutes, shaking the basket three times during cooking, until meatballs are brown and internal temperature has reached at least 165°F. Serve warm.

Thyme Sweet Potato Chips

Servings: 2
Cooking Time: 20 Minutes
Ingredients:
*   1 tbsp olive oil
*   1 sweet potato, sliced
*   ¼ tsp dried thyme
*   Salt to taste

Directions:
1. Preheat air fryer to 390°F. Spread the sweet potato slices in the greased basket and brush with olive oil. Air Fry for 6 minutes. Remove the basket, shake, and sprinkle with thyme and salt. Cook for 6 more minutes or until lightly browned. Serve warm and enjoy!

Eggplant Fries

Servings: 18
Cooking Time: 10 Minutes
Ingredients:
*   ¾ cup All-purpose flour or tapioca flour
*   1 Large egg(s), well beaten
*   1 cup Seasoned Italian-style dried bread crumbs (gluten-free, if a concern)
*   3 tablespoons (about ½ ounce) Finely grated Asiago or Parmesan cheese
*   3 Peeled ½-inch-thick eggplant slices
*   Olive oil spray

Directions:
1. Preheat the air fryer to 375°F.
2. Set up and fill three shallow soup plates or small pie plates on your counter: one for the flour, one for the egg(s), and one for the bread crumbs mixed with the cheese until well combined.
3. Cut each eggplant slice into six ½-inch-wide strips or sticks. Dip one strip in the flour, coating it well on all sides. Gently shake off the excess flour, then dip the strip in the beaten egg(s) to coat it without losing the flour. Let any excess egg slip back into the rest, then roll the strip in the bread-crumb mixture to coat evenly on all sides, even the ends. Set the strips aside on a cutting board and continue dipping and coating the remaining strips as you did the first one.

4. Generously coat the strips with olive oil spray on all sides. Set them in the basket in one layer and air-fry undisturbed for 10 minutes, or until golden brown and crisp. If the machine is at 390°F, the strips may be done in 8 minutes.
5. Remove the basket from the machine and cool for a couple of minutes. Then use kitchen tongs to transfer the eggplant fries to a wire rack to cool for only a minute or two more before serving.

Rumaki

Servings: 24
Cooking Time: 12 Minutes
Ingredients:
*   10 ounces raw chicken livers
*   1 can sliced water chestnuts, drained
*   ¼ cup low-sodium teriyaki sauce
*   12 slices turkey bacon
*   toothpicks

Directions:
1. Cut livers into 1½-inch pieces, trimming out tough veins as you slice.
2. Place livers, water chestnuts, and teriyaki sauce in small container with lid. If needed, add another tablespoon of teriyaki sauce to make sure livers are covered. Refrigerate for 1 hour.
3. When ready to cook, cut bacon slices in half crosswise.
4. Wrap 1 piece of liver and 1 slice of water chestnut in each bacon strip. Secure with toothpick.
5. When you have wrapped half of the livers, place them in the air fryer basket in a single layer.
6. Cook at 390°F for 12 minutes, until liver is done and bacon is crispy.
7. While first batch cooks, wrap the remaining livers. Repeat step 6 to cook your second batch.

Fried Dill Pickle Chips

Servings: 4
Cooking Time: 12 Minutes
Ingredients:
*   1 cup All-purpose flour or tapioca flour
*   1 Large egg white(s)
*   1 tablespoon Brine from a jar of dill pickles
*   1 cup Seasoned Italian-style dried bread crumbs (gluten-free, if a concern)
*   2 Large dill pickle(s), cut into ½-inch-thick rounds
*   Vegetable oil spray

Directions:
1. Preheat the air fryer to 400°F.
2. Set up and fill three shallow soup plates or small pie plates on your counter: one for the flour, one for the egg white(s) whisked with the pickle brine, and one for the bread crumbs.
3. Set a pickle round in the flour and turn it to coat all sides, even the edge. Gently shake off the excess flour, then

dip the round into the egg-white mixture and turn to coat both sides and the edge. Let any excess egg white mixture slip back into the rest, then set the round in the bread crumbs and turn it to coat both sides as well as the edge. Set aside on a cutting board and soldier on, dipping and coating the remaining rounds. Lightly coat the coated rounds on both sides with vegetable oil spray.

4. Set the pickle rounds in the basket in one layer. Air-fry undisturbed for 7 minutes, or until golden brown and crunchy. Cool in the basket for a few minutes before using kitchen tongs to transfer the rounds to a serving platter.

Halloumi Fries

Servings: 3
Cooking Time: 12 Minutes
Ingredients:
- 1½ tablespoons Olive oil
- 1½ teaspoons Minced garlic
- ⅛ teaspoon Dried oregano
- ⅛ teaspoon Dried thyme
- ⅛ teaspoon Table salt
- ⅛ teaspoon Ground black pepper
- ¾ pound Halloumi

Directions:
1. Preheat the air fryer to 400°F.
2. Whisk the oil, garlic, oregano, thyme, salt, and pepper in a medium bowl.
3. Lay the piece of halloumi flat on a cutting board. Slice it widthwise into ½-inch-thick sticks. Cut each stick lengthwise into ½-inch-thick batons.
4. Put these batons into the olive oil mixture. Toss gently but well to coat.
5. Place the batons in the basket in a single layer. Air-fry undisturbed for 12 minutes, or until lightly browned, particularly at the edges.
6. Dump the fries out onto a wire rack. They may need a little coaxing with a nonstick-safe spatula to come free. Cool for a couple of minutes before serving hot.

Cheese Arancini

Servings: 8
Cooking Time: 12 Minutes
Ingredients:
- 1 cup Water
- ½ cup Raw white Arborio rice
- 1½ teaspoons Butter
- ¼ teaspoon Table salt
- 8 ¾-inch semi-firm mozzarella cubes (not fresh mozzarella)
- 2 Large egg(s), well beaten
- 1 cup Seasoned Italian-style dried bread crumbs (gluten-free, if a concern)
- Olive oil spray

Directions:

1. Combine the water, rice, butter, and salt in a small saucepan. Bring to a boil over medium-high heat, stirring occasionally. Cover, reduce the heat to very low, and simmer very slowly for 20 minutes.
2. Take the saucepan off the heat and let it stand, covered, for 10 minutes. Uncover it and fluff the rice. Cool for 20 minutes.
3. Preheat the air fryer to 375°F .
4. Set up and fill two shallow soup plates or small bowls on your counter: one with the beaten egg(s) and one with the bread crumbs.
5. With clean but wet hands, scoop up about 2 tablespoons of the cooked rice and form it into a ball. Push a cube of mozzarella into the middle of the ball and seal the cheese inside. Dip the ball in the egg(s) to coat completely, letting any excess egg slip back into the rest. Roll the ball in the bread crumbs to coat evenly but lightly. Set aside and continue making more rice balls.
6. Generously spray the balls with olive oil spray, then set them in the basket in one layer. They must not touch. Air-fry undisturbed for 10 minutes, or until crunchy and golden brown. If the machine is at 360°F, you may need to add 2 minutes to the cooking time.
7. Use a nonstick-safe spatula, and maybe a flatware spoon for balance, to gently transfer the balls to a wire rack. Cool for at least 5 minutes or up to 20 minutes before serving.

Spinach Dip

Servings:2
Cooking Time: 15 Minutes
Ingredients:
- 8 ounces full-fat cream cheese, softened
- ½ cup mayonnaise
- 2 teaspoons minced garlic
- 1 cup grated Parmesan cheese
- 1 package frozen chopped spinach, thawed and drained

Directions:
1. Preheat the air fryer to 320°F.
2. In a large bowl, mix cream cheese, mayonnaise, garlic, and Parmesan.
3. Fold in spinach. Scrape mixture into a 6" round baking dish and place in the air fryer basket.
4. Cook 15 minutes until mixture is bubbling and top begins to turn brown. Serve warm.

Zucchini Chips

Servings: 3
Cooking Time: 17 Minutes
Ingredients:
- 1½ small Zucchini, washed but not peeled, and cut into ¼-inch-thick rounds
- Olive oil spray
- ¼ teaspoon Table salt

Directions:
1. Preheat the air fryer to 375°F.

2. Lay some paper towels on your work surface. Set the zucchini rounds on top, then set more paper towels over the rounds. Press gently to remove some of the moisture. Remove the top layer of paper towels and lightly coat the rounds with olive oil spray on both sides.

3. When the machine is at temperature, set the rounds in the basket, overlapping them a bit as needed. Air-fry for 15 minutes, tossing and rearranging the rounds at the 5- and 10-minute marks, until browned, soft, yet crisp at the edges.

4. Gently pour the contents of the basket onto a wire rack. Cool for at least 10 minutes or up to 2 hours before serving.

Chili Kale Chips

Servings:4
Cooking Time: 5 Minutes
Ingredients:
- 1 teaspoon nutritional yeast
- 1 teaspoon salt
- 2 cups kale, chopped
- ½ teaspoon chili flakes
- 1 teaspoon sesame oil

Directions:
1. Mix up kale leaves with nutritional yeast, salt, chili flakes, and sesame oil. Shake the greens well. Preheat the air fryer to 400°F and put the kale leaves in the air fryer basket. Cook them for 3 minutes and then give a good shake. Cook the kale leaves for 2 minutes more.

Chives Meatballs

Servings: 6
Cooking Time: 20 Minutes
Ingredients:
- 1 pound beef meat, ground
- 1 teaspoon onion powder
- 1 teaspoon garlic powder
- A pinch of salt and black pepper
- 2 tablespoons chives, chopped
- Cooking spray

Directions:
1. In a bowl, mix all the ingredients except the cooking spray, stir well and shape medium meatballs out of this mix. Pace them in your lined air fryer's basket, grease with cooking spray and cook at 360°F for 20 minutes. Serve as an appetizer.

Bacon-wrapped Jalapeño Poppers

Servings:4
Cooking Time: 12 Minutes
Ingredients:
- 3 ounces full-fat cream cheese
- ½ cup shredded sharp Cheddar cheese
- ¼ teaspoon garlic powder
- 6 jalapeño peppers, trimmed and halved lengthwise, seeded and membranes removed

- 12 slices bacon

Directions:
1. Preheat the air fryer to 400°F.
2. In a large microwave-safe bowl, place cream cheese, Cheddar, and garlic powder. Microwave 20 seconds until softened and stir. Spoon cheese mixture into hollow jalapeño halves.
3. Wrap a bacon slice around each jalapeño half, completely covering pepper.
4. Place in the air fryer basket and cook 12 minutes, turning halfway through cooking time. Serve warm.

Bacon Wrapped Onion Rings

Servings: 2
Cooking Time: 30 Minutes
Ingredients:
- 1 onion, cut into 1/2-inch slices
- 1 teaspoon curry powder
- 1 teaspoon cayenne pepper
- Salt and ground black pepper, to your liking
- 8 strips bacon
- 1/4 cup spicy ketchup

Directions:
1. Place the onion rings in the bowl with cold water; let them soak approximately 20 minutes; drain the onion rings and pat dry using a kitchen towel.
2. Sprinkle curry powder, cayenne pepper, salt, and black pepper over onion rings.
3. Wrap one layer of bacon around onion, trimming any excess. Secure the rings with toothpicks.
4. Spritz the Air Fryer basket with cooking spray; arrange the breaded onion rings in the Air Fryer basket.
5. Cook in the preheated Air Fryer at 360 °F for 15 minutes, turning them over halfway through the cooking time. Serve with spicy ketchup. Bon appétit!

Veggie Chips

Servings: X
Cooking Time: X
Ingredients:
- sweet potato
- large parsnip
- large carrot
- turnip
- large beet
- vegetable or canola oil, in a spray bottle
- salt

Directions:
1. You can do a medley of vegetable chips, or just select from the vegetables listed. Whatever you choose to do, scrub the vegetables well and then slice them paper-thin using a mandolin.
2. Preheat the air fryer to 400°F.
3. Air-fry the chips in batches, one type of vegetable at a time. Spray the chips lightly with oil and transfer them to the

air fryer basket. The key is to NOT over-load the basket. You can overlap the chips a little, but don't pile them on top of each other. Doing so will make it much harder to get evenly browned and crispy chips. Air-fry at 400°F for the time indicated below, shaking the basket several times during the cooking process for even cooking.

4. Sweet Potato – 8 to 9 minutes
5. Parsnips – 5 minutes
6. Carrot – 7 minutes
7. Turnips – 8 minutes
8. Beets – 9 minutes
9. Season the chips with salt during the last couple of minutes of air-frying. Check the chips as they cook until they are done to your liking. Some will start to brown sooner than others.
10. You can enjoy the chips warm out of the air fryer or cool them to room temperature for crispier chips.

Grilled Cheese Sandwich

Servings: 2
Cooking Time: 5 Minutes
Ingredients:
- 4 slices bread
- 4 ounces Cheddar cheese slices
- 2 teaspoons butter or oil

Directions:
1. Lay the four cheese slices on two of the bread slices and top with the remaining two slices of bread.
2. Brush both sides with butter or oil and cut the sandwiches in rectangular halves.
3. Place in air fryer basket and cook at 390°F for 5minutes until the outside is crisp and the cheese melts.

Cheese Bacon Jalapeno Poppers

Servings: 5
Cooking Time: 5 Minutes
Ingredients:
- 10 fresh jalapeno peppers, cut in half and remove seeds
- 2 bacon slices, cooked and crumbled
- 1/4 cup cheddar cheese, shredded
- 6 oz cream cheese, softened

Directions:
1. In a bowl, combine together bacon, cream cheese, and cheddar cheese.
2. Stuff each jalapeno half with bacon cheese mixture.
3. Spray air fryer basket with cooking spray.
4. Place stuffed jalapeno halved in air fryer basket and cook at 370°F for 5 minutes.
5. Serve and enjoy.

Onion Ring Nachos

Servings: 3
Cooking Time: 8 Minutes
Ingredients:

- ¾ pound Frozen breaded (not battered) onion rings (do not thaw)
- 1½ cups Shredded Cheddar, Monterey Jack, or Swiss cheese, or a purchased Tex-Mex blend
- Up to 12 Pickled jalapeño rings

Directions:
1. Preheat the air fryer to 400°F.
2. When the machine is at temperature, spread the onion rings in the basket in a fairly even layer. Air-fry undisturbed for 6 minutes, or until crisp. Remove the basket from the machine.
3. Cut a circle of parchment paper to line a 6-inch round cake pan for a small air fryer, a 7-inch round cake pan for a medium air fryer, or an 8-inch round cake pan for a large machine.
4. Pour the onion rings into a fairly even layer in the cake pan, then sprinkle the cheese evenly over them. Dot with the jalapeño rings.
5. Set the pan in the basket and air-fry undisturbed for 2 minutes, until the cheese has melted and is bubbling.
6. Remove the pan from the basket. Cool for 5 minutes before serving.

Corn Dog Bites

Servings: 3
Cooking Time: 12 Minutes
Ingredients:
- 3 cups Purchased cornbread stuffing mix
- ⅓ cup All-purpose flour
- 2 Large egg(s), well beaten
- 3 Hot dogs, cut into 2-inch pieces (vegetarian hot dogs, if preferred)
- Vegetable oil spray

Directions:
1. Preheat the air fryer to 375°F .
2. Put the cornbread stuffing mix in a food processor. Cover and pulse to grind into a mixture like fine bread crumbs.
3. Set up and fill three shallow soup plates or small pie plates on your counter: one for the flour, one for the egg(s), and one for the stuffing mix crumbs.
4. Dip a hot dog piece in the flour to coat it completely, then gently shake off any excess. Dip the hot dog piece into the egg(s) and gently roll it around to coat all surfaces, then pick it up and allow any excess egg to slip back into the rest. Set the hot dog piece in the stuffing mix crumbs and roll it gently to coat it evenly and well on all sides, even the ends. Set it aside on a cutting board and continue dipping and coating the remaining hot dog pieces.
5. Give the coated hot dog pieces a generous coating of vegetable oil spray on all sides, then set them in the basket in one layer with some space between them. Air-fry undisturbed for 10 minutes, or until golden brown and crunchy.

6. Use a nonstick-safe spatula, and perhaps a flatware fork for balance, to transfer the corn dog bites to a wire rack. Cool for 5 minutes before serving.

Buttered Corn On The Cob

Servings:2
Cooking Time:20 Minutes
Ingredients:
- 2 corn on the cob
- 2 tablespoons butter, softened and divided
- Salt and black pepper, to taste

Directions:
1. Preheat the Air fryer to 320°F and grease an Air fryer basket.
2. Season the cobs evenly with salt and black pepper and rub with 1 tablespoon butter.
3. Wrap the cobs in foil paper and arrange in the Air fryer basket.
4. Cook for about 20 minutes and top with remaining butter.
5. Dish out and serve warm.

Sweet Plantain Chips

Servings: 4
Cooking Time: 11 Minutes
Ingredients:
- 2 Very ripe plantain(s), peeled and sliced into 1-inch pieces
- Vegetable oil spray
- 3 tablespoons Maple syrup
- For garnishing Coarse sea salt or kosher salt

Directions:
1. Pour about ½ cup water into the bottom of your air fryer basket or into a metal tray on a lower rack in some models. Preheat the air fryer to 400°F.
2. Put the plantain pieces in a bowl, coat them with vegetable oil spray, and toss gently, spraying at least one more time and tossing repeatedly, until the pieces are well coated.
3. When the machine is at temperature, arrange the plantain pieces in the basket in one layer. Air-fry undisturbed for 5 minutes.
4. Remove the basket from the machine and spray the back of a metal spatula with vegetable oil spray. Use the spatula to press down on the plantain pieces, spraying it again as needed, to flatten the pieces to about half their original height. Brush the plantain pieces with maple syrup, then return the basket to the machine and continue air-frying undisturbed for 6 minutes, or until the plantain pieces are soft and caramelized.
5. Use kitchen tongs to transfer the pieces to a serving platter. Sprinkle the pieces with salt and cool for a couple of minutes before serving. Or cool to room temperature before serving, about 1 hour.

Crispy Tofu Bites

Servings: 4
Cooking Time: 20 Minutes
Ingredients:
- 1 pound Extra firm unflavored tofu
- Vegetable oil spray

Directions:
1. Wrap the piece of tofu in a triple layer of paper towels. Place it on a wooden cutting board and set a large pot on top of it to press out excess moisture. Set aside for 10 minutes.
2. Preheat the air fryer to 400°F.
3. Remove the pot and unwrap the tofu. Cut it into 1-inch cubes. Place these in a bowl and coat them generously with vegetable oil spray. Toss gently, then spray generously again before tossing, until all are glistening.
4. Gently pour the tofu pieces into the basket, spread them into as close to one layer as possible, and air-fry for 20 minutes, using kitchen tongs to gently rearrange the pieces at the 7- and 14-minute marks, until light brown and crisp.
5. Gently pour the tofu pieces onto a wire rack. Cool for 5 minutes before serving warm.

Ham And Cheese Sliders

Servings:3
Cooking Time: 10 Minutes
Ingredients:
- 6 Hawaiian sweet rolls
- 12 slices thinly sliced Black Forest ham
- 6 slices sharp Cheddar cheese
- ⅓ cup salted butter, melted
- 1 ½ teaspoons minced garlic

Directions:
1. Preheat the air fryer to 350°F.
2. For each slider, slice horizontally through the center of a roll without fully separating the two halves. Place 2 slices ham and 2 slices cheese inside roll and close. Repeat with remaining rolls, ham, and cheese.
3. In a small bowl, mix butter and garlic and brush over all sides of rolls.
4. Place in the air fryer and cook 10 minutes until rolls are golden on top and cheese is melted. Serve warm.

Italian Dip

Servings:8
Cooking Time: 12 Minutes
Ingredients:
- 8 oz cream cheese, softened
- 1 cup mozzarella cheese, shredded
- 1/2 cup roasted red peppers
- 1/3 cup basil pesto
- 1/4 cup parmesan cheese, grated

Directions:
1. Add parmesan cheese and cream cheese into the food processor and process until smooth.

2. Transfer cheese mixture into the air fryer pan and spread evenly.
3. Pour basil pesto on top of cheese layer.
4. Sprinkle roasted pepper on top of basil pesto layer.
5. Sprinkle mozzarella cheese on top of pepper layer and place dish in air fryer basket.
6. Cook dip at 250°F for 12 minutes.
7. Serve and enjoy.

Cheese Crackers

Servings:4
Cooking Time: 10 Minutes Per Batch
Ingredients:
- 4 ounces sharp Cheddar cheese, shredded
- ½ cup all-purpose flour
- 2 tablespoons salted butter, cubed
- ½ teaspoon salt
- 2 tablespoons cold water

Directions:
1. In a large bowl, using an electric hand mixer, mix all ingredients until dough forms. Pack dough together into a ball and wrap tightly in plastic wrap. Chill in the freezer 15 minutes.
2. Preheat the air fryer to 375°F. Cut parchment paper to fit the air fryer basket.
3. Spread a separate large sheet of parchment paper on a work surface. Remove dough from the freezer and roll out ¼" thick on parchment paper. Use a pizza cutter to cut dough into 1" squares.
4. Place crackers on precut parchment in the air fryer basket and cook 10 minutes, working in batches as necessary.
5. Allow crackers to cool at least 10 minutes before serving.

Beer-battered Onion Rings

Servings: 4
Cooking Time: 25 Minutes
Ingredients:
- 2 sliced onions, rings separated
- 1 cup flour
- Salt and pepper to taste
- 1 tsp garlic powder
- 1 cup beer

Directions:
1. Preheat air fryer to 350°F. In a mixing bowl, combine the flour, garlic powder, beer, salt, and black pepper. Dip the onion rings into the bowl and lay the coated rings in the frying basket. Air Fry for 15 minutes, shaking the basket several times during cooking to jostle the onion rings and ensure a good even fry. Once ready, the onions should be crispy and golden brown. Serve hot.

Buffalo Cauliflower Bites

Servings:6

Cooking Time: 15 Minutes
Ingredients:
- 1 medium head cauliflower, leaves and core removed, cut into bite-sized pieces
- 4 tablespoons salted butter, melted
- ¼ cup dry ranch seasoning
- ⅓ cup buffalo sauce

Directions:
1. Place cauliflower pieces into a large bowl. Pour butter over cauliflower and toss to coat. Sprinkle in ranch seasoning and toss to coat.
2. Place cauliflower into ungreased air fryer basket. Adjust the temperature to 350°F and set the timer for 12 minutes, shaking the basket three times during cooking.
3. When timer beeps, place cooked cauliflower in a clean large bowl. Toss with buffalo sauce, then return to air fryer basket to cook another 3 minutes. Cauliflower bites will be darkened at the edges and tender when done. Serve warm.

Onion Rings

Servings: 4
Cooking Time: 12 Minutes
Ingredients:
- 1 cup all-purpose flour
- 1 tablespoon seasoned salt
- 1 cup whole milk
- 1 large egg
- 1 cup panko bread crumbs
- 1 large Vidalia onion, peeled and sliced into ¼"-thick rings

Directions:
1. Preheat the air fryer to 350°F.
2. In a large bowl, whisk together flour and seasoned salt.
3. In a medium bowl, whisk together milk and egg. Place bread crumbs in a separate large bowl.
4. Dip onion rings into flour mixture to coat and set them aside. Pour milk mixture into the bowl of flour and stir to combine.
5. Dip onion rings into wet mixture and then press into bread crumbs to coat.
6. Place onion rings in the air fryer basket and spritz with cooking spray. Cook 12 minutes until the edges are crispy and golden. Serve warm.

Classic Potato Chips

Servings: 4
Cooking Time: 8 Minutes
Ingredients:
- 2 medium russet potatoes, washed
- 2 cups filtered water
- 1 tablespoon avocado oil
- ½ teaspoon salt

Directions:
1. Using a mandolin, slice the potatoes into ⅛-inch-thick pieces.

2. Pour the water into a large bowl. Place the potatoes in the bowl and soak for at least 30 minutes.

3. Preheat the air fryer to 350°F.

4. Drain the water and pat the potatoes dry with a paper towel or kitchen cloth. Toss with avocado oil and salt. Liberally spray the air fryer basket with olive oil mist.

5. Set the potatoes inside the air fryer basket, separating them so they're not on top of each other. Cook for 5 minutes, shake the basket, and cook another 5 minutes, or until browned.

6. Remove and let cool a few minutes prior to serving. Repeat until all the chips are cooked.

Plantain Chips

Servings: 2

Cooking Time: 14 Minutes

Ingredients:

- 1 large green plantain
- 2½ cups filtered water, divided
- 2 teaspoons sea salt, divided
- Cooking spray

Directions:

1. Slice the plantain into 1-inch pieces. Place the plantains into a large bowl, cover with 2 cups water and 1 teaspoon salt. Soak the plantains for 30 minutes; then remove and pat dry.

2. Preheat the air fryer to 390°F.

3. Place the plantain pieces into the air fryer basket, leaving space between the plantain rounds. Cook the plantains for 5 minutes, and carefully remove them from the air fryer basket.

4. Add the remaining water to a small bowl.

5. Using a small drinking glass, dip the bottom of the glass into the water and mash the warm plantains until they're ¼-inch thick. Return the plantains to the air fryer basket, sprinkle with the remaining sea salt, and spray lightly with cooking spray.

6. Cook for another 6 to 8 minutes, or until lightly golden brown edges appear.

Sweet Chili Peanuts

Servings: 6

Cooking Time: 5 Minutes

Ingredients:

- 2 cups Shelled raw peanuts
- 2 tablespoons Granulated white sugar
- 2 teaspoons Hot red pepper sauce, such as Cholula or Tabasco (gluten-free, if a concern)

Directions:

1. Preheat the air fryer to 400°F.

2. Toss the peanuts, sugar, and hot pepper sauce in a bowl until the peanuts are well coated.

3. When the machine is at temperature, pour the peanuts into the basket, spreading them into one layer as much as you can. Air-fry undisturbed for 3 minutes.

4. Shake the basket to rearrange the peanuts. Continue air-frying for 2 minutes more, shaking and stirring the peanuts every 30 seconds, until golden brown.

5. Pour the peanuts onto a large lipped baking sheet. Spread them into one layer and cool for 5 minutes before serving.

Crispy Curried Sweet Potato Fries

Servings: 4

Cooking Time: 20 Minutes

Ingredients:

- ½ cup sour cream
- ½ cup peach chutney
- 3 tsp curry powder
- 2 sweet potatoes, julienned
- 1 tbsp olive oil
- Salt and pepper to taste

Directions:

1. Preheat air fryer to 390°F. Mix together sour cream, peach chutney, and 1 ½ tsp curry powder in a small bowl. Set aside. In a medium bowl, add sweet potatoes, olive oil, the rest of the curry powder, salt, and pepper. Toss to coat. Place the potatoes in the frying basket. Bake for about 6 minutes, then shake the basket once. Cook for an additional 4 -6 minutes or until the potatoes are golden and crispy. Serve the fries hot in a basket along with the chutney sauce for dipping.

Individual Pizzas

Servings: 2

Cooking Time: 7 Minutes

Ingredients:

- 6 ounces Purchased fresh pizza dough (not a prebaked crust)
- Olive oil spray
- 4½ tablespoons Purchased pizza sauce or purchased pesto
- ½ cup Shredded semi-firm mozzarella

Directions:

1. Preheat the air fryer to 400°F.

2. Press the pizza dough into a 5-inch circle for a small air fryer, a 6-inch circle for a medium air fryer, or a 7-inch circle for a large machine. Generously coat the top of the dough with olive oil spray.

3. Remove the basket from the machine and set the dough oil side down in the basket. Smear the sauce or pesto over the dough, then sprinkle with the cheese.

4. Return the basket to the machine and air-fry undisturbed for 7 minutes, or until the dough is puffed and browned and the cheese has melted.

5. Remove the basket from the machine and cool the pizza in it for 5 minutes. Use a large nonstick-safe spatula to transfer the pizza from the basket to a wire rack. Cool for 5 minutes more before serving.

Crispy Deviled Eggs

Servings:12
Cooking Time: 25 Minutes
Ingredients:

- 7 large eggs, divided
- 1 ounce plain pork rinds, finely crushed
- 2 tablespoons mayonnaise
- ¼ teaspoon salt
- ¼ teaspoon ground black pepper

Directions:

1. Place 6 whole eggs into ungreased air fryer basket. Adjust the temperature to 220°F and set the timer for 20 minutes. When done, place eggs into a bowl of ice water to cool 5 minutes.
2. Peel cool eggs, then cut in half lengthwise. Remove yolks and place aside in a medium bowl.
3. In a separate small bowl, whisk remaining raw egg. Place pork rinds in a separate medium bowl. Dip each egg white into whisked egg, then gently coat with pork rinds. Spritz with cooking spray and place into ungreased air fryer basket. Adjust the temperature to 400°F and set the timer for 5 minutes, turning eggs halfway through cooking. Eggs will be golden when done.
4. Mash yolks in bowl with mayonnaise until smooth. Sprinkle with salt and pepper and mix.
5. Spoon 2 tablespoons yolk mixture into each fried egg white. Serve warm.

Cucumber Sushi

Servings:10
Cooking Time: 10 Minutes
Ingredients:

- 10 bacon slices
- 2 tablespoons cream cheese
- 1 cucumber

Directions:

1. Place the bacon slices in the air fryer in one layer and cook for 10 minutes at 400°F. Meanwhile, cut the cucumber into small wedges. When the bacon is cooked, cool it to the room temperature and spread with cream cheese. Then place the cucumber wedges over the cream cheese and roll the bacon into the sushi.

Cheesy Tortellini Bites

Servings: 8
Cooking Time: 10 Minutes
Ingredients:

- 1 large egg
- ½ teaspoon black pepper
- ½ teaspoon garlic powder
- 1 teaspoon Italian seasoning
- 12 ounces frozen cheese tortellini
- ½ cup panko breadcrumbs

Directions:

1. Preheat the air fryer to 380°F.
2. Spray the air fryer basket with an olive-oil-based spray.
3. In a medium bowl, whisk the egg with the pepper, garlic powder, and Italian seasoning.
4. Dip the tortellini in the egg batter and then coat with the breadcrumbs. Place each tortellini in the basket, trying not to overlap them. You may need to cook in batches to ensure the even crisp all around.
5. Bake for 5 minutes, shake the basket, and bake another 5 minutes.
6. Remove and let cool 5 minutes. Serve with marinara sauce, ranch, or your favorite dressing.

Tater Tots

Servings: 4
Cooking Time: 25 Minutes
Ingredients:

- 4 cups water
- 1 pound russet potatoes, peeled
- ½ teaspoon salt
- ½ teaspoon ground black pepper

Directions:

1. In a large saucepan over medium-high heat, bring the water to a boil. Add potatoes and boil about 10 minutes until a fork can be easily inserted into them. Drain potatoes and let cool.
2. Preheat the air fryer to 350°F.
3. Grate potatoes into a large bowl. Add salt and pepper and mix gently by hand.
4. Form potatoes into sixteen 1-tablespoon tater tot–shaped balls. Place tater tots in the air fryer basket and spray lightly with cooking spray.
5. Cook 15 minutes, shaking the basket halfway through cooking time, until crispy and brown. Serve warm.

Roasted Carrots

Servings: 2
Cooking Time: 20 Minutes
Ingredients:

- 1 tbsp. olive oil
- 3 cups baby carrots or carrots, cut into large chunks
- 1 tbsp. honey
- Salt and pepper to taste

Directions:

1. In a bowl, coat the carrots with the honey and olive oil before sprinkling on some salt and pepper.
2. Place into the Air Fryer and cook at 390°F for 12 minutes. Serve hot.

Bbq Chicken Wings

Servings: 4
Cooking Time: 15 Minutes
Ingredients:
- 1 lb chicken wings
- 1/2 cup BBQ sauce, sugar-free
- 1/4 tsp garlic powder
- Pepper

Directions:
1. Preheat the air fryer to 400 F.
2. Season chicken wings with garlic powder and pepper and place into the air fryer basket.
3. Cook chicken wings for 15 minutes. Shake basket 3-4 times while cooking.
4. Transfer cooked chicken wings in a large mixing bowl. Pour BBQ sauce over chicken wings and toss to coat.
5. Serve and enjoy.

Lemon Tofu Cubes

Servings:2
Cooking Time: 7 Minutes
Ingredients:
- ½ teaspoon ground coriander
- 1 tablespoon avocado oil
- 1 teaspoon lemon juice
- ½ teaspoon chili flakes
- 6 oz tofu

Directions:
1. In the shallow bowl mix up ground coriander, avocado oil, lemon juice, and chili flakes. Chop the tofu into cubes and sprinkle with coriander mixture. Shake the tofu. After this, preheat the air fryer to 400°F and put the tofu cubes in it. Cook the tofu for 4 minutes. Then flip the tofu on another side and cook for 3 minutes more.

Fried Pickles

Servings: 2
Cooking Time: 15 Minutes
Ingredients:
- 1 egg
- 1 tablespoon milk
- ¼ teaspoon hot sauce
- 2 cups sliced dill pickles, well drained
- ¾ cup breadcrumbs
- oil for misting or cooking spray

Directions:
1. Preheat air fryer to 390°F.
2. Beat together egg, milk, and hot sauce in a bowl large enough to hold all the pickles.
3. Add pickles to the egg wash and stir well to coat.
4. Place breadcrumbs in a large plastic bag or container with lid.
5. Drain egg wash from pickles and place them in bag with breadcrumbs. Shake to coat.
6. Pile pickles into air fryer basket and spray with oil.
7. Cook for 5 minutes. Shake basket and spray with oil.
8. Cook 5 more minutes. Shake and spray again. Separate any pickles that have stuck together and mist any spots you've missed.
9. Cook for 5 minutes longer or until dark golden brown and crispy.

Bacon, Sausage And Bell Pepper Skewers

Servings: 4
Cooking Time: 20 Minutes
Ingredients:
- 16 cocktail sausages, halved
- 4 ounces bacon, diced
- 1 red bell pepper, cut into 1 ½-inch pieces
- 1 green bell pepper, cut into 1 ½-inch pieces
- Salt and cracked black pepper, to taste
- 1/2 cup tomato chili sauce

Directions:
1. Thread the cocktail sausages, bacon, and peppers alternately onto skewers. Sprinkle with salt and black pepper.
2. Cook in the preheated Air Fryer at 380°F for 15 minutes, turning the skewers over once or twice to ensure even cooking.
3. Serve with the tomato chili sauce on the side. Enjoy!

Cheddar Cheese Lumpia Rolls

Servings: 5
Cooking Time: 20 Minutes
Ingredients:
- 5 ounces mature cheddar cheese, cut into 15 sticks
- 15 pieces spring roll lumpia wrappers
- 2 tablespoons sesame oil

Directions:
1. Wrap the cheese sticks in the lumpia wrappers. Transfer to the Air Fryer basket. Brush with sesame oil.
2. Bake in the preheated Air Fryer at 395°F for 10 minutes or until the lumpia wrappers turn golden brown. Work in batches.
3. Shake the Air Fryer basket occasionally to ensure even cooking. Bon appétit!

Cheesy Pigs In A Blanket

Servings: 4
Cooking Time: 7 Minutes
Ingredients:
- 24 cocktail size smoked sausages
- 6 slices deli-sliced Cheddar cheese, each cut into 8 rectangular pieces
- 1 tube refrigerated crescent roll dough
- ketchup or mustard for dipping

Directions:

1. Unroll the crescent roll dough into one large sheet. If your crescent roll dough has perforated seams, pinch or roll all the perforated seams together. Cut the large sheet of dough into 4 rectangles. Then cut each rectangle into 6 pieces by making one slice lengthwise in the middle and 2 slices horizontally. You should have 24 pieces of dough.
2. Make a deep slit lengthwise down the center of the cocktail sausage. Stuff two pieces of cheese into the slit in the sausage. Roll one piece of crescent dough around the stuffed cocktail sausage leaving the ends of the sausage exposed. Pinch the seam together. Repeat with the remaining sausages.
3. Preheat the air fryer to 350°F.
4. Air-fry in 2 batches, placing the sausages seam side down in the basket. Air-fry for 7 minutes. Serve hot with ketchup or your favorite mustard for dipping.

Bacon-wrapped Goat Cheese Poppers

Servings: 10
Cooking Time: 10 Minutes
Ingredients:
- 10 large jalapeño peppers
- 8 ounces goat cheese
- 10 slices bacon

Directions:
1. Preheat the air fryer to 380°F.
2. Slice the jalapeños in half. Carefully remove the veins and seeds of the jalapeños with a spoon.
3. Fill each jalapeño half with 2 teaspoons goat cheese.
4. Cut the bacon in half lengthwise to make long strips. Wrap the jalapeños with bacon, trying to cover the entire length of the jalapeño.
5. Place the bacon-wrapped jalapeños into the air fryer basket. Cook the stuffed jalapeños for 10 minutes or until bacon is crispy.

Fiery Bacon-wrapped Dates

Servings: 16
Cooking Time: 6 Minutes
Ingredients:
- 8 Thin-cut bacon strips, halved widthwise (gluten-free, if a concern)
- 16 Medium or large Medjool dates, pitted
- 3 tablespoons (about ¾ ounce) Shredded semi-firm mozzarella
- 32 Pickled jalapeño rings

Directions:
1. Preheat the air fryer to 400°F.
2. Lay a bacon strip half on a clean, dry work surface. Split one date lengthwise without cutting through it, so that it opens like a pocket. Set it on one end of the bacon strip and open it a bit. Place 1 teaspoon of the shredded cheese and 2 pickled jalapeño rings in the date, then gently squeeze it

together without fully closing it. Roll up the date in the bacon strip and set it bacon seam side down on a cutting board. Repeat this process with the remaining bacon strip halves, dates, cheese, and jalapeño rings.
3. Place the bacon-wrapped dates bacon seam side down in the basket. Air-fry undisturbed for 6 minutes, or until crisp and brown.
4. Use kitchen tongs to gently transfer the wrapped dates to a wire rack or serving platter. Cool for a few minutes before serving.

Garlic Parmesan Kale Chips

Servings: 2
Cooking Time: 6 Minutes
Ingredients:
- 16 large kale leaves, washed and thick stems removed
- 1 tablespoon avocado oil
- ½ teaspoon garlic powder
- 1 teaspoon soy sauce or tamari
- ¼ cup grated Parmesan cheese

Directions:
1. Preheat the air fryer to 370°F.
2. Make a stack of kale leaves and cut them into 4 pieces.
3. Place the kale pieces into a large bowl. Drizzle the avocado oil onto the kale and rub to coat. Add the garlic powder, soy sauce or tamari, and cheese, tossing to coat.
4. Pour the chips into the air fryer basket and cook for 3 minutes, shake the basket, and cook another 3 minutes, checking for crispness every minute. When done cooking, pour the kale chips onto paper towels and cool at least 5 minutes before serving.

Herbed Cheese Brittle

Servings: 4
Cooking Time: 5 Minutes
Ingredients:
- ½ cup shredded Parmesan cheese
- ½ cup shredded white cheddar cheese
- 1 tablespoon fresh chopped rosemary
- 1 teaspoon garlic powder
- 1 large egg white

Directions:
1. Preheat the air fryer to 400°F.
2. In a large bowl, mix the cheeses, rosemary, and garlic powder. Mix in the egg white. Then pour the batter into a 7-inch pan. Place the pan in the air fryer basket and cook for 4 to 5 minutes, or until the cheese is melted and slightly browned.
3. Remove the pan from the air fryer, and let it cool for 2 minutes. Invert the pan before the cheese brittle completely cools but is semi-hardened to allow it to easily slide out of the pan.
4. Let the pan cool another 5 minutes. Break into pieces and serve.

Asian Five-spice Wings

Servings: 4
Cooking Time: 15 Minutes
Ingredients:
- 2 pounds chicken wings
- ½ cup Asian-style salad dressing
- 2 tablespoons Chinese five-spice powder

Directions:
1. Cut off wing tips and discard or freeze for stock. Cut remaining wing pieces in two at the joint.
2. Place wing pieces in a large sealable plastic bag. Pour in the Asian dressing, seal bag, and massage the marinade into the wings until well coated. Refrigerate for at least an hour.
3. Remove wings from bag, drain off excess marinade, and place wings in air fryer basket.
4. Cook at 360°F for 15minutes or until juices run clear. About halfway through cooking time, shake the basket or stir wings for more even cooking.
5. Transfer cooked wings to plate in a single layer. Sprinkle half of the Chinese five-spice powder on the wings, turn, and sprinkle other side with remaining seasoning.

Chapter 4. Beef,pork & Lamb Recipes

Pork Meatballs

Servings:18
Cooking Time: 12 Minutes
Ingredients:
- 1 pound ground pork
- 1 large egg, whisked
- ½ teaspoon garlic powder
- ½ teaspoon salt
- ½ teaspoon ground ginger
- ¼ teaspoon crushed red pepper flakes
- 1 medium scallion, trimmed and sliced

Directions:
1. Combine all ingredients in a large bowl. Spoon out 2 tablespoons mixture and roll into a ball. Repeat to form eighteen meatballs total.
2. Place meatballs into ungreased air fryer basket. Adjust the temperature to 400°F and set the timer for 12 minutes, shaking the basket three times throughout cooking. Meatballs will be browned and have an internal temperature of at least 145°F when done. Serve warm.

Teriyaki Country-style Pork Ribs

Servings: 3
Cooking Time: 30 Minutes
Ingredients:
- 3 tablespoons Regular or low-sodium soy sauce or gluten-free tamari sauce
- 3 tablespoons Honey
- ¾ teaspoon Ground dried ginger
- ¾ teaspoon Garlic powder
- 3 8-ounce boneless country-style pork ribs
- Vegetable oil spray

Directions:
1. Preheat the air fryer to 350°F .
2. Mix the soy or tamari sauce, honey, ground ginger, and garlic powder in another bowl until uniform.
3. Smear about half of this teriyaki sauce over all sides of the country-style ribs. Reserve the remainder of the teriyaki sauce. Generously coat the meat with vegetable oil spray.
4. When the machine is at temperature, place the country-style ribs in the basket with as much air space between them as possible. Air-fry undisturbed for 15 minutes. Turn the country-style ribs and brush them all over with the remaining teriyaki sauce. Continue air-frying undisturbed for 15 minutes, or until an instant-read meat thermometer inserted into the center of one rib registers at least 145°F.
5. Use kitchen tongs to transfer the country-style ribs to a wire rack. Cool for 5 minutes before serving.

Rib Eye Steak Seasoned With Italian Herb

Servings:4
Cooking Time: 45 Minutes
Ingredients:
- 1 packet Italian herb mix
- 1 tablespoon olive oil
- 2 pounds bone-in rib eye steak
- Salt and pepper to taste

Directions:
1. Preheat the air fryer to 390°F.
2. Place the grill pan accessory in the air fryer.
3. Season the steak with salt, pepper, Italian herb mix, and olive oil. Cover top with foil.
4. Grill for 45 minutes and flip the steak halfway through the cooking time.

Cheddar Bacon Ranch Pinwheels

Servings:5
Cooking Time: 12 Minutes Per Batch
Ingredients:

- 4 ounces full-fat cream cheese, softened
- 1 tablespoon dry ranch seasoning
- ½ cup shredded Cheddar cheese
- 1 sheet frozen puff pastry dough, thawed
- 6 slices bacon, cooked and crumbled

Directions:

1. Preheat the air fryer to 320°F. Cut parchment paper to fit the air fryer basket.
2. In a medium bowl, mix cream cheese, ranch seasoning, and Cheddar. Unfold puff pastry and gently spread cheese mixture over pastry.
3. Sprinkle crumbled bacon on top. Starting from a long side, roll dough into a log, pressing in the edges to seal.
4. Cut log into ten pieces, then place on parchment in the air fryer basket, working in batches as necessary.
5. Cook 12 minutes, turning each piece after 7 minutes. Let cool 5 minutes before serving.

Easy-peasy Beef Sliders

Servings:4
Cooking Time: 25 Minutes
Ingredients:

- 1 lb ground beef
- ¼ tsp cumin
- ¼ tsp mustard power
- 1/3 cup grated yellow onion
- ½ tsp smoked paprika
- Salt and pepper to taste

Directions:

1. Preheat air fryer to 350°F. Combine the ground beef, cumin, mustard, onion, paprika, salt, and black pepper in a bowl. Form mixture into 8 patties and make a slight indentation in the middle of each. Place beef patties in the greased frying basket and Air Fry for 8-10 minutes, flipping once. Serve right away and enjoy!

Rib Eye Steak

Servings:4
Cooking Time: 15 Minutes
Ingredients:

- 4 rib eye steaks
- 1 teaspoon salt
- ½ teaspoon ground black pepper
- 2 tablespoons salted butter

Directions:

1. Preheat the air fryer to 400°F.
2. Sprinkle steaks with salt and pepper and place in the air fryer basket.

3. Cook 15 minutes, turning halfway through cooking time, until edges are firm, and the internal temperature reaches at least 160°F for well-done.
4. Top each steak with ½ tablespoon butter immediately after removing from the air fryer. Let rest 5 minutes before cutting. Serve warm.

Boneless Ribeyes

Servings: 2
Cooking Time: 10-15 Minutes
Ingredients:

- 2 8-ounce boneless ribeye steaks
- 4 teaspoons Worcestershire sauce
- ½ teaspoon garlic powder
- pepper
- 4 teaspoons extra virgin olive oil
- salt

Directions:

1. Season steaks on both sides with Worcestershire sauce. Use the back of a spoon to spread evenly.
2. Sprinkle both sides of steaks with garlic powder and coarsely ground black pepper to taste.
3. Drizzle both sides of steaks with olive oil, again using the back of a spoon to spread evenly over surfaces.
4. Allow steaks to marinate for 30minutes.
5. Place both steaks in air fryer basket and cook at 390°F for 5minutes.
6. Turn steaks over and cook until done: medium rare: additional 5 minutes, medium: additional 7 minutes, well done: additional 10 minutes.
7. Remove steaks from air fryer basket and let sit 5minutes. Salt to taste and serve.

Jerk Pork

Servings: 4
Cooking Time: 20 Minutes
Ingredients:

- 1 1/2 lbs pork butt, chopped into pieces
- 3 tbsp jerk paste

Directions:

1. Add meat and jerk paste into the bowl and coat well. Place in the fridge for overnight.
2. Spray air fryer basket with cooking spray.
3. Preheat the air fryer to 390°F.
4. Add marinated meat into the air fryer and cook for 20 minutes. Turn halfway through.
5. Serve and enjoy.

Honey-sriracha Pork Ribs

Servings:4
Cooking Time: 25 Minutes
Ingredients:

- 3 pounds pork back ribs, white membrane removed
- 2 teaspoons salt
- 1 teaspoon ground black pepper

- ½ cup sriracha
- ⅓ cup honey
- 1 tablespoon lemon juice

Directions:

1. Preheat the air fryer to 400°F.
2. Place ribs on a work surface and cut the rack into two pieces to fit in the air fryer basket.
3. Sprinkle ribs with salt and pepper and place in the air fryer basket meat side down. Cook 15 minutes.
4. In a small bowl, combine the sriracha, honey, and lemon juice to make a sauce.
5. Remove ribs from the air fryer basket and pour sauce over both sides. Return them to the air fryer basket meat side up and cook an additional 10 minutes until brown and the internal temperature reaches at least 190°F. Serve warm.

Pesto Coated Rack Of Lamb

Servings:4
Cooking Time:15 Minutes

Ingredients:

- ½ bunch fresh mint
- 1 rack of lamb
- 1 garlic clove
- ¼ cup extra-virgin olive oil
- ½ tablespoon honey
- Salt and black pepper, to taste

Directions:

1. Preheat the Air fryer to 200°F and grease an Air fryer basket.
2. Put the mint, garlic, oil, honey, salt, and black pepper in a blender and pulse until smooth to make pesto.
3. Coat the rack of lamb with this pesto on both sides and arrange in the Air fryer basket.
4. Cook for about 15 minutes and cut the rack into individual chops to serve.

Fajita Flank Steak Rolls

Servings:4
Cooking Time: 12 Minutes

Ingredients:

- 1 pound flank steak
- 4 slices pepper jack cheese
- 1 medium green bell pepper, seeded and chopped
- ½ medium red bell pepper, seeded and chopped
- ¼ cup finely chopped yellow onion
- 1 teaspoon salt
- ½ teaspoon ground black pepper
- Cooking spray

Directions:

1. Preheat the air fryer to 400°F.
2. Carefully butterfly steak, leaving the two halves connected. Place slices of cheese on top of steak. Scatter bell peppers and onion over cheese in an even layer.

3. Place steak so that the grain runs horizontally. Tightly roll up steak and secure it with eight evenly spaced toothpicks or eight sections of butcher's twine.
4. Slice steak into four even rolls. Spritz with cooking spray, then sprinkle with salt and black pepper. Place in the air fryer basket and cook 12 minutes until steak is brown on the edges and internal temperature reaches at least 160°F for well-done. Serve.

Mustard And Rosemary Pork Tenderloin With Fried Apples

Servings: 2
Cooking Time: 26 Minutes

Ingredients:

- 1 pork tenderloin
- 2 tablespoons coarse brown mustard
- salt and freshly ground black pepper
- 1½ teaspoons finely chopped fresh rosemary, plus sprigs for garnish
- 2 apples, cored and cut into 8 wedges
- 1 tablespoon butter, melted
- 1 teaspoon brown sugar

Directions:

1. Preheat the air fryer to 370°F.
2. Cut the pork tenderloin in half so that you have two pieces that fit into the air fryer basket. Brush the mustard onto both halves of the pork tenderloin and then season with salt, pepper and the fresh rosemary. Place the pork tenderloin halves into the air fryer basket and air-fry for 10 minutes. Turn the pork over and air-fry for an additional 8 minutes or until the internal temperature of the pork registers 155°F on an instant read thermometer. If your pork tenderloin is especially thick, you may need to add a minute or two, but it's better to check the pork and add time, than to overcook it.
3. Let the pork rest for 5 minutes. In the meantime, toss the apple wedges with the butter and brown sugar and air-fry at 400°F for 8 minutes, shaking the basket once or twice during the cooking process so the apples cook and brown evenly.
4. Slice the pork on the bias. Serve with the fried apples scattered over the top and a few sprigs of rosemary as garnish.

Mexican-style Shredded Beef

Servings:6
Cooking Time: 35 Minutes

Ingredients:

- 1 beef chuck roast, cut into 2" cubes
- 1 teaspoon salt
- ½ teaspoon ground black pepper
- ½ cup no-sugar-added chipotle sauce

Directions:

1. In a large bowl, sprinkle beef cubes with salt and pepper and toss to coat. Place beef into ungreased air fryer basket.

Adjust the temperature to 400°F and set the timer for 30 minutes, shaking the basket halfway through cooking. Beef will be done when internal temperature is at least 160°F.

2. Place cooked beef into a large bowl and shred with two forks. Pour in chipotle sauce and toss to coat.

3. Return beef to air fryer basket for an additional 5 minutes at 400°F to crisp with sauce. Serve warm.

Fried Spam

Servings: 2
Cooking Time: 12 Minutes
Ingredients:
- ½ cup All-purpose flour or gluten-free all-purpose flour
- 1 Large egg(s)
- 1 tablespoon Wasabi paste
- 1⅓ cups Plain panko bread crumbs (gluten-free, if a concern)
- 4 ½-inch-thick Spam slices
- Vegetable oil spray

Directions:
1. Preheat the air fryer to 400°F.
2. Set up and fill three shallow soup plates or small pie plates on your counter: one for the flour; one for the egg(s), whisked with the wasabi paste until uniform; and one for the bread crumbs.
3. Dip a slice of Spam in the flour, coating both sides. Slip it into the egg mixture and turn to coat on both sides, even along the edges. Let any excess egg mixture slip back into the rest, then set the slice in the bread crumbs. Turn it several times, pressing gently to make an even coating on both sides. Generously coat both sides of the slice with vegetable oil spray. Set aside so you can dip, coat, and spray the remaining slice(s).
4. Set the slices in the basket in a single layer so that they don't touch. Air-fry undisturbed for 12 minutes, or until very brown and quite crunchy.
5. Use kitchen tongs to transfer the slices to a wire rack. Cool for a minute or two before serving.

Lamb Burgers

Servings: 2
Cooking Time: 16 Minutes
Ingredients:
- 8 oz lamb, minced
- ½ teaspoon salt
- ½ teaspoon ground black pepper
- ½ teaspoon dried cilantro
- 1 tablespoon water
- Cooking spray

Directions:
1. In the mixing bowl mix up minced lamb, salt, ground black pepper, dried cilantro, and water.
2. Stir the meat mixture carefully with the help of the spoon and make 2 burgers.
3. Preheat the air fryer to 375°F.

4. Spray the air fryer basket with cooking spray and put the burgers inside.
5. Cook them for 8 minutes from each side.

Peppered Steak Bites

Servings: 4
Cooking Time: 14 Minutes
Ingredients:
- 1 pound sirloin steak, cut into 1-inch cubes
- ½ teaspoon coarse sea salt
- 1 teaspoon coarse black pepper
- 2 teaspoons Worcestershire sauce
- ½ teaspoon garlic powder
- ¼ teaspoon red pepper flakes
- ¼ cup chopped parsley

Directions:
1. Preheat the air fryer to 390°F.
2. In a large bowl, place the steak cubes and toss with the salt, pepper, Worcestershire sauce, garlic powder, and red pepper flakes.
3. Pour the steak into the air fryer basket and cook for 10 to 14 minutes, depending on how well done you prefer your bites. Starting at the 8-minute mark, toss the steak bites every 2 minutes to check for doneness.
4. When the steak is cooked, remove it from the basket to a serving bowl and top with the chopped parsley. Allow the steak to rest for 5 minutes before serving.

Air-fried Roast Beef With Rosemary Roasted Potatoes

Servings: 8
Cooking Time: 60 Minutes
Ingredients:
- 1 top sirloin roast
- salt and freshly ground black pepper
- 1 teaspoon dried thyme
- 2 pounds red potatoes, halved or quartered
- 2 teaspoons olive oil
- 1 teaspoon very finely chopped fresh rosemary, plus more for garnish

Directions:
1. Start by making sure your roast will fit into the air fryer basket without touching the top element. Trim it if you have to in order to get it to fit nicely in your air fryer.
2. Preheat the air fryer to 360°F.
3. Season the beef all over with salt, pepper and thyme. Transfer the seasoned roast to the air fryer basket.
4. Air-fry at 360°F for 20 minutes. Turn the roast over and continue to air-fry at 360°F for another 20 minutes.
5. Toss the potatoes with the olive oil, salt, pepper and fresh rosemary. Turn the roast over again in the air fryer basket and toss the potatoes in around the sides of the roast. Air-fry the roast and potatoes at 360°F for another 20 minutes. Check the internal temperature of the roast with an

instant-read thermometer, and continue to roast until the beef is 5° lower than your desired degree of doneness. Let the roast rest for 5 to 10 minutes before slicing and serving. While the roast is resting, continue to air-fry the potatoes if desired for extra browning and crispiness.

6.   Slice the roast and serve with the potatoes, adding a little more fresh rosemary if desired.

Roast Beef

Servings:6
Cooking Time: 60 Minutes
Ingredients:
- 1 top round beef roast
- 1 teaspoon salt
- ½ teaspoon ground black pepper
- 1 teaspoon dried rosemary
- ½ teaspoon garlic powder
- 1 tablespoon coconut oil, melted

Directions:
1.   Sprinkle all sides of roast with salt, pepper, rosemary, and garlic powder. Drizzle with coconut oil. Place roast into ungreased air fryer basket, fatty side down. Adjust the temperature to 375°F and set the timer for 60 minutes, turning the roast halfway through cooking. Roast will be done when no pink remains and internal temperature is at least 180°F. Serve warm.

Meatloaf

Servings:4
Cooking Time: 40 Minutes
Ingredients:
- 1 pound 80/20 lean ground beef
- 1 large egg
- 3 tablespoons Italian bread crumbs
- 1 teaspoon salt
- 2 tablespoons ketchup
- 2 tablespoons brown sugar

Directions:
1.   Preheat the air fryer to 350°F.
2.   In a large bowl, combine beef, egg, bread crumbs, and salt.
3.   In a small bowl, mix ketchup and brown sugar.
4.   Form meat mixture into a 6" × 3" loaf and brush with ketchup mixture.
5.   Place in the air fryer basket and cook 40 minutes until internal temperature reaches at least 160°F. Serve warm.

Cheese-stuffed Steak Burgers

Servings:4
Cooking Time: 10 Minutes
Ingredients:
- 1 pound 80/20 ground sirloin
- 4 ounces mild Cheddar cheese, cubed
- ½ teaspoon salt

- ¼ teaspoon ground black pepper

Directions:
1.   Form ground sirloin into four equal balls, then separate each ball in half and flatten into two thin patties, for eight total patties. Place 1 ounce Cheddar into center of one patty, then top with a second patty and press edges to seal burger closed. Repeat with remaining patties and Cheddar to create four burgers.
2.   Sprinkle salt and pepper over both sides of burgers and carefully place burgers into ungreased air fryer basket. Adjust the temperature to 350°F and set the timer for 10 minutes. Burgers will be done when browned on the edges and top. Serve warm.

Beef Short Ribs

Servings:4
Cooking Time: 25 Minutes
Ingredients:
- 3 pounds beef short ribs
- 2 tablespoons olive oil
- 3 teaspoons salt
- 3 teaspoons ground black pepper
- ½ cup barbecue sauce

Directions:
1.   Preheat the air fryer to 375°F.
2.   Place short ribs in a large bowl. Drizzle with oil and sprinkle both sides with salt and pepper.
3.   Place in the air fryer basket and cook 20 minutes. Remove from basket and brush with barbecue sauce. Return to the air fryer basket and cook 5 additional minutes until sauce is dark brown and internal temperature reaches at least 160°F. Serve warm.

Grilled Prosciutto Wrapped Fig

Servings:2
Cooking Time: 8 Minutes
Ingredients:
- 2 whole figs, sliced in quarters
- 8 prosciutto slices
- Pepper and salt to taste

Directions:
1.   Wrap a prosciutto slice around one slice of figs and then thread into skewer. Repeat process for remaining Ingredients. Place on skewer rack in air fryer.
2.   For 8 minutes, cook on 390°F. Halfway through cooking time, turnover skewers.
3.   Serve and enjoy.

Crispy Pork Belly

Servings:4
Cooking Time: 20 Minutes
Ingredients:
- 1 pound pork belly, cut into 1" cubes
- ¼ cup soy sauce
- 1 tablespoon Worcestershire sauce

- 2 teaspoons sriracha hot chili sauce
- ½ teaspoon salt
- ¼ teaspoon ground black pepper

Directions:

1. Place pork belly into a medium sealable bowl or bag and pour in soy sauce, Worcestershire sauce, and sriracha. Seal and let marinate 30 minutes in the refrigerator.
2. Remove pork from marinade, pat dry with a paper towel, and sprinkle with salt and pepper.
3. Place pork in ungreased air fryer basket. Adjust the temperature to 360°F and set the timer for 20 minutes, shaking the basket halfway through cooking. Pork belly will be done when it has an internal temperature of at least 145°F and is golden brown.
4. Let pork belly rest on a large plate 10 minutes. Serve warm.

Herbed Beef Roast

Servings:5
Cooking Time:45 Minutes
Ingredients:

- 2 pounds beef roast
- 1 tablespoon olive oil
- 1 teaspoon dried rosemary, crushed
- 1 teaspoon dried thyme, crushed
- Salt, to taste

Directions:

1. Preheat the Air fryer to 360°F and grease an Air fryer basket.
2. Rub the roast generously with herb mixture and coat with olive oil.
3. Arrange the roast in the Air fryer basket and cook for about 45 minutes.
4. Dish out the roast and cover with foil for about 10 minutes.
5. Cut into desired size slices and serve.

Bourbon-bbq Sauce Marinated Beef Bbq

Servings:4
Cooking Time: 60 Minutes
Ingredients:

- ¼ cup bourbon
- ¼ cup barbecue sauce
- 1 tablespoon Worcestershire sauce
- 2 pounds beef steak, pounded
- Salt and pepper to taste

Directions:

1. Place all ingredients in a Ziploc bag and allow to marinate in the fridge for at least 2 hours.
2. Preheat the air fryer to 390°F.
3. Place the grill pan accessory in the air fryer.
4. Place on the grill pan and cook for 20 minutes per batch.

5. Halfway through the cooking time, give a stir to cook evenly.
6. Meanwhile, pour the marinade on a saucepan and allow to simmer until the sauce thickens.
7. Serve beef with the bourbon sauce.

Crouton-breaded Pork Chops

Servings:4
Cooking Time: 14 Minutes
Ingredients:

- 4 boneless pork chops
- 1 teaspoon salt
- ½ teaspoon ground black pepper
- 2 cups croutons
- ½ teaspoon dried thyme
- ¼ teaspoon dried sage
- 1 large egg, whisked
- Cooking spray

Directions:

1. Preheat the air fryer to 400°F.
2. Sprinkle pork chops with salt and pepper on both sides.
3. In a food processor, add croutons, thyme, and sage. Pulse five times until croutons are mostly broken down with a few medium-sized pieces remaining. Transfer to a medium bowl.
4. In a separate medium bowl, place egg. Dip each pork chop into egg, then press into crouton mixture to coat both sides. Spritz with cooking spray.
5. Place pork in the air fryer basket and cook 14 minutes, turning halfway through cooking time, until chops are golden brown and internal temperature reaches at least 145°F. Serve warm.

Bjorn's Beef Steak

Servings: 1
Cooking Time: 15 Minutes
Ingredients:

- 1 steak, 1-inch thick
- 1 tbsp. olive oil
- Black pepper to taste
- Sea salt to taste

Directions:

1. Place the baking tray inside the Air Fryer and pre-heat for about 5 minutes at 390°F.
2. Brush or spray both sides of the steak with the oil.
3. Season both sides with salt and pepper.
4. Take care when placing the steak in the baking tray and allow to cook for 3 minutes. Flip the meat over, and cook for an additional 3 minutes.
5. Take it out of the fryer and allow to sit for roughly 3 minutes before serving.

London Broil

Servings:4
Cooking Time: 12 Minutes
Ingredients:
- 1 pound top round steak
- 1 tablespoon Worcestershire sauce
- ¼ cup soy sauce
- 2 cloves garlic, peeled and finely minced
- ½ teaspoon ground black pepper
- ½ teaspoon salt
- 2 tablespoons salted butter, melted

Directions:
1. Place steak in a large sealable bowl or bag. Pour in Worcestershire sauce and soy sauce, then add garlic, pepper, and salt. Toss to coat. Seal and place into refrigerator to let marinate 2 hours.
2. Remove steak from marinade and pat dry. Drizzle top side with butter, then place into ungreased air fryer basket. Adjust the temperature to 375°F and set the timer for 12 minutes, turning steak halfway through cooking. Steak will be done when browned at the edges and it has an internal temperature of 150°F for medium or 180°F for well-done.
3. Let steak rest on a large plate 10 minutes before slicing into thin pieces. Serve warm.

Mozzarella-stuffed Meatloaf

Servings:6
Cooking Time: 30 Minutes
Ingredients:
- 1 pound 80/20 ground beef
- ½ medium green bell pepper, seeded and chopped
- ¼ medium yellow onion, peeled and chopped
- ½ teaspoon salt
- ¼ teaspoon ground black pepper
- 2 ounces mozzarella cheese, sliced into ¼"-thick slices
- ¼ cup low-carb ketchup

Directions:
1. In a large bowl, combine ground beef, bell pepper, onion, salt, and black pepper. Cut a piece of parchment to fit air fryer basket. Place half beef mixture on ungreased parchment and form a 9" × 4" loaf, about ½" thick.
2. Center mozzarella slices on beef loaf, leaving at least ¼" around each edge.
3. Press remaining beef into a second 9" × 4" loaf and place on top of mozzarella, pressing edges of loaves together to seal.
4. Place parchment with meatloaf into air fryer basket. Adjust the temperature to 350°F and set the timer for 30 minutes, carefully turning loaf and brushing top with ketchup halfway through cooking. Loaf will be browned and have an internal temperature of at least 180°F when done. Slice and serve warm.

Bacon And Cheese–stuffed Pork Chops

Servings:4
Cooking Time: 12 Minutes
Ingredients:
- ½ ounce plain pork rinds, finely crushed
- ½ cup shredded sharp Cheddar cheese
- 4 slices cooked sugar-free bacon, crumbled
- 4 boneless pork chops
- ½ teaspoon salt
- ¼ teaspoon ground black pepper

Directions:
1. In a small bowl, mix pork rinds, Cheddar, and bacon.
2. Make a 3" slit in the side of each pork chop and stuff with ¼ pork rind mixture. Sprinkle each side of pork chops with salt and pepper.
3. Place pork chops into ungreased air fryer basket, stuffed side up. Adjust the temperature to 400°F and set the timer for 12 minutes. Pork chops will be browned and have an internal temperature of at least 145°F when done. Serve warm.

Salty Lamb Chops

Servings: 4
Cooking Time: 8 Minutes
Ingredients:
- 1-pound lamb chops
- 1 egg, beaten
- ½ teaspoon salt
- ½ cup coconut flour
- Cooking spray

Directions:
1. Chop the lamb chops into small pieces (popcorn) and sprinkle with salt. Then add a beaten egg and stir the meat well. After this, add coconut flour and shake the lamb popcorn until all meat pieces are coated. Preheat the air fryer to 380°F. Put the lamb popcorn in the air fryer and spray it with cooking spray. Cook the lamb popcorn for 4 minutes. Then shake the meat well and cook it for 4 minutes more.

Blackened Steak Nuggets

Servings:2
Cooking Time: 7 Minutes
Ingredients:
- 1 pound rib eye steak, cut into 1" cubes
- 2 tablespoons salted butter, melted
- ½ teaspoon paprika
- ½ teaspoon salt
- ¼ teaspoon garlic powder
- ¼ teaspoon onion powder
- ¼ teaspoon ground black pepper
- ⅛ teaspoon cayenne pepper

Directions:

1. Place steak into a large bowl and pour in butter. Toss to coat. Sprinkle with remaining ingredients.
2. Place bites into ungreased air fryer basket. Adjust the temperature to 400°F and set the timer for 7 minutes, shaking the basket three times during cooking. Steak will be crispy on the outside and browned when done and internal temperature is at least 150°F for medium and 180°F for well-done. Serve warm.

Corn Dogs

Servings:4
Cooking Time: 8 Minutes
Ingredients:
- 1½ cups shredded mozzarella cheese
- 1 ounce cream cheese
- ½ cup blanched finely ground almond flour
- 4 beef hot dogs

Directions:
1. Place mozzarella, cream cheese, and flour in a large microwave-safe bowl. Microwave on high 45 seconds, then stir with a fork until a soft ball of dough forms.
2. Press dough out into a 12" × 6" rectangle, then use a knife to separate into four smaller rectangles.
3. Wrap each hot dog in one rectangle of dough and place into ungreased air fryer basket. Adjust the temperature to 400°F and set the timer for 8 minutes, turning corn dogs halfway through cooking. Corn dogs will be golden brown when done. Serve warm.

Simple Air Fryer Steak

Servings: 2
Cooking Time: 18 Minutes
Ingredients:
- 12 oz steaks, 3/4-inch thick
- 1 tsp garlic powder
- 1 tsp olive oil
- Pepper
- Salt

Directions:
1. Coat steaks with oil and season with garlic powder, pepper, and salt.
2. Preheat the air fryer to 400°F.
3. Place steaks in air fryer basket and cook for 15-18 minutes. Turn halfway through.
4. Serve and enjoy.

Pepperoni Pockets

Servings: 4
Cooking Time: 8 Minutes
Ingredients:
- 4 bread slices, 1-inch thick
- olive oil for misting
- 24 slices pepperoni
- 1 ounce roasted red peppers, drained and patted dry
- 1 ounce Pepper Jack cheese cut into 4 slices

- pizza sauce (optional)

Directions:
1. Spray both sides of bread slices with olive oil.
2. Stand slices upright and cut a deep slit in the top to create a pocket—almost to the bottom crust but not all the way through.
3. Stuff each bread pocket with 6 slices of pepperoni, a large strip of roasted red pepper, and a slice of cheese.
4. Place bread pockets in air fryer basket, standing up. Cook at 360°F for 8 minutes, until filling is heated through and bread is lightly browned. Serve while hot as is or with pizza sauce for dipping.

Crispy Smoked Pork Chops

Servings: 3
Cooking Time: 8 Minutes
Ingredients:
- ⅔ cup All-purpose flour or tapioca flour
- 1 Large egg white(s)
- 2 tablespoons Water
- 1½ cups Corn flake crumbs (gluten-free, if a concern)
- 3 ½-pound, ½-inch-thick bone-in smoked pork chops

Directions:
1. Preheat the air fryer to 375°F.
2. Set up and fill three shallow soup plates or small pie plates on your counter: one for the flour; one for the egg white(s), whisked with the water until foamy; and one for the corn flake crumbs.
3. Set a chop in the flour and turn it several times, coating both sides and the edges. Gently shake off any excess flour, then set it in the beaten egg white mixture. Turn to coat both sides as well as the edges. Let any excess egg white slip back into the rest, then set the chop in the corn flake crumbs. Turn it several times, pressing gently to coat the chop evenly on both sides and around the edge. Set the chop aside and continue coating the remaining chop(s) in the same way.
4. Set the chops in the basket with as much air space between them as possible. Air-fry undisturbed for 8 minutes, or until the coating is crunchy and the chops are heated through.
5. Use kitchen tongs to transfer the chops to a wire rack and cool for a couple of minutes before serving.

Crunchy Fried Pork Loin Chops

Servings: 3
Cooking Time: 12 Minutes
Ingredients:
- 1 cup All-purpose flour or tapioca flour
- 1 Large egg(s), well beaten
- 1½ cups Seasoned Italian-style dried bread crumbs (gluten-free, if a concern)
- 3 4- to 5-ounce boneless center-cut pork loin chops
- Vegetable oil spray

Directions:
1. Preheat the air fryer to 350°F .

2. Set up and fill three shallow soup plates or small pie plates on your counter: one for the flour, one for the beaten egg(s), and one for the bread crumbs.

3. Dredge a pork chop in the flour, coating both sides as well as around the edge. Gently shake off any excess, then dip the chop in the egg(s), again coating both sides and the edge. Let any excess egg slip back into the rest, then set the chop in the bread crumbs, turning it and pressing gently to coat well on both sides and the edge. Coat the pork chop all over with vegetable oil spray and set aside so you can dredge, coat, and spray the additional chop(s).

4. Set the chops in the basket with as much air space between them as possible. Air-fry undisturbed for 12 minutes, or until brown and crunchy and an instant-read meat thermometer inserted into the center of a chop registers 145°F.

5. Use kitchen tongs to transfer the chops to a wire rack. Cool for 5 minutes before serving.

Spinach And Mushroom Steak Rolls

Servings:4
Cooking Time: 19 Minutes
Ingredients:
- ½ medium yellow onion, peeled and chopped
- ½ cup chopped baby bella mushrooms
- 1 cup chopped fresh spinach
- 1 pound flank steak
- 8 slices provolone cheese
- 1 teaspoon salt
- ½ teaspoon ground black pepper
- Cooking spray

Directions:
1. In a medium skillet over medium heat, sauté onion 2 minutes until fragrant and beginning to soften. Add mushrooms and spinach and continue cooking 5 more minutes until spinach is wilted and mushrooms are soft.

2. Preheat the air fryer to 400°F.

3. Carefully butterfly steak, leaving the two halves connected. Place slices of cheese on top of steak, then top with cooked vegetables.

4. Place steak so that the grain runs horizontally. Tightly roll up steak and secure it closed with eight evenly placed toothpicks or eight sections of butcher's twine.

5. Slice steak into four rolls. Spritz with cooking spray, then sprinkle with salt and pepper. Place in the air fryer basket and cook 12 minutes until steak is brown on the edges and internal temperature reaches at least 160°F for well-done. Serve.

Mustard-crusted Rib-eye

Servings: 2
Cooking Time: 9 Minutes
Ingredients:
- Two 6-ounce rib-eye steaks, about 1-inch thick
- 1 teaspoon coarse salt

- ½ teaspoon coarse black pepper
- 2 tablespoons Dijon mustard

Directions:
1. Rub the steaks with the salt and pepper. Then spread the mustard on both sides of the steaks. Cover with foil and let the steaks sit at room temperature for 30 minutes.

2. Preheat the air fryer to 390°F.

3. Cook the steaks for 9 minutes. Check for an internal temperature of 140°F and immediately remove the steaks and let them rest for 5 minutes before slicing.

Maple'n Soy Marinated Beef

Servings:4
Cooking Time: 45 Minutes
Ingredients:
- 2 pounds sirloin flap steaks, pounded
- 3 tablespoons balsamic vinegar
- 3 tablespoons maple syrup
- 3 tablespoons soy sauce
- 4 cloves of garlic, minced

Directions:
1. Preheat the air fryer to 390°F.

2. Place the grill pan accessory in the air fryer.

3. On a deep dish, place the flap steaks and season with soy sauce, balsamic vinegar, and maple syrup, and garlic.

4. Place on the grill pan and cook for 15 minutes in batches.

Air Fried Thyme Garlic Lamb Chops

Servings: 4
Cooking Time: 12 Minutes
Ingredients:
- 4 lamb chops
- 4 garlic cloves, minced
- 3 tbsp olive oil
- 1 tbsp dried thyme
- Pepper
- Salt

Directions:
1. Preheat the air fryer to 390°F.

2. Season lamb chops with pepper and salt.

3. In a small bowl, mix together thyme, oil, and garlic and rub over lamb chops.

4. Place lamb chops into the air fryer and cook for 12 minutes. Turn halfway through.

5. Serve and enjoy.

Barbecue-style Beef Cube Steak

Servings: 2
Cooking Time: 14 Minutes
Ingredients:

- 2 4-ounce beef cube steak(s)
- 2 cups Fritos (original flavor) or a generic corn chip equivalent, crushed to crumbs
- 6 tablespoons Purchased smooth barbecue sauce, any flavor (gluten-free, if a concern)

Directions:

1. Preheat the air fryer to 375°F.
2. Spread the Fritos crumbs in a shallow soup plate or a small pie plate. Rub the barbecue sauce onto both sides of the steak(s). Dredge the steak(s) in the Fritos crumbs to coat well and thoroughly, turning several times and pressing down to get the little bits to adhere to the meat.
3. When the machine is at temperature, set the steak(s) in the basket. Leave as much air space between them as possible if you're working with more than one piece of beef. Air-fry undisturbed for 12 minutes, or until lightly brown and crunchy. If the machine is at 360°F, you may need to add 2 minutes to the cooking time.
4. Use kitchen tongs to transfer the steak(s) to a wire rack. Cool for 5 minutes before serving.

Marinated Steak Kebabs

Servings:4
Cooking Time: 5 Minutes
Ingredients:

- 1 pound strip steak, fat trimmed, cut into 1" cubes
- ½ cup soy sauce
- ¼ cup olive oil
- 1 tablespoon granular brown erythritol
- ½ teaspoon salt
- ¼ teaspoon ground black pepper
- 1 medium green bell pepper, seeded and chopped into 1" cubes

Directions:

1. Place steak into a large sealable bowl or bag and pour in soy sauce and olive oil. Add erythritol, then stir to coat steak. Marinate at room temperature 30 minutes.
2. Remove streak from marinade and sprinkle with salt and black pepper.
3. Place meat and vegetables onto 6" skewer sticks, alternating between steak and bell pepper.
4. Place kebabs into ungreased air fryer basket. Adjust the temperature to 400°F and set the timer for 5 minutes. Steak will be done when crispy at the edges and peppers are tender. Serve warm.

Champagne-vinegar Marinated Skirt Steak

Servings:2
Cooking Time: 40 Minutes

Ingredients:

- ¼ cup Dijon mustard
- 1 tablespoon rosemary leaves
- 1-pound skirt steak, trimmed
- 2 tablespoons champagne vinegar
- Salt and pepper to taste

Directions:

1. Place all ingredients in a Ziploc bag and marinate in the fridge for 2 hours.
2. Preheat the air fryer to 390°F.
3. Place the grill pan accessory in the air fryer.
4. Grill the skirt steak for 20 minutes per batch.
5. Flip the beef halfway through the cooking time.

Quick & Simple Bratwurst With Vegetables

Servings: 6
Cooking Time: 20 Minutes
Ingredients:

- 1 package bratwurst, sliced 1/2-inch rounds
- 1/2 tbsp Cajun seasoning
- 1/4 cup onion, diced
- 2 bell pepper, sliced

Directions:

1. Add all ingredients into the large mixing bowl and toss well.
2. Line air fryer basket with foil.
3. Add vegetable and bratwurst mixture into the air fryer basket and cook at 390°F for 10 minutes.
4. Toss well and cook for 10 minutes more.
5. Serve and enjoy.

Sweet Potato–crusted Pork Rib Chops

Servings: 2
Cooking Time: 14 Minutes
Ingredients:

- 2 Large egg white(s), well beaten
- 1½ cups Crushed sweet potato chips (certified gluten-free, if a concern)
- 1 teaspoon Ground cinnamon
- 1 teaspoon Ground dried ginger
- 1 teaspoon Table salt (optional)
- 2 10-ounce, 1-inch-thick bone-in pork rib chop(s)

Directions:

1. Preheat the air fryer to 375°F .
2. Set up and fill two shallow soup plates or small pie plates on your counter: one for the beaten egg white(s); and one for the crushed chips, mixed with the cinnamon, ginger, and salt.
3. Dip a chop in the egg white(s), coating it on both sides as well as the edges. Let the excess egg white slip back into the rest, then set it in the crushed chip mixture. Turn it

several times, pressing gently, until evenly coated on both sides and the edges. If necessary, set the chop aside and coat the remaining chop(s).

4. Set the chop(s) in the basket with as much air space between them as possible. Air-fry undisturbed for 12 minutes, or until crunchy and browned and an instant-read meat thermometer inserted into the center of a chop registers 145°F. If the machine is at 360°F, you may need to add 2 minutes to the cooking time.

5. Use kitchen tongs to transfer the chop(s) to a wire rack. Cool for 2 or 3 minutes before serving.

Steakhouse Filets Mignons

Servings: 3
Cooking Time: 12-15 Minutes
Ingredients:
- ¾ ounce Dried porcini mushrooms
- ¼ teaspoon Granulated white sugar
- ¼ teaspoon Ground white pepper
- ¼ teaspoon Table salt
- 6 ¼-pound filets mignons or beef tenderloin steaks
- 6 Thin-cut bacon strips (gluten-free, if a concern)

Directions:
1. Preheat the air fryer to 400°F.
2. Grind the dried mushrooms in a clean spice grinder until powdery. Add the sugar, white pepper, and salt. Grind to blend.
3. Rub this mushroom mixture into both cut sides of each filet. Wrap the circumference of each filet with a strip of bacon.
4. Set the filets mignons in the basket on their sides with the bacon seam side down. Do not let the filets touch; keep at least ¼ inch open between them. Air-fry undisturbed for 12 minutes for rare, or until an instant-read meat thermometer inserted into the center of a filet registers 125°F; 13 minutes for medium-rare, or until an instant-read meat thermometer inserted into the center of a filet registers 132°F; or 15 minutes for medium, or until an instant-read meat thermometer inserted into the center of a filet registers 145°F.
5. Use kitchen tongs to transfer the filets to a wire rack, setting them cut side down. Cool for 5 minutes before serving.

Spice-coated Steaks

Servings:2
Cooking Time: 15 Minutes
Ingredients:
- ½ tsp cayenne pepper
- 1 tbsp olive oil
- ½ tsp ground paprika
- Salt and black pepper to taste

Directions:
1. Preheat air fryer to 390°F. Mix olive oil, black pepper, cayenne, paprika, and salt and rub onto steaks. Spread

evenly. Put the steaks in the fryer, and cook for 6 minutes, turning them halfway through.

Salted 'n Peppered Scored Beef Chuck

Servings:6
Cooking Time: 1 Hour And 30 Minutes
Ingredients:
- 2 ounces black peppercorns
- 2 tablespoons olive oil
- 3 pounds beef chuck roll, scored with knife
- 3 tablespoons salt

Directions:
1. Preheat the air fryer to 390°F.
2. Place the grill pan accessory in the air fryer.
3. Season the beef chuck roll with black peppercorns and salt.
4. Brush with olive oil and cover top with foil.
5. Grill for 1 hour and 30 minutes.
6. Flip the beef every 30 minutes for even grilling on all sides.

Beef Al Carbon (street Taco Meat)

Servings: 6
Cooking Time: 8 Minutes
Ingredients:
- 1½ pounds sirloin steak, cut into ½-inch cubes
- ¾ cup lime juice
- ½ cup extra-virgin olive oil
- 1 teaspoon ground cumin
- 2 teaspoons garlic powder
- 1 teaspoon salt

Directions:
1. In a large bowl, toss together the steak, lime juice, olive oil, cumin, garlic powder, and salt. Allow the meat to marinate for 30 minutes. Drain off all the marinade and pat the meat dry with paper towels.
2. Preheat the air fryer to 400°F.
3. Place the meat in the air fryer basket and spray with cooking spray. Cook the meat for 5 minutes, toss the meat, and continue cooking another 3 minutes, until slightly crispy.

Egg Stuffed Pork Meatballs

Servings: 2
Cooking Time: 40 Minutes
Ingredients:
- 3 soft boiled eggs, peeled
- 8 oz ground pork
- 2 tsp dried tarragon
- ½ tsp hot paprika
- 2 tsp garlic powder
- Salt and pepper to taste

Directions:

1. Preheat air fryer to 350°F. Combine the pork, tarragon, hot paprika, garlic powder, salt, and pepper in a bowl and stir until all spices are evenly spread throughout the meat. Divide the meat mixture into three equal portions in the mixing bowl, and shape each into balls.

2. Flatten one of the meatballs on top to make a wide, flat meat circle. Place an egg in the middle. Use your hands to mold the mixture up and around to enclose the egg. Repeat with the remaining eggs. Place the stuffed balls in the air fryer. Air Fry for 18-20 minutes, shaking the basket once until the meat is crispy and golden brown. Serve.

Easy & The Traditional Beef Roast Recipe

Servings:12
Cooking Time: 2 Hours
Ingredients:
- 1 cup organic beef broth
- 3 pounds beef round roast
- 4 tablespoons olive oil
- Salt and pepper to taste

Directions:
1. Place in a Ziploc bag all the ingredients and allow to marinate in the fridge for 2 hours.
2. Preheat the air fryer for 5 minutes.
3. Transfer all ingredients in a baking dish that will fit in the air fryer.
4. Place in the air fryer and cook for 2 hours for 400°F.

Delicious Cheeseburgers

Servings: 4
Cooking Time: 12 Minutes
Ingredients:
- 1 lb ground beef
- 4 cheddar cheese slices
- 1/2 tsp Italian seasoning
- Pepper
- Salt
- Cooking spray

Directions:
1. Spray air fryer basket with cooking spray.
2. In a bowl, mix together ground beef, Italian seasoning, pepper, and salt.
3. Make four equal shapes of patties from meat mixture and place into the air fryer basket.
4. Cook at 375°F for 5 minutes. Turn patties to another side and cook for 5 minutes more.
5. Place cheese slices on top of each patty and cook for 2 minutes more.
6. Serve and enjoy.

Honey Mesquite Pork Chops

Servings: 2
Cooking Time: 10 Minutes

Ingredients:
- 2 tablespoons mesquite seasoning
- ¼ cup honey
- 1 tablespoon olive oil
- 1 tablespoon water
- freshly ground black pepper
- 2 bone-in center cut pork chops

Directions:
1. Whisk the mesquite seasoning, honey, olive oil, water and freshly ground black pepper together in a shallow glass dish. Pierce the chops all over and on both sides with a fork or meat tenderizer. Add the pork chops to the marinade and massage the marinade into the chops. Cover and marinate for 30 minutes.
2. Preheat the air fryer to 330°F.
3. Transfer the pork chops to the air fryer basket and pour half of the marinade over the chops, reserving the remaining marinade. Air-fry the pork chops for 6 minutes. Flip the pork chops over and pour the remaining marinade on top. Air-fry for an additional 3 minutes at 330°F. Then, increase the air fryer temperature to 400°F and air-fry the pork chops for an additional minute.
4. Transfer the pork chops to a serving plate, and let them rest for 5 minutes before serving. If you'd like a sauce for these chops, pour the cooked marinade from the bottom of the air fryer over the top.

Crispy Lamb Shoulder Chops

Servings: 3
Cooking Time: 28 Minutes
Ingredients:
- ¾ cup All-purpose flour or gluten-free all-purpose flour
- 2 teaspoons Mild paprika
- 2 teaspoons Table salt
- 1½ teaspoons Garlic powder
- 1½ teaspoons Dried sage leaves
- 3 6-ounce bone-in lamb shoulder chops, any excess fat trimmed
- Olive oil spray

Directions:
1. Whisk the flour, paprika, salt, garlic powder, and sage in a large bowl until the mixture is of a uniform color. Add the chops and toss well to coat. Transfer them to a cutting board.
2. Preheat the air fryer to 375°F .
3. When the machine is at temperature, again dredge the chops one by one in the flour mixture. Lightly coat both sides of each chop with olive oil spray before putting it in the basket. Continue on with the remaining chop(s), leaving air space between them in the basket.
4. Air-fry, turning once, for 25 minutes, or until the chops are well browned and tender when pierced with the point of a paring knife. If the machine is at 360°F, you may need to add up to 3 minutes to the cooking time.
5. Use kitchen tongs to transfer the chops to a wire rack. Cool for 5 minutes before serving.

Lamb Chops

Servings: 2

Cooking Time: 20 Minutes

Ingredients:

- 2 teaspoons oil
- ½ teaspoon ground rosemary
- ½ teaspoon lemon juice
- 1 pound lamb chops, approximately 1-inch thick
- salt and pepper
- cooking spray

Directions:

1. Mix the oil, rosemary, and lemon juice together and rub into all sides of the lamb chops. Season to taste with salt and pepper.
2. For best flavor, cover lamb chops and allow them to rest in the fridge for 20 minutes.
3. Spray air fryer basket with nonstick spray and place lamb chops in it.
4. Cook at 360°F for approximately 20minutes. This will cook chops to medium. The meat will be juicy but have no remaining pink. Cook for a minute or two longer for well done chops. For rare chops, stop cooking after about 12minutes and check for doneness.

Air Fried Grilled Steak

Servings:2

Cooking Time: 45 Minutes

Ingredients:

- 2 top sirloin steaks
- 3 tablespoons butter, melted
- 3 tablespoons olive oil
- Salt and pepper to taste

Directions:

1. Preheat the air fryer for 5 minutes.
2. Season the sirloin steaks with olive oil, salt and pepper.
3. Place the beef in the air fryer basket.
4. Cook for 45 minutes at 350°F.
5. Once cooked, serve with butter.

Perfect Pork Chops

Servings: 3

Cooking Time: 10 Minutes

Ingredients:

- ¾ teaspoon Mild paprika
- ¾ teaspoon Dried thyme
- ¾ teaspoon Onion powder
- ¼ teaspoon Garlic powder
- ¼ teaspoon Table salt
- ¼ teaspoon Ground black pepper
- 3 6-ounce boneless center-cut pork loin chops
- Vegetable oil spray

Directions:

1. Preheat the air fryer to 400°F.

2. Mix the paprika, thyme, onion powder, garlic powder, salt, and pepper in a small bowl until well combined. Massage this mixture into both sides of the chops. Generously coat both sides of the chops with vegetable oil spray.
3. When the machine is at temperature, set the chops in the basket with as much air space between them as possible. Air-fry undisturbed for 10 minutes, or until an instant-read meat thermometer inserted into the thickest part of a chop registers 145°F.
4. Use kitchen tongs to transfer the chops to a cutting board or serving plates. Cool for 5 minutes before serving.

Bacon With Shallot And Greens

Servings: 2

Cooking Time: 10 Minutes

Ingredients:

- 7 ounces mixed greens
- 8 thick slices pork bacon
- 2 shallots, peeled and diced
- Nonstick cooking spray

Directions:

1. Begin by preheating the air fryer to 345°F.
2. Now, add the shallot and bacon to the Air Fryer cooking basket; set the timer for 2 minutes. Spritz with a nonstick cooking spray.
3. After that, pause the Air Fryer; throw in the mixed greens; give it a good stir and cook an additional 5 minutes. Serve warm.

Caramelized Pork

Servings:6

Cooking Time:17 Minutes

Ingredients:

- 2 pounds pork shoulder, cut into 1½-inch thick slices
- 1/3 cup soy sauce
- 2 tablespoons sugar
- 1 tablespoon honey

Directions:

1. Preheat the Air fryer to 335°F and grease an Air fryer basket.
2. Mix all the ingredients in a large bowl and coat chops well.
3. Cover and refrigerate for about 8 hours.
4. Arrange the chops in the Air fryer basket and cook for about 10 minutes, flipping once in between.
5. Set the Air fryer to 390°F and cook for 7 more minutes.
6. Dish out in a platter and serve hot.

Simple Lamb Chops

Servings:2
Cooking Time:6 Minutes
Ingredients:
- 4 lamb chops
- Salt and black pepper, to taste
- 1 tablespoon olive oil

Directions:
1. Preheat the Air fryer to 390°F and grease an Air fryer basket.
2. Mix the olive oil, salt, and black pepper in a large bowl and add chops.
3. Arrange the chops in the Air fryer basket and cook for about 6 minutes.
4. Dish out the lamb chops and serve hot.

Pork Spare Ribs

Servings:4
Cooking Time: 30 Minutes
Ingredients:
- 1 rack pork spare ribs
- 1 teaspoon ground cumin
- 2 teaspoons salt
- 1 teaspoon ground black pepper
- 1 teaspoon garlic powder
- ½ teaspoon dry ground mustard
- ½ cup low-carb barbecue sauce

Directions:
1. Place ribs on ungreased aluminum foil sheet. Carefully use a knife to remove membrane and sprinkle meat evenly on both sides with cumin, salt, pepper, garlic powder, and ground mustard.
2. Cut rack into portions that will fit in your air fryer, and wrap each portion in one layer of aluminum foil, working in batches if needed.
3. Place ribs into ungreased air fryer basket. Adjust the temperature to 400°F and set the timer for 25 minutes.
4. When the timer beeps, carefully remove ribs from foil and brush with barbecue sauce. Return to air fryer and cook at 400°F for an additional 5 minutes to brown. Ribs will be done when no pink remains and internal temperature is at least 180°F. Serve warm.

Chapter 5. Poultry Recipes

15-minute Chicken

Servings:4
Cooking Time: 15 Minutes
Ingredients:
- 4 boneless, skinless chicken breasts
- 2 tablespoons olive oil
- 1 teaspoon salt
- 1 teaspoon garlic powder
- 1 teaspoon paprika
- ½ teaspoon ground black pepper

Directions:
1. Preheat the air fryer to 375°F.
2. Carefully butterfly chicken breasts lengthwise, leaving the two halves connected. Drizzle chicken with oil, then sprinkle with salt, garlic powder, paprika, and pepper.
3. Place in the air fryer basket and cook 15 minutes, turning halfway through cooking time, until chicken is golden brown and the internal temperature reaches at least 165°F. Serve warm.

Jerk Chicken Wings

Servings:4
Cooking Time: 1 Hour 20 Minutes
Ingredients:
- ¼ cup Jamaican jerk marinade
- 1 teaspoon onion powder
- 1 teaspoon garlic powder
- 1 teaspoon salt
- 2 pounds chicken wings, flats and drums separated

Directions:
1. In a large bowl, combine jerk seasoning, onion powder, garlic powder, and salt. Add chicken wings and toss to coat well. Cover and let marinate in refrigerator at least 1 hour.
2. Preheat the air fryer to 400°F.
3. Place wings in the air fryer basket in a single layer, working in batches as necessary. Cook wings 20 minutes, turning halfway through cooking time, until internal temperature reaches at least 165°F. Cool 5 minutes before serving.

Crispy "fried" Chicken

Servings: 4
Cooking Time: 14 Minutes
Ingredients:
- ¾ cup all-purpose flour
- ½ teaspoon paprika
- ¼ teaspoon black pepper

- ¼ teaspoon salt
- 2 large eggs
- 1½ cups panko breadcrumbs
- 1 pound boneless, skinless chicken tenders

Directions:
1. Preheat the air fryer to 400°F.
2. In a shallow bowl, mix the flour with the paprika, pepper, and salt.
3. In a separate bowl, whisk the eggs; set aside.
4. In a third bowl, place the breadcrumbs.
5. Liberally spray the air fryer basket with olive oil spray.
6. Pat the chicken tenders dry with a paper towel. Dredge the tenders one at a time in the flour, then dip them in the egg, and toss them in the breadcrumb coating. Repeat until all tenders are coated.
7. Set each tender in the air fryer, leaving room on each side of the tender to allow for flipping.
8. When the basket is full, cook 4 to 7 minutes, flip, and cook another 4 to 7 minutes.
9. Remove the tenders and let cool 5 minutes before serving. Repeat until all tenders are cooked.

Paprika Duck

Servings: 6
Cooking Time: 28 Minutes
Ingredients:
- 10 oz duck skin
- 1 teaspoon sunflower oil
- ½ teaspoon salt
- ½ teaspoon ground paprika

Directions:
1. Preheat the air fryer to 375°F. Then sprinkle the duck skin with sunflower oil, salt, and ground paprika. Put the duck skin in the air fryer and cook it for 18 minutes. Then flip it on another side and cook for 10 minutes more or until it is crunchy from both sides.

Creamy Chicken Tenders

Servings:8
Cooking Time:20 Minutes
Ingredients:
- 2 pounds chicken tenders
- 1 cup feta cheese
- 4 tablespoons olive oil
- 1 cup cream
- Salt and black pepper, to taste

Directions:
1. Preheat the Air fryer to 340°F and grease an Air fryer basket.
2. Season the chicken tenders with salt and black pepper.
3. Arrange the chicken tenderloins in the Air fryer basket and drizzle with olive oil.
4. Cook for about 15 minutes and set the Air fryer to 390°F.

5. Cook for about 5 more minutes and dish out to serve warm.
6. Repeat with the remaining mixture and dish out to serve hot.

Cajun-breaded Chicken Bites

Servings:4
Cooking Time: 12 Minutes
Ingredients:
- 1 pound boneless, skinless chicken breasts, cut into 1" cubes
- ½ cup heavy whipping cream
- ½ teaspoon salt
- ¼ teaspoon ground black pepper
- 1 ounce plain pork rinds, finely crushed
- ¼ cup unflavored whey protein powder
- ½ teaspoon Cajun seasoning

Directions:
1. Place chicken in a medium bowl and pour in cream. Stir to coat. Sprinkle with salt and pepper.
2. In a separate large bowl, combine pork rinds, protein powder, and Cajun seasoning. Remove chicken from cream, shaking off any excess, and toss in dry mix until fully coated.
3. Place bites into ungreased air fryer basket. Adjust the temperature to 400°F and set the timer for 12 minutes, shaking the basket twice during cooking. Bites will be done when golden brown and have an internal temperature of at least 165°F. Serve warm.

Cheesy Chicken Nuggets

Servings:4
Cooking Time: 15 Minutes
Ingredients:
- 1 pound ground chicken thighs
- ½ cup shredded mozzarella cheese
- 1 large egg, whisked
- ½ teaspoon salt
- ¼ teaspoon dried oregano
- ¼ teaspoon garlic powder

Directions:
1. In a large bowl, combine all ingredients. Form mixture into twenty nugget shapes, about 2 tablespoons each.
2. Place nuggets into ungreased air fryer basket, working in batches if needed. Adjust the temperature to 375°F and set the timer for 15 minutes, turning nuggets halfway through cooking. Let cool 5 minutes before serving.

Baked Chicken Nachos

Servings:4
Cooking Time: 7 Minutes
Ingredients:
- 50 tortilla chips
- 2 cups shredded cooked chicken breast, divided
- 2 cups shredded Mexican-blend cheese, divided

- ½ cup sliced pickled jalapeño peppers, divided
- ½ cup diced red onion, divided

Directions:
1. Preheat the air fryer to 300°F.
2. Use foil to make a bowl shape that fits the shape of the air fryer basket. Place half tortilla chips in the bottom of foil bowl, then top with 1 cup chicken, 1 cup cheese, ¼ cup jalapeños, and ¼ cup onion. Repeat with remaining chips and toppings.
3. Place foil bowl in the air fryer basket and cook 7 minutes until cheese is melted and toppings heated through. Serve warm.

Herb Seasoned Turkey Breast

Servings: 4
Cooking Time: 35 Minutes

Ingredients:
- 2 lbs turkey breast
- 1 tsp fresh sage, chopped
- 1 tsp fresh rosemary, chopped
- 1 tsp fresh thyme, chopped
- Pepper
- Salt

Directions:
1. Spray air fryer basket with cooking spray.
2. In a small bowl, mix together sage, rosemary, and thyme.
3. Season turkey breast with pepper and salt and rub with herb mixture.
4. Place turkey breast in air fryer basket and cook at 390°F for 30-35 minutes.
5. Slice and serve.

Tuscan Stuffed Chicken

Servings: 4
Cooking Time: 30 Minutes

Ingredients:
- 1/3 cup ricotta cheese
- 1 cup Tuscan kale, chopped
- 4 chicken breasts
- 1 tbsp chicken seasoning
- Salt and pepper to taste
- 1 tsp paprika

Directions:
1. Preheat air fryer to 370°F. Soften the ricotta cheese in a microwave-safe bowl for 15 seconds. Combine in a bowl along with Tuscan kale. Set aside. Cut 4-5 slits in the top of each chicken breast about ¾ of the way down. Season with chicken seasoning, salt, and pepper.
2. Place the chicken with the slits facing up in the greased frying basket. Lightly spray the chicken with oil. Bake for 6-8 minutes. Slide-out and stuff the cream cheese mixture into the chicken slits. Sprinkle ½ tsp of paprika and cook for another 3 minutes. Serve and enjoy!

Buttermilk Brined Turkey Breast

Servings:8
Cooking Time:20 Minutes

Ingredients:
- ¾ cup brine from a can of olives
- 3½ pounds boneless, skinless turkey breast
- 2 fresh thyme sprigs
- 1 fresh rosemary sprig
- ½ cup buttermilk

Directions:
1. Preheat the Air fryer to 350°F and grease an Air fryer basket.
2. Mix olive brine and buttermilk in a bowl until well combined.
3. Place the turkey breast, buttermilk mixture and herb sprigs in a resealable plastic bag.
4. Seal the bag and refrigerate for about 12 hours.
5. Remove the turkey breast from bag and arrange the turkey breast into the Air fryer basket.
6. Cook for about 20 minutes, flipping once in between.
7. Dish out the turkey breast onto a cutting board and cut into desired size slices to serve.

Pretzel-crusted Chicken

Servings:4
Cooking Time: 12 Minutes

Ingredients:
- 2 cups mini twist pretzels
- ½ cup mayonnaise
- 2 tablespoons honey
- 2 tablespoons yellow mustard
- 4 boneless, skinless chicken breasts, sliced in half lengthwise
- 1 teaspoon salt
- ½ teaspoon ground black pepper
- Cooking spray

Directions:
1. Preheat the air fryer to 375°F.
2. In a food processor, place pretzels and pulse ten times.
3. In a medium bowl, mix mayonnaise, honey, and mustard.
4. Sprinkle chicken with salt and pepper, then brush with sauce mixture until well coated.
5. Pour pretzel crumbs onto a shallow plate and press each piece of chicken into them until well coated.
6. Spritz chicken with cooking spray and place in the air fryer basket. Cook 12 minutes, turning halfway through cooking time, until edges are golden brown and the internal temperature reaches at least 165°F. Serve warm.

Dill Pickle–ranch Wings

Servings:4
Cooking Time: 2 Hours 20 Minutes
Ingredients:
- 1 cup pickle juice
- 2 pounds chicken wings, flats and drums separated
- ½ teaspoon salt
- ½ teaspoon ground black pepper
- 2 teaspoons dry ranch seasoning

Directions:
1. In a large bowl or resealable plastic bag, combine pickle juice and wings. Cover and let marinate in refrigerator 2 hours.
2. Preheat the air fryer to 400°F.
3. In a separate bowl, mix salt, pepper, and ranch seasoning. Remove wings from marinade and toss in dry seasoning.
4. Place wings in the air fryer basket in a single layer, working in batches as necessary. Cook 20 minutes, turning halfway through cooking time, until wings reach an internal temperature of at least 165°F. Cool 5 minutes before serving.

Roasted Chicken

Servings: 6
Cooking Time: 90 Minutes
Ingredients:
- 6 lb. whole chicken
- 1 tsp. olive oil
- 1 tbsp. minced garlic
- 1 white onion, peeled and halved
- 3 tbsp. butter

Directions:
1. Pre-heat the fryer at 360°F.
2. Massage the chicken with the olive oil and the minced garlic.
3. Place the peeled and halved onion, as well as the butter, inside of the chicken.
4. Cook the chicken in the fryer for seventy-five minutes.
5. Take care when removing the chicken from the fryer, then carve and serve.

Crispy 'n Salted Chicken Meatballs

Servings:6
Cooking Time: 20 Minutes
Ingredients:
- ½ cup almond flour
- ¾ pound skinless boneless chicken breasts, ground
- 1 ½ teaspoon herbs de Provence
- 1 tablespoon coconut milk
- 2 eggs, beaten
- Salt and pepper to taste

Directions:
1. Mix all ingredient in a bowl.
2. Form small balls using the palms of your hands.

3. Place in the fridge to set for at least 2 hours.
4. Preheat the air fryer for 5 minutes.
5. Place the chicken balls in the fryer basket.
6. Cook for 20 minutes at 325°F.
7. Halfway through the cooking time, give the fryer basket a shake to cook evenly on all sides.

Crispy Tender Parmesan Chicken

Servings:2
Cooking Time: 20 Minutes
Ingredients:
- 1 tablespoon butter, melted
- 2 chicken breasts
- 2 tablespoons parmesan cheese
- 6 tablespoons almond flour

Directions:
1. Preheat the air fryer for 5 minutes.
2. Combine the almond flour and parmesan cheese in a plate.
3. Drizzle the chicken breasts with butter.
4. Dredge in the almond flour mixture.
5. Place in the fryer basket.
6. Cook for 20 minutes at 350°F.

Chicken Wrapped In Bacon

Servings: 6
Cooking Time: 25 Minutes
Ingredients:
- 6 rashers unsmoked back bacon
- 1 small chicken breast
- 1 tbsp. garlic soft cheese

Directions:
1. Cut the chicken breast into six bite-sized pieces.
2. Spread the soft cheese across one side of each slice of bacon.
3. Put the chicken on top of the cheese and wrap the bacon around it, holding it in place with a toothpick.
4. Transfer the wrapped chicken pieces to the Air Fryer and cook for 15 minutes at 350°F.

Butter And Bacon Chicken

Servings:6
Cooking Time: 65 Minutes
Ingredients:
- 1 whole chicken
- 2 tablespoons salted butter, softened
- 1 teaspoon dried thyme
- ½ teaspoon garlic powder
- 1 teaspoon salt
- ½ teaspoon ground black pepper
- 6 slices sugar-free bacon

Directions:
1. Pat chicken dry with a paper towel, then rub with butter on all sides. Sprinkle thyme, garlic powder, salt, and pepper over chicken.

2. Place chicken into ungreased air fryer basket, breast side up. Lay strips of bacon over chicken and secure with toothpicks.

3. Adjust the temperature to 350°F and set the timer for 65 minutes. Halfway through cooking, remove and set aside bacon and flip chicken over. Chicken will be done when the skin is golden and crispy and the internal temperature is at least 165°F. Serve warm with bacon.

Crispy Cajun Fried Chicken

Servings: 4
Cooking Time: 50 Minutes
Ingredients:
- 4 boneless, skinless chicken thighs
- ¾ cup buttermilk
- ⅓ cup hot sauce
- 1 ½ tablespoons Cajun seasoning, divided
- 1 cup all-purpose flour
- 1 large egg

Directions:
1. Preheat the air fryer to 375°F.
2. In a large bowl, combine chicken thighs, buttermilk, hot sauce, and ½ tablespoon Cajun seasoning, and toss to coat. Cover and let marinate in refrigerator at least 30 minutes.
3. In a large bowl, whisk flour with ½ tablespoon Cajun seasoning. In a medium bowl, whisk egg.
4. Remove chicken from marinade and sprinkle with remaining ½ tablespoon Cajun seasoning.
5. Dredge chicken by dipping into egg, then pressing into flour to fully coat. Spritz with cooking spray and place into the air fryer basket.
6. Cook 20 minutes, turning halfway through cooking time, until chicken is golden brown and internal temperature reaches at least 165°F. Serve warm.

Easy & Crispy Chicken Wings

Servings: 8
Cooking Time: 20 Minutes
Ingredients:
- 1 1/2 lbs chicken wings
- 2 tbsp olive oil
- Pepper
- Salt

Directions:
1. Toss chicken wings with oil and place in the air fryer basket.
2. Cook chicken wings at 370°F for 15 minutes.
3. Shake basket and cook at 400 F for 5 minutes more.
4. Season chicken wings with pepper and salt.
5. Serve and enjoy.

Teriyaki Chicken Legs

Servings: 2
Cooking Time: 20 Minutes
Ingredients:

- 4 tablespoons teriyaki sauce
- 1 tablespoon orange juice
- 1 teaspoon smoked paprika
- 4 chicken legs
- cooking spray

Directions:
1. Mix together the teriyaki sauce, orange juice, and smoked paprika. Brush on all sides of chicken legs.
2. Spray air fryer basket with nonstick cooking spray and place chicken in basket.
3. Cook at 360°F for 6minutes. Turn and baste with sauce. Cook for 6 moreminutes, turn and baste. Cook for 8 minutes more, until juices run clear when chicken is pierced with a fork.

Surprisingly Tasty Chicken

Servings:4
Cooking Time:1 Hour
Ingredients:
- 1 whole chicken
- 1 pound small potatoes
- Salt and black pepper, to taste
- 1 tablespoon olive oil, scrubbed

Directions:
1. Preheat the Air fryer to 390°F and grease an Air fryer basket.
2. Season the chicken with salt and black pepper and transfer into the Air fryer.
3. Cook for about 40 minutes and dish out in a plate, covering with a foil paper.
4. Mix potato, oil, salt and black pepper in a bowl and toss to coat well
5. Arrange the potatoes into the Air fryer basket and cook for 20 minutes.
6. Dish out and serve warm.

Jerk Chicken Kebabs

Servings:4
Cooking Time: 14 Minutes
Ingredients:
- 8 ounces boneless, skinless chicken thighs, cut into 1" cubes
- 2 tablespoons jerk seasoning
- 2 tablespoons coconut oil
- ½ medium red bell pepper, seeded and cut into 1" pieces
- ¼ medium red onion, peeled and cut into 1" pieces
- ½ teaspoon salt

Directions:
1. Place chicken in a medium bowl and sprinkle with jerk seasoning and coconut oil. Toss to coat on all sides.
2. Using eight 6" skewers, build skewers by alternating chicken, pepper, and onion pieces, about three repetitions per skewer.

3. Sprinkle salt over skewers and place into ungreased air fryer basket. Adjust the temperature to 370°F and set the timer for 14 minutes, turning skewers halfway through cooking. Chicken will be golden and have an internal temperature of at least 165°F when done. Serve warm.

Crunchy Chicken Strips

Servings: 4
Cooking Time: 40 Minutes
Ingredients:
- 1 chicken breast, sliced into strips
- 1 tbsp grated Parmesan cheese
- 1 cup breadcrumbs
- 1 tbsp chicken seasoning
- 2 eggs, beaten
- Salt and pepper to taste

Directions:
1. Preheat air fryer to 350°F. Mix the breadcrumbs, Parmesan cheese, chicken seasoning, salt, and pepper in a mixing bowl. Coat the chicken with the crumb mixture, then dip in the beaten eggs. Finally, coat again with the dry ingredients. Arrange the coated chicken pieces on the greased frying basket and Air Fry for 15 minutes. Turn over halfway through cooking and cook for another 15 minutes. Serve immediately.

Pecan-crusted Chicken Tenders

Servings:4
Cooking Time: 12 Minutes
Ingredients:
- 2 tablespoons mayonnaise
- 1 teaspoon Dijon mustard
- 1 pound boneless, skinless chicken tenders
- ½ teaspoon salt
- ¼ teaspoon ground black pepper
- ½ cup chopped roasted pecans, finely ground

Directions:
1. In a small bowl, whisk mayonnaise and mustard until combined. Brush mixture onto chicken tenders on both sides, then sprinkle tenders with salt and pepper.
2. Place pecans in a medium bowl and press each tender into pecans to coat each side.
3. Place tenders into ungreased air fryer basket in a single layer, working in batches if needed. Adjust the temperature to 375°F and set the timer for 12 minutes, turning tenders halfway through cooking. Tenders will be golden brown and have an internal temperature of at least 165°F when done. Serve warm.

Sweet Nutty Chicken Breasts

Servings:4
Cooking Time: 30 Minutes
Ingredients:
- 2 chicken breasts, halved lengthwise
- ¼ cup honey mustard

- ¼ cup chopped pecans
- 1 tbsp olive oil
- 1 tbsp parsley, chopped

Directions:
1. Preheat air fryer to 350°F. Brush chicken breasts with honey mustard and olive oil on all sides. Place the pecans in a bowl. Add and coat the chicken breasts. Place the breasts in the greased frying basket and Air Fry for 25 minutes, turning once. Let chill onto a serving plate for 5 minutes. Sprinkle with parsley and serve.

Fantasy Sweet Chili Chicken Strips

Servings: 2
Cooking Time: 20 Minutes
Ingredients:
- 1 lb chicken strips
- 1 cup sweet chili sauce
- ½ cup bread crumbs
- ½ cup cornmeal

Directions:
1. Preheat air fryer at 350°F. Combine chicken strips and sweet chili sauce in a bowl until fully coated. In another bowl, mix the remaining ingredients. Dredge strips in the mixture. Shake off any excess. Place chicken strips in the greased frying basket and Air Fry for 10 minutes, tossing once. Serve right away.

Ginger Turmeric Chicken Thighs

Servings:4
Cooking Time: 25 Minutes
Ingredients:
- 4 boneless, skin-on chicken thighs
- 2 tablespoons coconut oil, melted
- ½ teaspoon ground turmeric
- ½ teaspoon salt
- ½ teaspoon garlic powder
- ½ teaspoon ground ginger
- ¼ teaspoon ground black pepper

Directions:
1. Place chicken thighs in a large bowl and drizzle with coconut oil. Sprinkle with remaining ingredients and toss to coat both sides of thighs.
2. Place thighs skin side up into ungreased air fryer basket. Adjust the temperature to 400°F and set the timer for 25 minutes. After 10 minutes, turn thighs. When 5 minutes remain, flip thighs once more. Chicken will be done when skin is golden brown and the internal temperature is at least 165°F. Serve warm.

Pulled Turkey Quesadillas

Servings: 4
Cooking Time: 15 Minutes
Ingredients:
- ¾ cup pulled cooked turkey breast
- 6 tortilla wraps
- 1/3 cup grated Swiss cheese
- 1 small red onion, sliced
- 2 tbsp Mexican chili sauce

Directions:
1. Preheat air fryer to 400°F. Lay 3 tortilla wraps on a clean workspace, then spoon equal amounts of Swiss cheese, turkey, Mexican chili sauce, and red onion on the tortillas. Spritz the exterior of the tortillas with cooking spray. Air Fry the quesadillas, one at a time, for 5-8 minutes. The cheese should be melted and the outsides crispy. Serve.

Stuffed Chicken

Servings: 2
Cooking Time: 11 Minutes
Ingredients:
- 8 oz chicken fillet
- 3 oz Blue cheese
- ½ teaspoon salt
- ½ teaspoon thyme
- 1 teaspoon sesame oil

Directions:
1. Cut the fillet into halves and beat them gently with the help of the kitchen hammer. After this, make the horizontal cut in every fillet. Sprinkle the chicken with salt and thyme. Then fill it with Blue cheese and secure the cut with the help of the toothpick. Sprinkle the stuffed chicken fillets with sesame oil. Preheat the air fryer to 385°F. Put the chicken fillets in the air fryer and cook them for 7 minutes. Then carefully flip the chicken fillets on another side and cook for 4 minutes more.

Basic Chicken Breasts.

Servings:4
Cooking Time: 15 Minutes
Ingredients:
- 2 tsp olive oil
- 2 chicken breasts
- Salt and pepper to taste
- ½ tsp garlic powder
- ½ tsp rosemary

Directions:
1. Preheat air fryer to 350ºF. Rub the chicken breasts with olive oil over tops and bottom and sprinkle with garlic powder, rosemary, salt, and pepper. Place the chicken in the frying basket and Air Fry for 9 minutes, flipping once. Let rest onto a serving plate for 5 minutes before cutting into cubes. Serve and enjoy!

Buffalo Chicken Meatballs

Servings:5
Cooking Time: 12 Minutes
Ingredients:
- 1 pound ground chicken breast
- 1 packet dry ranch seasoning
- ⅓ cup plain bread crumbs
- 3 tablespoons mayonnaise
- 5 tablespoons buffalo sauce, divided

Directions:
1. Preheat the air fryer to 370°F.
2. In a large bowl, mix chicken, ranch seasoning, bread crumbs, and mayonnaise. Pour in 2 tablespoons buffalo sauce and stir to combine.
3. Roll meat mixture into balls, about 2 tablespoons for each, to make twenty meatballs.
4. Place meatballs in the air fryer basket and cook 12 minutes, shaking the basket twice during cooking, until brown and internal temperature reaches at least 165°F.
5. Toss meatballs in remaining buffalo sauce and serve.

Chicken & Pepperoni Pizza

Servings: 6
Cooking Time: 20 Minutes
Ingredients:
- 2 cups cooked chicken, cubed
- 20 slices pepperoni
- 1 cup sugar-free pizza sauce
- 1 cup mozzarella cheese, shredded
- ¼ cup parmesan cheese, grated

Directions:
1. Place the chicken into the base of a four-cup baking dish and add the pepperoni and pizza sauce on top. Mix well so as to completely coat the meat with the sauce.
2. Add the parmesan and mozzarella on top of the chicken, then place the baking dish into your fryer.
3. Cook for 15 minutes at 375°F.
4. When everything is bubbling and melted, remove from the fryer. Serve hot.

Buttermilk-fried Chicken Thighs

Servings:4
Cooking Time: 1 Hour
Ingredients:
- 1 cup buttermilk
- 2 tablespoons seasoned salt, divided
- 1 pound bone-in, skin-on chicken thighs
- 1 cup all-purpose flour
- ¼ cup cornstarch

Directions:
1. In a large bowl, combine buttermilk and 1 tablespoon seasoned salt. Add chicken. Cover and let marinate in refrigerator 30 minutes.
2. Preheat the air fryer to 375°F.

3. In a separate bowl, mix flour, cornstarch, and remaining seasoned salt. Dredge chicken thighs, one at a time, in flour mixture, covering completely.

4. Spray chicken generously with cooking spray, being sure that no dry spots remain. Place chicken in the air fryer basket and cook 30 minutes, turning halfway through cooking time and spraying any dry spots, until chicken is dark golden brown and crispy and internal temperature reaches at least 165°F.

5. Serve warm.

Harissa Chicken Wings

Servings: 4
Cooking Time: 25 Minutes
Ingredients:
- 8 whole chicken wings
- 1 tsp garlic powder
- ¼ tsp dried oregano
- 1 tbsp harissa seasoning

Directions:
1. Preheat air fryer to 400°F. Season the wings with garlic, harissa seasoning, and oregano. Place them in the greased frying basket and spray with cooking oil spray. Air Fry for 10 minutes, shake the basket, and cook for another 5-7 minutes until golden and crispy. Serve warm.

Broccoli And Cheese–stuffed Chicken

Servings:4
Cooking Time: 20 Minutes
Ingredients:
- 2 ounces cream cheese, softened
- 1 cup chopped fresh broccoli, steamed
- ½ cup shredded sharp Cheddar cheese
- 4 boneless, skinless chicken breasts
- 2 tablespoons mayonnaise
- ¼ teaspoon salt
- ¼ teaspoon garlic powder
- ⅛ teaspoon ground black pepper

Directions:
1. In a medium bowl, combine cream cheese, broccoli, and Cheddar. Cut a 4" pocket into each chicken breast. Evenly divide mixture between chicken breasts; stuff the pocket of each chicken breast with the mixture.

2. Spread ¼ tablespoon mayonnaise per side of each chicken breast, then sprinkle both sides of breasts with salt, garlic powder, and pepper.

3. Place stuffed chicken breasts into ungreased air fryer basket so that the open seams face up. Adjust the temperature to 350°F and set the timer for 20 minutes, turning chicken halfway through cooking. When done, chicken will be golden and have an internal temperature of at least 165°F. Serve warm.

Tangy Mustard Wings

Servings:4
Cooking Time: 25 Minutes
Ingredients:
- 1 pound bone-in chicken wings, separated at joints
- ¼ cup yellow mustard
- ½ teaspoon salt
- ¼ teaspoon ground black pepper

Directions:
1. Place wings in a large bowl and toss with mustard to fully coat. Sprinkle with salt and pepper.

2. Place wings into ungreased air fryer basket. Adjust the temperature to 400°F and set the timer for 25 minutes, shaking the basket three times during cooking. Wings will be done when browned and cooked to an internal temperature of at least 165°F. Serve warm.

Garlic Dill Wings

Servings:4
Cooking Time: 25 Minutes
Ingredients:
- 2 pounds bone-in chicken wings, separated at joints
- ½ teaspoon salt
- ½ teaspoon ground black pepper
- ½ teaspoon onion powder
- ½ teaspoon garlic powder
- 1 teaspoon dried dill

Directions:
1. In a large bowl, toss wings with salt, pepper, onion powder, garlic powder, and dill until evenly coated. Place wings into ungreased air fryer basket in a single layer, working in batches if needed.

2. Adjust the temperature to 400°F and set the timer for 25 minutes, shaking the basket every 7 minutes during cooking. Wings should have an internal temperature of at least 165°F and be golden brown when done. Serve warm.

Rosemary Partridge

Servings: 4
Cooking Time: 14 Minutes
Ingredients:
- 10 oz partridges
- 1 teaspoon dried rosemary
- 1 tablespoon butter, melted
- 1 teaspoon salt

Directions:
1. Cut the partridges into the halves and sprinkle with dried rosemary and salt. Then brush them with melted butter. Preheat the air fryer to 385°F. Put the partridge halves in the air fryer and cook them for 8 minutes. Then flip the poultry on another side and cook for 6 minutes more.

Betty's Baked Chicken

Servings: 1
Cooking Time: 70 Minutes
Ingredients:
- ½ cup butter
- 1 tsp. pepper
- 3 tbsp. garlic, minced
- 1 whole chicken

Directions:
1. Pre-heat your fryer at 350°F.
2. Allow the butter to soften at room temperature, then mix well in a small bowl with the pepper and garlic.
3. Massage the butter into the chicken. Any remaining butter can go inside the chicken.
4. Cook the chicken in the fryer for half an hour. Flip, then cook on the other side for another thirty minutes.
5. Test the temperature of the chicken by sticking a meat thermometer into the fat of the thigh to make sure it has reached 165°F. Take care when removing the chicken from the fryer. Let sit for ten minutes before you carve it and serve.

Basic Chicken Breasts

Servings: 4
Cooking Time: 15 Minutes
Ingredients:
- 2 tsp olive oil
- 4 chicken breasts
- Salt and pepper to taste
- 1 tbsp Italian seasoning

Directions:
1. Preheat air fryer at 350ºF. Rub olive oil over chicken breasts and sprinkle with salt, Italian seasoning and black pepper. Place them in the frying basket and Air Fry for 8-10 minutes. Let rest for 5 minutes before cutting. Store it covered in the fridge for up to 1 week.

Garlic Ginger Chicken

Servings:4
Cooking Time: 12 Minutes
Ingredients:
- 1 pound boneless, skinless chicken thighs, cut into 1" pieces
- ¼ cup soy sauce
- 2 cloves garlic, peeled and finely minced
- 1 tablespoon minced ginger
- ¼ teaspoon salt

Directions:
1. Place all ingredients in a large sealable bowl or bag. Place sealed bowl or bag into refrigerator and let marinate at least 30 minutes up to overnight.
2. Remove chicken from marinade and place into ungreased air fryer basket. Adjust the temperature to 375°F and set the timer for 12 minutes, shaking the basket twice

during cooking. Chicken will be golden and have an internal temperature of at least 165°F when done. Serve warm.

Grilled Chicken Pesto

Servings:8
Cooking Time: 30 Minutes
Ingredients:
- 1 ¾ cup commercial pesto
- 8 chicken thighs
- Salt and pepper to taste

Directions:
1. Place all Ingredients in the Ziploc bag and allow to marinate in the fridge for at least 2 hours.
2. Preheat the air fryer to 390°F.
3. Place the grill pan accessory in the air fryer.
4. Grill the chicken for at least 30 minutes.
5. Make sure to flip the chicken every 10 minutes for even grilling.

Chicken Fajita Poppers

Servings:18
Cooking Time: 20 Minutes
Ingredients:
- 1 pound ground chicken thighs
- ½ medium green bell pepper, seeded and finely chopped
- ¼ medium yellow onion, peeled and finely chopped
- ½ cup shredded pepper jack cheese
- 1 packet gluten-free fajita seasoning

Directions:
1. In a large bowl, combine all ingredients. Form mixture into eighteen 2" balls and place in a single layer into ungreased air fryer basket, working in batches if needed.
2. Adjust the temperature to 350°F and set the timer for 20 minutes. Carefully use tongs to turn poppers halfway through cooking. When 5 minutes remain on timer, increase temperature to 400°F to give the poppers a dark golden-brown color. Shake air fryer basket once more when 2 minutes remain on timer. Serve warm.

Buffalo Chicken Sandwiches

Servings:4
Cooking Time: 20 Minutes
Ingredients:
- 4 boneless, skinless chicken thighs
- 1 packet dry ranch seasoning
- ¼ cup buffalo sauce
- 4 slices pepper jack cheese
- 4 sandwich buns

Directions:
1. Preheat the air fryer to 375°F.
2. Sprinkle each chicken thigh with ranch seasoning and spritz with cooking spray.
3. Place chicken in the air fryer basket and cook 20 minutes, turning chicken halfway through, until chicken is

brown at the edges and internal temperature reaches at least 165°F.

4. Drizzle buffalo sauce over chicken, top with a slice of cheese, and place on buns to serve.

Buttermilk-fried Drumsticks

Servings: 2
Cooking Time: 25 Minutes
Ingredients:
- 1 egg
- ½ cup buttermilk
- ¾ cup self-rising flour
- ¾ cup seasoned panko breadcrumbs
- 1 teaspoon salt
- ¼ teaspoon ground black pepper (to mix into coating)
- 4 chicken drumsticks, skin on
- oil for misting or cooking spray

Directions:
1. Beat together egg and buttermilk in shallow dish.
2. In a second shallow dish, combine the flour, panko crumbs, salt, and pepper.
3. Sprinkle chicken legs with additional salt and pepper to taste.
4. Dip legs in buttermilk mixture, then roll in panko mixture, pressing in crumbs to make coating stick. Mist with oil or cooking spray.
5. Spray air fryer basket with cooking spray.
6. Cook drumsticks at 360°F for 10 minutes. Turn pieces over and cook an additional 10minutes.
7. Turn pieces to check for browning. If you have any white spots that haven't begun to brown, spritz them with oil or cooking spray. Continue cooking for 5 more minutes or until crust is golden brown and juices run clear. Larger, meatier drumsticks will take longer to cook than small ones.

Crispy Italian Chicken Thighs

Servings:4
Cooking Time: 25 Minutes
Ingredients:
- ½ cup mayonnaise
- 4 bone-in, skin-on chicken thighs
- 1 teaspoon salt
- ½ teaspoon ground black pepper
- 2 teaspoons Italian seasoning
- 1 cup Italian bread crumbs

Directions:
1. Preheat the air fryer to 370°F.
2. Brush mayonnaise over chicken thighs on both sides.
3. Sprinkle thighs with salt, pepper, and Italian seasoning.
4. Place bread crumbs into a resealable plastic bag and add thighs. Shake to coat.
5. Remove thighs from bag and spritz with cooking spray. Place in the air fryer basket and cook 25 minutes, turning thighs after 15 minutes, until skin is golden and crispy and internal temperature reaches at least 165°F.

6. Serve warm.

Chicken Adobo

Servings: 6
Cooking Time: 12 Minutes
Ingredients:
- 6 boneless chicken thighs
- ¼ cup soy sauce or tamari
- ½ cup rice wine vinegar
- 4 cloves garlic, minced
- ⅛ teaspoon crushed red pepper flakes
- ½ teaspoon black pepper

Directions:
1. Place the chicken thighs into a resealable plastic bag with the soy sauce or tamari, the rice wine vinegar, the garlic, and the crushed red pepper flakes. Seal the bag and let the chicken marinate at least 1 hour in the refrigerator.
2. Preheat the air fryer to 400°F.
3. Drain the chicken and pat dry with a paper towel. Season the chicken with black pepper and liberally spray with cooking spray.
4. Place the chicken in the air fryer basket and cook for 9 minutes, turn over at 9 minutes and check for an internal temperature of 165°F, and cook another 3 minutes.

Chicken Sausage In Dijon Sauce

Servings: 4
Cooking Time: 20 Minutes
Ingredients:
- 4 chicken sausages
- 1/4 cup mayonnaise
- 2 tablespoons Dijon mustard
- 1 tablespoon balsamic vinegar
- 1/2 teaspoon dried rosemary

Directions:
1. Arrange the sausages on the grill pan and transfer it to the preheated Air Fryer.
2. Grill the sausages at 350°F for approximately 13 minutes. Turn them halfway through cooking.
3. Meanwhile, prepare the sauce by mixing the remaining ingredients with a wire whisk. Serve the warm sausages with chilled Dijon sauce. Enjoy!

Thyme Turkey Nuggets

Servings:2
Cooking Time: 20 Minutes
Ingredients:
- 1 egg, beaten
- 1 cup breadcrumbs
- 1 tbsp dried thyme
- ½ tbsp dried parsley
- Salt and pepper, to taste

Directions:

1. Preheat air fryer to 350°F. In a bowl, mix ground chicken, thyme, parsley, salt and pepper. Shape the mixture into balls. Dip in the breadcrumbs, then egg, then in the breadcrumbs again. Place the nuggets in the air fryer basket, spray with cooking spray cook for 10 minutes, shaking once.

Sweet Lime 'n Chili Chicken Barbecue

Servings:2
Cooking Time: 40 Minutes
Ingredients:
- ¼ cup soy sauce
- 1 cup sweet chili sauce
- 1-pound chicken breasts
- Juice from 2 limes, freshly squeezed

Directions:
1. In a Ziploc bag, combine all Ingredients and give a good shake. Allow to marinate for at least 2 hours in the fridge.
2. Preheat the air fryer to 390°F.
3. Place the grill pan accessory in the air fryer.
4. Place chicken on the grill and cook for 30 to 40 minutes. Make sure to flip the chicken every 10 minutes to cook evenly.
5. Meanwhile, use the remaining marinade and put it in a saucepan. Simmer until the sauce thickens.
6. Once the chicken is cooked, brush with the thickened marinade.

Hot Chicken Skin

Servings: 4
Cooking Time: 30 Minutes
Ingredients:
- ½ teaspoon chili paste
- 8 oz chicken skin
- 1 teaspoon sesame oil
- ½ teaspoon chili powder
- ½ teaspoon salt

Directions:
1. In the shallow bowl mix up chili paste, sesame oil, chili powder, and salt. Then brush the chicken skin with chili mixture well and leave for 10 minutes to marinate. Meanwhile, preheat the air fryer to 365°F. Put the marinated chicken skin in the air fryer and cook it for 20 minutes. When the time is finished, flip the chicken skin on another side and cook it for 10 minutes more or until the chicken skin is crunchy.

Chipotle Aioli Wings

Servings:6
Cooking Time: 25 Minutes
Ingredients:
- 2 pounds bone-in chicken wings
- ½ teaspoon salt
- ¼ teaspoon ground black pepper

- 2 tablespoons mayonnaise
- 2 teaspoons chipotle powder
- 2 tablespoons lemon juice

Directions:
1. In a large bowl, toss wings in salt and pepper, then place into ungreased air fryer basket. Adjust the temperature to 400°F and set the timer for 25 minutes, shaking the basket twice while cooking. Wings will be done when golden and have an internal temperature of at least 165°F.
2. In a small bowl, whisk together mayonnaise, chipotle powder, and lemon juice. Place cooked wings into a large serving bowl and drizzle with aioli. Toss to coat. Serve warm.

Creamy Onion Chicken

Servings:4
Cooking Time: 20 Minutes
Ingredients:
- 1 ½ cup onion soup mix
- 1 cup mushroom soup
- ½ cup cream

Directions:
1. Preheat Fryer to 400°F. Add mushrooms, onion mix and cream in a frying pan. Heat on low heat for 1 minute. Pour the warm mixture over chicken slices and allow to sit for 25 minutes. Place the marinated chicken in the air fryer cooking basket and cook for 15 minutes. Serve with the remaining cream.

Air Fried Chicken Tenderloin

Servings:8
Cooking Time: 15 Minutes
Ingredients:
- ½ cup almond flour
- 1 egg, beaten
- 2 tablespoons coconut oil
- 8 chicken tenderloins
- Salt and pepper to taste

Directions:
1. Preheat the air fryer for 5 minutes.
2. Season the chicken tenderloin with salt and pepper to taste.
3. Soak in beaten eggs then dredge in almond flour.
4. Place in the air fryer and brush with coconut oil.
5. Cook for 15 minutes at 375°F.
6. Halfway through the cooking time, give the fryer basket a shake to cook evenly.

Sticky Drumsticks

Servings: 4
Cooking Time: 45 Minutes
Ingredients:
- 1 lb chicken drumsticks
- 1 tbsp chicken seasoning
- 1 tsp dried chili flakes

- Salt and pepper to taste
- ¼ cup honey
- 1 cup barbecue sauce

Directions:

1. Preheat air fryer to 390°F. Season drumsticks with chicken seasoning, chili flakes, salt, and pepper. Place one batch of drumsticks in the greased frying basket and Air Fry for 18-20 minutes, flipping once until golden.

2. While the chicken is cooking, combine honey and barbecue sauce in a small bowl. Remove the drumsticks to a serving dish. Drizzle honey-barbecue sauce over and serve.

Perfect Grill Chicken Breast

Servings: 2
Cooking Time: 12 Minutes

Ingredients:

- 2 chicken breast, skinless and boneless
- 2 tsp olive oil
- Pepper
- Salt

Directions:

1. Remove air fryer basket and replace it with air fryer grill pan.

2. Place chicken breast to the grill pan. Season chicken with pepper and salt. Drizzle with oil.

3. Cook chicken for 375°F for 12 minutes.

4. Serve and enjoy.

Turkey-hummus Wraps

Servings: 4
Cooking Time: 7 Minutes Per Batch

Ingredients:

- 4 large whole wheat wraps
- ½ cup hummus
- 16 thin slices deli turkey
- 8 slices provolone cheese
- 1 cup fresh baby spinach (or more to taste)

Directions:

1. To assemble, place 2 tablespoons of hummus on each wrap and spread to within about a half inch from edges. Top with 4 slices of turkey and 2 slices of provolone. Finish with ¼ cup of baby spinach—or pile on as much as you like.

2. Roll up each wrap. You don't need to fold or seal the ends.

3. Place 2 wraps in air fryer basket, seam side down.

4. Cook at 360°F for 4minutes to warm filling and melt cheese. If you like, you can continue cooking for 3 more minutes, until the wrap is slightly crispy.

5. Repeat step 4 to cook remaining wraps.

Family Chicken Fingers

Servings: 4
Cooking Time: 30 Minutes

Ingredients:

- 1 lb chicken breast fingers

- 1 tbsp chicken seasoning
- ½ tsp mustard powder
- Salt and pepper to taste
- 2 eggs
- 1 cup bread crumbs

Directions:

1. Preheat air fryer to 400°F. Add the chicken fingers to a large bowl along with chicken seasoning, mustard, salt, and pepper; mix well. Set up two small bowls. In one bowl, beat the eggs. In the second bowl, add the bread crumbs. Dip the chicken in the egg, then dredge in breadcrumbs. Place the nuggets in the air fryer. Lightly spray with cooking oil, then Air Fry for 8 minutes, shaking the basket once until crispy and cooked through. Serve warm.

Za'atar Chicken Drumsticks

Servings: 4
Cooking Time: 45 Minutes

Ingredients:

- 2 tbsp butter, melted
- 8 chicken drumsticks
- 1 ½ tbsp Za'atar seasoning
- Salt and pepper to taste
- 1 lemon, zested
- 2 tbsp parsley, chopped

Directions:

1. Preheat air fryer to 390°F. Mix the Za'atar seasoning, lemon zest, parsley, salt, and pepper in a bowl. Add the chicken drumsticks and toss to coat. Place them in the air fryer and brush them with butter. Air Fry for 18-20 minutes, flipping once until crispy. Serve and enjoy!

Gingered Chicken Drumsticks

Servings:3
Cooking Time:25 Minutes

Ingredients:

- ¼ cup full-fat coconut milk
- 3 chicken drumsticks
- 2 teaspoons fresh ginger, minced
- 2 teaspoons galangal, minced
- 2 teaspoons ground turmeric
- Salt, to taste

Directions:

1. Preheat the Air fryer to 375°F and grease an Air fryer basket.

2. Mix the coconut milk, galangal, ginger, and spices in a bowl.

3. Add the chicken drumsticks and coat generously with the marinade.

4. Refrigerate to marinate for at least 8 hours and transfer into the Air fryer basket.

5. Cook for about 25 minutes and dish out the chicken drumsticks onto a serving platter.

Barbecue Chicken Drumsticks

Servings:4
Cooking Time: 25 Minutes
Ingredients:

- 1 teaspoon salt
- 1 teaspoon chili powder
- 1 teaspoon garlic powder
- ½ teaspoon ground black pepper
- ½ teaspoon onion powder
- 8 chicken drumsticks
- 1 cup barbecue sauce, divided

Directions:
1. Preheat the air fryer to 375°F.
2. In a large bowl, combine salt, chili powder, garlic powder, pepper, and onion powder. Add drumsticks and toss to fully coat.
3. Brush drumsticks with ¾ cup barbecue sauce to coat.
4. Place in the air fryer basket and cook 25 minutes, turning three times during cooking, until drumsticks are brown and internal temperature reaches at least 165°F.
5. Before serving, brush remaining ¼ cup barbecue sauce over drumsticks. Serve warm.

Chapter 6. Fish And Seafood Recipes

Super-simple Scallops

Servings:2
Cooking Time:4 Minutes
Ingredients:

- ¾ pound sea scallops
- 1 tablespoon butter, melted
- ½ tablespoon fresh thyme, minced
- Salt and black pepper, to taste

Directions:
1. Preheat the Air fryer to 390°F and grease an Air fryer basket.
2. Mix all the ingredients in a bowl and toss to coat well.
3. Arrange the scallops in the Air fryer basket and cook for about 4 minutes.
4. Dish out and serve warm.

Honey-glazed Salmon

Servings:4
Cooking Time: 30 Minutes
Ingredients:

- 2 tablespoons soy sauce
- 1 teaspoon sriracha
- ½ teaspoon minced garlic
- 4 skin-on salmon fillets
- 2 teaspoons honey

Directions:
1. In a large bowl, whisk together soy sauce, sriracha, and garlic. Place salmon in bowl. Cover and let marinate in refrigerator at least 20 minutes.
2. Preheat the air fryer to 375°F.
3. Place salmon in the air fryer basket and cook 8 minutes. Open air fryer and brush honey on salmon. Continue cooking 2 more minutes until salmon flakes easily and internal temperature reaches at least 145°F. Serve warm.

Air Fried Cod With Basil Vinaigrette

Servings:4
Cooking Time: 15 Minutes
Ingredients:

- ¼ cup olive oil
- 4 cod fillets
- A bunch of basil, torn
- Juice from 1 lemon, freshly squeezed
- Salt and pepper to taste

Directions:
1. Preheat the air fryer for 5 minutes.
2. Season the cod fillets with salt and pepper to taste.
3. Place in the air fryer and cook for 15 minutes at 350°F.
4. Meanwhile, mix the rest of the ingredients in a bowl and toss to combine.
5. Serve the air fried cod with the basil vinaigrette.

Garlic-lemon Steamer Clams

Servings:2
Cooking Time: 30 Minutes
Ingredients:

- 25 Manila clams, scrubbed
- 2 tbsp butter, melted
- 1 garlic clove, minced
- 2 lemon wedges

Directions:
1. Add the clams to a large bowl filled with water and let sit for 10 minutes. Drain. Pour more water and let sit for 10 more minutes. Drain. Preheat air fryer to 350°F. Place clams in the basket and Air Fry for 7 minutes. Discard any clams that don´t open. Remove clams from shells and place them

into a large serving dish. Drizzle with melted butter and garlic and squeeze lemon on top. Serve.

Tilapia Fish Fillets

Servings: 2
Cooking Time: 7 Minutes
Ingredients:
- 2 tilapia fillets
- 1 tsp old bay seasoning
- 1/2 tsp butter
- 1/4 tsp lemon pepper
- Pepper
- Salt

Directions:
1. Spray air fryer basket with cooking spray.
2. Place fish fillets into the air fryer basket and season with lemon pepper, old bay seasoning, pepper, and salt.
3. Spray fish fillets with cooking spray and cook at 400°F for 7 minutes.
4. Serve and enjoy.

Fish Taco Bowl

Servings:4
Cooking Time: 12 Minutes
Ingredients:
- 2 cups finely shredded cabbage
- ½ cup mayonnaise
- Juice of 1 medium lime, divided
- 4 boneless, skinless tilapia fillets
- 2 teaspoons chili powder
- 1 teaspoon salt
- ½ teaspoon ground black pepper

Directions:
1. In a large bowl, mix cabbage, mayonnaise, and half of lime juice to make a slaw. Cover and refrigerate while the fish cooks.
2. Preheat the air fryer to 400°F.
3. Sprinkle tilapia with chili powder, salt, and pepper. Spritz each side with cooking spray.
4. Place fillets in the air fryer basket and cook 12 minutes, turning halfway through cooking time, until fish is opaque, flakes easily, and reaches an internal temperature of 145°F.
5. Allow fish to cool 5 minutes before chopping into bite-sized pieces. To serve, place ½ cup slaw into each bowl and top with one-fourth of fish. Squeeze remaining lime juice over fish. Serve warm.

Mediterranean-style Cod

Servings:4
Cooking Time: 12 Minutes
Ingredients:
- 4 cod fillets
- 3 tablespoons fresh lemon juice
- 1 tablespoon olive oil
- ¼ teaspoon salt
- 6 cherry tomatoes, halved
- ¼ cup pitted and sliced kalamata olives

Directions:
1. Place cod into an ungreased 6" round nonstick baking dish. Pour lemon juice into dish and drizzle cod with olive oil. Sprinkle with salt. Place tomatoes and olives around baking dish in between fillets.
2. Place dish into air fryer basket. Adjust the temperature to 350°F and set the timer for 12 minutes, carefully turning cod halfway through cooking. Fillets will be lightly browned, easily flake, and have an internal temperature of at least 145°F when done. Serve warm.

Horseradish-crusted Salmon Fillets

Servings:3
Cooking Time: 8 Minutes
Ingredients:
- ½ cup Fresh bread crumbs
- 4 tablespoons (¼ cup/½ stick) Butter, melted and cooled
- ¼ cup Jarred prepared white horseradish
- Vegetable oil spray
- 4 6-ounce skin-on salmon fillets

Directions:
1. Preheat the air fryer to 400°F.
2. Mix the bread crumbs, butter, and horseradish in a bowl until well combined.
3. Take the basket out of the machine. Generously spray the skin side of each fillet. Pick them up one by one with a nonstick-safe spatula and set them in the basket skin side down with as much air space between them as possible. Divide the bread-crumb mixture between the fillets, coating the top of each fillet with an even layer. Generously coat the bread-crumb mixture with vegetable oil spray.
4. Return the basket to the machine and air-fry undisturbed for 8 minutes, or until the topping has lightly browned and the fish is firm but not hard.
5. Use a nonstick-safe spatula to transfer the salmon fillets to serving plates. Cool for 5 minutes before serving. Because of the butter in the topping, it will stay very hot for quite a while. Take care, especially if you're serving these fillets to children.

Ham Tilapia

Servings: 4
Cooking Time: 10 Minutes
Ingredients:
- 16 oz tilapia fillet
- 4 ham slices
- 1 teaspoon sunflower oil
- ½ teaspoon salt
- 1 teaspoon dried rosemary

Directions:
1. Cut the tilapia on 4 servings. Sprinkle every fish serving with salt, dried rosemary, and sunflower oil. Then carefully

wrap the fish fillets in the ham slices and secure with toothpicks. Preheat the air fryer to 400°F. Put the wrapped tilapia in the air fryer basket in one layer and cook them for 10 minutes. Gently flip the fish on another side after 5 minutes of cooking.

Perfect Soft-shelled Crabs

Servings:2
Cooking Time: 12 Minutes
Ingredients:
- ½ cup All-purpose flour
- 1 tablespoon Old Bay seasoning
- 1 Large egg(s), well beaten
- 1 cup Ground oyster crackers
- 2 2½-ounce cleaned soft-shelled crab(s), about 4 inches across
- Vegetable oil spray

Directions:
1. Preheat the air fryer to 375°F.
2. Set up and fill three shallow soup plates or small pie plates on your counter: one for the flour, whisked with the Old Bay until well combined; one for the beaten egg(s); and one for the cracker crumbs.
3. Set a soft-shelled crab in the flour mixture and turn to coat evenly and well on all sides, even inside the legs. Dip the crab into the egg(s) and coat well, turning at least once, again getting some of the egg between the legs. Let any excess egg slip back into the rest, then set the crab in the cracker crumbs. Turn several times, pressing very gently to get the crab evenly coated with crumbs, even between the legs. Generously coat the crab on all sides with vegetable oil spray. Set it aside if you're making more than one and coat these in the same way.
4. Set the crab(s) in the basket with as much air space between them as possible. They may overlap slightly, particularly at the ends of their legs, depending on the basket's size. Air-fry undisturbed for 12 minutes, or until very crisp and golden brown. If the machine is at 390°F, the crabs may be done in only 10 minutes.
5. Use kitchen tongs to gently transfer the crab(s) to a wire rack. Cool for a couple of minutes before serving.

Coconut Jerk Shrimp

Servings:3
Cooking Time: 8 Minutes
Ingredients:
- 1 Large egg white(s)
- 1 teaspoon Purchased or homemade jerk dried seasoning blend
- ¾ cup Plain panko bread crumbs (gluten-free, if a concern)
- ¾ cup Unsweetened shredded coconut
- 12 Large shrimp, peeled and deveined
- Coconut oil spray

Directions:

1. Preheat the air fryer to 375°F .
2. Whisk the egg white(s) and seasoning blend in a bowl until foamy. Add the shrimp and toss well to coat evenly.
3. Mix the bread crumbs and coconut on a dinner plate until well combined. Use kitchen tongs to pick up a shrimp, letting the excess egg white mixture slip back into the rest. Set the shrimp in the bread-crumb mixture. Turn several times to coat evenly and thoroughly. Set on a cutting board and continue coating the remainder of the shrimp.
4. Lightly coat all the shrimp on both sides with the coconut oil spray. Set them in the basket in one layer with as much space between them as possible. Air-fry undisturbed for 6 minutes, or until the coating is lightly browned. If the air fryer is at 360°F, you may need to add 2 minutes to the cooking time.
5. Use clean kitchen tongs to transfer the shrimp to a wire rack. Cool for only a minute or two before serving.

Mahi-mahi "burrito" Fillets

Servings:3
Cooking Time: 10 Minutes
Ingredients:
- 1 Large egg white
- 1½ cups Crushed corn tortilla chips (gluten-free, if a concern)
- 1 tablespoon Chile powder
- 3 5-ounce skinless mahi-mahi fillets
- 6 tablespoons Canned refried beans
- Vegetable oil spray

Directions:
1. Preheat the air fryer to 400°F.
2. Set up and fill two shallow soup plates or small pie plates on your counter: one with the egg white, beaten until foamy; and one with the crushed tortilla chips.
3. Gently rub ½ teaspoon chile powder on each side of each fillet.
4. Spread 1 tablespoon refried beans over both sides and the edges of a fillet. Dip the fillet in the egg white, turning to coat it on both sides. Let any excess egg white slip back into the rest, then set the fillet in the crushed tortilla chips. Turn several times, pressing gently to coat it evenly. Coat the fillet on all sides with the vegetable oil spray, then set it aside. Prepare the remaining fillet(s) in the same way.
5. When the machine is at temperature, set the fillets in the basket with as much air space between them as possible. Air-fry undisturbed for 10 minutes, or until crisp and browned.
6. Use a nonstick-safe spatula to transfer the fillets to a serving platter or plates. Cool for only a minute or so, then serve hot.

Better Fish Sticks

Servings: 3
Cooking Time: 8 Minutes
Ingredients:
- ¾ cup Seasoned Italian-style dried bread crumbs (gluten-free, if a concern)
- 3 tablespoons (about ½ ounce) Finely grated Parmesan cheese
- 10 ounces Skinless cod fillets, cut lengthwise into 1-inch-wide pieces
- 3 tablespoons Regular or low-fat mayonnaise (not fat-free; gluten-free, if a concern)
- Vegetable oil spray

Directions:
1. Preheat the air fryer to 400°F.
2. Mix the bread crumbs and grated Parmesan in a shallow soup bowl or a small pie plate.
3. Smear the fish fillet sticks completely with the mayonnaise, then dip them one by one in the bread-crumb mixture, turning and pressing gently to make an even and thorough coating. Coat each stick on all sides with vegetable oil spray.
4. Set the fish sticks in the basket with at least ¼ inch between them. Air-fry undisturbed for 8 minutes, or until golden brown and crisp.
5. Use a nonstick-safe spatula to gently transfer them from the basket to a wire rack. Cool for only a minute or two before serving.

Fried Catfish Fillets

Servings: 2
Cooking Time: 40 Minutes
Ingredients:
- 3 tbsp breadcrumbs
- 1 tsp cayenne pepper
- 1 tsp dry fish seasoning, of choice
- 2 sprigs parsley, chopped
- Salt to taste, optional
- Cooking spray

Directions:
1. Preheat air fryer to 400°F. Pour all the dry ingredients, except the parsley, in a zipper bag. Pat dry and add the fish pieces. Close the bag and shake to coat the fish well. Do this with one fish piece at a time.
2. Lightly spray the fish with olive oil. Arrange them in the fryer basket, one at a time depending on the size of the fish. Close the air fryer and cook for 10 minutes. Flip the fish and cook further for 10 minutes. For extra crispiness, cook for 3 more minutes. Garnish with parsley and serve.

Timeless Garlic-lemon Scallops

Servings: 2
Cooking Time: 15 Minutes
Ingredients:

- 2 tbsp butter, melted
- 1 garlic clove, minced
- 1 tbsp lemon juice
- 1 lb jumbo sea scallops

Directions:
1. Preheat air fryer to 400ºF. Whisk butter, garlic, and lemon juice in a bowl. Roll scallops in the mixture to coat all sides. Place scallops in the frying basket and Air Fry for 4 minutes, flipping once. Brush the tops of each scallop with butter mixture and cook for 4 more minutes, flipping once. Serve and enjoy!

Italian Shrimp

Servings: 4
Cooking Time: 12 Minutes
Ingredients:
- 1 pound shrimp, peeled and deveined
- A pinch of salt and black pepper
- 1 tablespoon sesame seeds, toasted
- ½ teaspoon Italian seasoning
- 1 tablespoon olive oil

Directions:
1. In a bowl, mix the shrimp with the rest of the ingredients and toss well. Put the shrimp in the air fryer's basket, cook at 370°F for 12 minutes, divide into bowls and serve,

Stevia Cod

Servings: 4
Cooking Time: 14 Minutes
Ingredients:
- 1/3 cup stevia
- 2 tablespoons coconut aminos
- 4 cod fillets, boneless
- A pinch of salt and black pepper

Directions:
1. In a pan that fits the air fryer, combine all the ingredients and toss gently. Introduce the pan in the fryer and cook at 350°F for 14 minutes, flipping the fish halfway. Divide everything between plates and serve.

Butternut Squash–wrapped Halibut Fillets

Servings: 3
Cooking Time: 11 Minutes
Ingredients:
- 15 Long spiralized peeled and seeded butternut squash strands
- 3 5- to 6-ounce skinless halibut fillets
- 3 tablespoons Butter, melted
- ¾ teaspoon Mild paprika
- ¾ teaspoon Table salt
- ¾ teaspoon Ground black pepper

Directions:

1. Preheat the air fryer to 375°F .
2. Hold 5 long butternut squash strands together and wrap them around a fillet. Set it aside and wrap any remaining fillet(s).
3. Mix the melted butter, paprika, salt, and pepper in a small bowl. Brush this mixture over the squash-wrapped fillets on all sides.
4. When the machine is at temperature, set the fillets in the basket with as much air space between them as possible. Air-fry undisturbed for 10 minutes, or until the squash strands have browned but not burned. If the machine is at 360°F, you may need to add 1 minute to the cooking time. In any event, watch the fish carefully after the 8-minute mark.
5. Use a nonstick-safe spatula to gently transfer the fillets to a serving platter or plates. Cool for only a minute or so before serving.

Crunchy And Buttery Cod With Ritz Cracker Crust

Servings: 2
Cooking Time: 10 Minutes
Ingredients:
- 4 tablespoons butter, melted
- 8 to 10 RITZ crackers, crushed into crumbs
- 2 cod fillets
- salt and freshly ground black pepper
- 1 lemon

Directions:
1. Preheat the air fryer to 380°F.
2. Melt the butter in a small saucepan on the stovetop or in a microwavable dish in the microwave, and then transfer the butter to a shallow dish. Place the crushed RITZ crackers into a second shallow dish.
3. Season the fish fillets with salt and freshly ground black pepper. Dip them into the butter and then coat both sides with the RITZ crackers.
4. Place the fish into the air fryer basket and air-fry at 380°F for 10 minutes, flipping the fish over halfway through the cooking time.
5. Serve with a wedge of lemon to squeeze over the top.

Cajun Lobster Tails

Servings:4
Cooking Time: 10 Minutes
Ingredients:
- 4 lobster tails
- 2 tablespoons salted butter, melted
- 2 teaspoons lemon juice
- 1 tablespoon Cajun seasoning

Directions:
1. Preheat the air fryer to 400°F.
2. Carefully cut open lobster tails with kitchen scissors and pull back the shell a little to expose the meat. Drizzle butter

and lemon juice over each tail, then sprinkle with Cajun seasoning.
3. Place tails in the air fryer basket and cook 10 minutes until lobster shells are bright red and internal temperature reaches at least 145°F. Serve warm.

Kid´s Flounder Fingers

Servings: 4
Cooking Time: 45 Minutes
Ingredients:
- 1 lb catfish flounder fillets, cut into 1-inch chunks
- ½ cup seasoned fish fry breading mix

Directions:
1. Preheat air fryer to 400°F. In a resealable bag, add flounder and breading mix. Seal bag and shake until the fish is coated. Place the nuggets in the greased frying basket and Air Fry for 18-20 minutes, shaking the basket once until crisp. Serve warm and enjoy!

Chili Blackened Shrimp

Servings: 4
Cooking Time: 15 Minutes
Ingredients:
- 1 lb peeled shrimp, deveined
- 1 tsp paprika
- ½ tsp dried dill
- ½ tsp red chili flakes
- ½ lemon, juiced
- Salt and pepper to taste

Directions:
1. Preheat air fryer to 400°F. In a resealable bag, add shrimp, paprika, dill, red chili flakes, lemon juice, salt and pepper. Seal and shake well. Place the shrimp in the greased frying basket and Air Fry for 7-8 minutes, shaking the basket once until blackened. Let cool slightly and serve.

Sweet Potato–wrapped Shrimp

Servings:3
Cooking Time: 6 Minutes
Ingredients:
- 24 Long spiralized sweet potato strands
- Olive oil spray
- ¼ teaspoon Garlic powder
- ¼ teaspoon Table salt
- Up to a ⅛ teaspoon Cayenne
- 12 Large shrimp, peeled and deveined

Directions:
1. Preheat the air fryer to 400°F.
2. Lay the spiralized sweet potato strands on a large swath of paper towels and straighten out the strands to long ropes. Coat them with olive oil spray, then sprinkle them with the garlic powder, salt, and cayenne.
3. Pick up 2 strands and wrap them around the center of a shrimp, with the ends tucked under what now becomes the

bottom side of the shrimp. Continue wrapping the remainder of the shrimp.

4. Set the shrimp bottom side down in the basket with as much air space between them as possible. Air-fry undisturbed for 6 minutes, or until the sweet potato strands are crisp and the shrimp are pink and firm.

5. Use kitchen tongs to transfer the shrimp to a wire rack. Cool for only a minute or two before serving.

Spicy Prawns

Servings: 2
Cooking Time: 8 Minutes
Ingredients:
- 6 prawns
- 1/4 tsp pepper
- 1/2 tsp chili powder
- 1 tsp chili flakes
- 1/4 tsp salt

Directions:
1. Preheat the air fryer to 350°F.
2. In a bowl, mix together spices add prawns.
3. Spray air fryer basket with cooking spray.
4. Transfer prawns into the air fryer basket and cook for 8 minutes.
5. Serve and enjoy.

Rainbow Salmon Kebabs

Servings:2
Cooking Time: 8 Minutes
Ingredients:
- 6 ounces boneless, skinless salmon, cut into 1" cubes
- ¼ medium red onion, peeled and cut into 1" pieces
- ½ medium yellow bell pepper, seeded and cut into 1" pieces
- ½ medium zucchini, trimmed and cut into ½" slices
- 1 tablespoon olive oil
- ½ teaspoon salt
- ¼ teaspoon ground black pepper

Directions:
1. Using onc 6" skewer, skewer 1 piece salmon, then 1 piece onion, 1 piece bell pepper, and finally 1 piece zucchini. Repeat this pattern with additional skewers to make four kebabs total. Drizzle with olive oil and sprinkle with salt and black pepper.
2. Place kebabs into ungreased air fryer basket. Adjust the temperature to 400°F and set the timer for 8 minutes, turning kebabs halfway through cooking. Salmon will easily flake and have an internal temperature of at least 145°F when done; vegetables will be tender. Serve warm.

Italian Baked Cod

Servings:4
Cooking Time: 12 Minutes
Ingredients:
- 4 cod fillets

- 2 tablespoons salted butter, melted
- 1 teaspoon Italian seasoning
- ¼ teaspoon salt
- ½ cup low-carb marinara sauce

Directions:
1. Place cod into an ungreased 6" round nonstick baking dish. Pour butter over cod and sprinkle with Italian seasoning and salt. Top with marinara.
2. Place dish into air fryer basket. Adjust the temperature to 350°F and set the timer for 12 minutes. Fillets will be lightly browned, easily flake, and have an internal temperature of at least 145°F when done. Serve warm.

Flounder Fillets

Servings: 4
Cooking Time: 8 Minutes
Ingredients:
- 1 egg white
- 1 tablespoon water
- 1 cup panko breadcrumbs
- 2 tablespoons extra-light virgin olive oil
- 4 4-ounce flounder fillets
- salt and pepper
- oil for misting or cooking spray

Directions:
1. Preheat air fryer to 390°F.
2. Beat together egg white and water in shallow dish.
3. In another shallow dish, mix panko crumbs and oil until well combined and crumbly.
4. Season flounder fillets with salt and pepper to taste. Dip each fillet into egg mixture and then roll in panko crumbs, pressing in crumbs so that fish is nicely coated.
5. Spray air fryer basket with nonstick cooking spray and add fillets. Cook at 390°F for 3minutes.
6. Spray fish fillets but do not turn. Cook 5 minutes longer or until golden brown and crispy. Using a spatula, carefully remove fish from basket and serve.

Lemon Butter Cod

Servings:4
Cooking Time: 12 Minutes
Ingredients:
- 4 cod fillets
- 2 tablespoons salted butter, melted
- 1 teaspoon Old Bay Seasoning
- ½ medium lemon, cut into 4 slices

Directions:
1. Place cod fillets into an ungreased 6" round nonstick baking dish. Brush tops of fillets with butter and sprinkle with Old Bay Seasoning. Lay 1 lemon slice on each fillet.
2. Cover dish with aluminum foil and place into air fryer basket. Adjust the temperature to 350°F and set the timer for 12 minutes, turning fillets halfway through cooking. Fish

will be opaque and have an internal temperature of at least 145°F when done. Serve warm.

Fish Fillet Sandwich

Servings:4
Cooking Time: 18 Minutes
Ingredients:
- 4 cod fillets
- ½ teaspoon salt
- ¼ teaspoon ground black pepper
- 2 cups unsweetened cornflakes, crushed
- 1 cup Italian bread crumbs
- 2 large eggs
- 4 sandwich buns

Directions:
1. Preheat the air fryer to 375°F.
2. Sprinkle cod with salt and pepper on both sides.
3. In a large bowl, combine cornflakes and bread crumbs.
4. In a medium bowl, whisk eggs. Press each piece of cod into eggs to coat, shaking off excess, then into cornflake mixture to coat evenly on both sides. Spritz with cooking spray.
5. Place in the air fryer basket and cook 18 minutes, turning halfway through cooking time, until fillets are brown and internal temperature reaches at least 145°F. Place on buns to serve.

Spicy Fish Taco Bowl

Servings:4
Cooking Time: 12 Minutes
Ingredients:
- ½ teaspoon salt
- ¼ teaspoon garlic powder
- ¼ teaspoon ground cumin
- 4 cod fillets
- 4 cups finely shredded green cabbage
- ⅓ cup mayonnaise
- ¼ teaspoon ground black pepper
- ¼ cup chopped pickled jalapeños

Directions:
1. Sprinkle salt, garlic powder, and cumin over cod and place into ungreased air fryer basket. Adjust the temperature to 350°F and set the timer for 12 minutes, turning fillets halfway through cooking. Cod will flake easily and have an internal temperature of at least 145°F when done.
2. In a large bowl, toss cabbage with mayonnaise, pepper, and jalapeños until fully coated. Serve cod warm over cabbage slaw on four medium plates.

Garlic And Dill Salmon

Servings: 2
Cooking Time: 8 Minutes
Ingredients:
- 12 ounces salmon filets with skin

- 2 tablespoons melted butter
- 1 tablespoon extra-virgin olive oil
- 2 garlic cloves, minced
- 1 tablespoon fresh dill
- ½ teaspoon sea salt
- ½ lemon

Directions:
1. Pat the salmon dry with paper towels.
2. In a small bowl, mix together the melted butter, olive oil, garlic, and dill.
3. Sprinkle the top of the salmon with sea salt. Brush all sides of the salmon with the garlic and dill butter.
4. Preheat the air fryer to 350°F.
5. Place the salmon, skin side down, in the air fryer basket. Cook for 6 to 8 minutes, or until the fish flakes in the center.
6. Remove the salmon and plate on a serving platter. Squeeze fresh lemon over the top of the salmon. Serve immediately.

Air Fried Calamari

Servings:3
Cooking Time: 30 Minutes
Ingredients:
- ½ cup cornmeal or cornstarch
- 2 large eggs, beaten
- 2 mashed garlic cloves
- 1 cup breadcrumbs
- lemon juice

Directions:
1. Coat calamari with the cornmeal. The first mixture is prepared by mixing the eggs and garlic. Dip the calamari in the eggs' mixture. Then dip them in the breadcrumbs. Put the rings in the fridge for 2 hours.
2. Then, line them in the air fryer and add oil generously. Fry for 10 to 13 minutes at 390°F, shaking once halfway through. Serve with garlic mayonnaise and top with lemon juice.

Sweet And Sour Glazed Cod

Servings:2
Cooking Time:12 Minutes
Ingredients:
- 1 teaspoon water
- 4 cod fillets
- 1/3 cup soy sauce
- 1/3 cup honey
- 3 teaspoons rice wine vinegar

Directions:
1. Preheat the Air fryer to 355°F and grease an Air fryer basket.
2. Mix the soy sauce, honey, vinegar and water in a small bowl.
3. Reserve about half of the mixture in another bowl.

4. Stir the cod fillets in the remaining mixture until well coated.

5. Cover and refrigerate to marinate for about 3 hours.

6. Arrange the cod fillets into the Air fryer basket and cook for about 12 minutes, flipping once in between.

7. Coat with the reserved marinade and dish out the cod to serve hot.

Coriander Cod And Green Beans

Servings: 4

Cooking Time: 15 Minutes

Ingredients:

- 12 oz cod fillet
- ½ cup green beans, trimmed and halved
- 1 tablespoon avocado oil
- 1 teaspoon salt
- 1 teaspoon ground coriander

Directions:

1. Cut the cod fillet on 4 servings and sprinkle every serving with salt and ground coriander. After this, place the fish on 4 foil squares. Top them with green beans and avocado oil and wrap them into parcels. Preheat the air fryer to 400°F. Place the cod parcels in the air fryer and cook them for 15 minutes.

Lemon And Thyme Sea Bass

Servings: 3

Cooking Time: 15 Minutes

Ingredients:

- 8 oz sea bass, trimmed, peeled
- 4 lemon slices
- 1 tablespoon thyme
- 2 teaspoons sesame oil
- 1 teaspoon salt

Directions:

1. Fill the sea bass with lemon slices and rub with thyme, salt, and sesame oil. Then preheat the air fryer to 385°F and put the fish in the air fryer basket. Cook it for 12 minutes. Then flip the fish on another side and cook it for 3 minutes more.

Easy-peasy Shrimp

Servings:2

Cooking Time: 15 Minutes

Ingredients:

- 1 lb tail-on shrimp, deveined
- 2 tbsp butter, melted
- 1 tbsp lemon juice
- 1 tbsp dill, chopped

Directions:

1. Preheat air fryer to 350ºF. Combine shrimp and butter in a bowl. Place shrimp in the greased frying basket and Air Fry for 6 minutes, flipping once. Squeeze lemon juice over and top with dill. Serve hot.

Tuna-stuffed Tomatoes

Servings:2

Cooking Time: 5 Minutes

Ingredients:

- 2 medium beefsteak tomatoes, tops removed, seeded, membranes removed
- 2 pouches tuna packed in water, drained
- 1 medium stalk celery, trimmed and chopped
- 2 tablespoons mayonnaise
- ¼ teaspoon salt
- ¼ teaspoon ground black pepper
- 2 teaspoons coconut oil
- ¼ cup shredded mild Cheddar cheese

Directions:

1. Scoop pulp out of each tomato, leaving ½" shell.

2. In a medium bowl, mix tuna, celery, mayonnaise, salt, and pepper. Drizzle with coconut oil. Spoon ½ mixture into each tomato and top each with 2 tablespoons Cheddar.

3. Place tomatoes into ungreased air fryer basket. Adjust the temperature to 320°F and set the timer for 5 minutes. Cheese will be melted when done. Serve warm.

Miso Fish

Servings: 2

Cooking Time: 10 Minutes

Ingredients:

- 2 cod fish fillets
- 1 tbsp garlic, chopped
- 2 tsp swerve
- 2 tbsp miso

Directions:

1. Add all ingredients to the zip-lock bag. Shake well place in the refrigerator for overnight.

2. Place marinated fish fillets into the air fryer basket and cook at 350°F for 10 minutes.

3. Serve and enjoy.

Lime Flaming Halibut

Servings:2

Cooking Time: 20 Minutes

Ingredients:

- 2 tbsp butter, melted
- ½ tsp chili powder
- ½ cup bread crumbs
- 2 halibut fillets

Directions:

1. Preheat air fryer to 350ºF. In a bowl, mix the butter, chili powder and bread crumbs. Press mixture onto tops of halibut fillets. Place halibut in the greased frying basket and Air Fry for 10 minutes or until the fish is opaque and flake easily with a fork. Serve right away.

Creamy Salmon

Servings: 2
Cooking Time: 20 Minutes
Ingredients:
- ¾ lb. salmon, cut into 6 pieces
- ¼ cup yogurt
- 1 tbsp. olive oil
- 1 tbsp. dill, chopped
- 3 tbsp. sour cream
- Salt to taste

Directions:
1. Sprinkle some salt on the salmon.
2. Put the salmon slices in the Air Fryer basket and add in a drizzle of olive oil.
3. Air fry the salmon at 285°F for 10 minutes.
4. In the meantime, combine together the cream, dill, yogurt, and salt.
5. Plate up the salmon and pour the creamy sauce over it. Serve hot.

Crab-stuffed Avocado Boats

Servings:4
Cooking Time: 7 Minutes
Ingredients:
- 2 medium avocados, halved and pitted
- 8 ounces cooked crabmeat
- ¼ teaspoon Old Bay Seasoning
- 2 tablespoons peeled and diced yellow onion
- 2 tablespoons mayonnaise

Directions:
1. Scoop out avocado flesh in each avocado half, leaving ½" around edges to form a shell. Chop scooped-out avocado.
2. In a medium bowl, combine crabmeat, Old Bay Seasoning, onion, mayonnaise, and chopped avocado. Place ¼ mixture into each avocado shell.
3. Place avocado boats into ungreased air fryer basket. Adjust the temperature to 350°F and set the timer for 7 minutes. Avocado will be browned on the top and mixture will be bubbling when done. Serve warm.

Crispy Smelts

Servings:3
Cooking Time: 20 Minutes
Ingredients:
- 1 pound Cleaned smelts
- 3 tablespoons Tapioca flour
- Vegetable oil spray
- To taste Coarse sea salt or kosher salt

Directions:
1. Preheat the air fryer to 400°F.
2. Toss the smelts and tapioca flour in a large bowl until the little fish are evenly coated.
3. Lay the smelts out on a large cutting board. Lightly coat both sides of each fish with vegetable oil spray.

4. When the machine is at temperature, set the smelts close together in the basket, with a few even overlapping on top. Air-fry undisturbed for 20 minutes, until lightly browned and crisp.
5. Remove the basket from the machine and turn out the fish onto a wire rack. The smelts will most likely come out as one large block, or maybe in a couple of large pieces. Cool for a minute or two, then sprinkle the smelts with salt and break the block(s) into much smaller sections or individual fish to serve.

Maple Balsamic Glazed Salmon

Servings: 4
Cooking Time: 10 Minutes
Ingredients:
- 4 fillets of salmon
- salt and freshly ground black pepper
- vegetable oil
- ¼ cup pure maple syrup
- 3 tablespoons balsamic vinegar
- 1 teaspoon Dijon mustard

Directions:
1. Preheat the air fryer to 400°F.
2. Season the salmon well with salt and freshly ground black pepper. Spray or brush the bottom of the air fryer basket with vegetable oil and place the salmon fillets inside. Air-fry the salmon for 5 minutes.
3. While the salmon is air-frying, combine the maple syrup, balsamic vinegar and Dijon mustard in a small saucepan over medium heat and stir to blend well. Let the mixture simmer while the fish is cooking. It should start to thicken slightly, but keep your eye on it so it doesn't burn.
4. Brush the glaze on the salmon fillets and air-fry for an additional 5 minutes. The salmon should feel firm to the touch when finished and the glaze should be nicely browned on top. Brush a little more glaze on top before removing and serving with rice and vegetables, or a nice green salad.

Great Cat Fish

Servings:4
Cooking Time: 25 Minutes
Ingredients:
- ¼ cup seasoned fish fry
- 1 tbsp olive oil
- 1 tbsp parsley, chopped

Directions:
1. Preheat your air fryer to 400°F, and add seasoned fish fry, and fillets in a large Ziploc bag; massage well to coat. Place the fillets in your air fryer's cooking basket and cook for 10 minutes. Flip the fish and cook for 2-3 more minutes. Top with parsley and serve.

Easy Lobster Tail With Salted Butetr

Servings:4
Cooking Time: 6 Minutes
Ingredients:
- 2 tablespoons melted butter
- 4 lobster tails
- Salt and pepper to taste

Directions:
1. Preheat the air fryer to 390°F.
2. Place the grill pan accessory.
3. Cut the lobster through the tail section using a pair of kitchen scissors.
4. Brush the lobster tails with melted butter and season with salt and pepper to taste.
5. Place on the grill pan and cook for 6 minutes.

Panko-breaded Cod Fillets

Servings:2
Cooking Time: 20 Minutes
Ingredients:
- 1 lemon wedge, juiced and zested
- ½ cup panko bread crumbs
- Salt to taste
- 1 tbsp Dijon mustard
- 1 tbsp butter, melted
- 2 cod fillets

Directions:
1. Preheat air fryer to 350ºF. Combine all ingredients, except for the fish, in a bowl. Press mixture evenly across tops of cod fillets. Place fillets in the greased frying basket and Air Fry for 10 minutes until the cod is opaque and flakes easily with a fork. Serve immediately.

Italian Tuna Roast

Servings: 8
Cooking Time: 21 Minutes
Ingredients:
- cooking spray
- 1 tablespoon Italian seasoning
- ⅛ teaspoon ground black pepper
- 1 tablespoon extra-light olive oil
- 1 teaspoon lemon juice
- 1 tuna loin

Directions:
1. Spray baking dish with cooking spray and place in air fryer basket. Preheat air fryer to 390°F.
2. Mix together the Italian seasoning, pepper, oil, and lemon juice.
3. Using a dull table knife or butter knife, pierce top of tuna about every half inch: Insert knife into top of tuna roast and pierce almost all the way to the bottom.
4. Spoon oil mixture into each of the holes and use the knife to push seasonings into the tuna as deeply as possible.

5. Spread any remaining oil mixture on all outer surfaces of tuna.
6. Place tuna roast in baking dish and cook at 390°F for 20 minutes. Check temperature with a meat thermometer. Cook for an additional 1 minutes or until temperature reaches 145°F.
7. Remove basket from fryer and let tuna sit in basket for 10minutes.

Seared Scallops In Beurre Blanc

Servings: 4
Cooking Time: 15 Minutes
Ingredients:
- 1 lb sea scallops
- Salt and pepper to taste
- 2 tbsp butter, melted
- 1 lemon, zested and juiced
- 2 tbsp dry white wine

Directions:
1. Preheat the air fryer to 400°F. Sprinkle the scallops with salt and pepper, then set in a bowl. Combine the butter, lemon zest, lemon juice, and white wine in another bowl; mix well. Put the scallops in a baking pan and drizzle over them the mixture. Air Fry for 8-11 minutes, flipping over at about 5 minutes until opaque. Serve and enjoy!

Shrimp Burgers

Servings:4
Cooking Time: 10 Minutes
Ingredients:
- 10 ounces medium shrimp, peeled and deveined
- ¼ cup mayonnaise
- ½ cup panko bread crumbs
- ½ teaspoon Old Bay Seasoning
- ¼ teaspoon salt
- ⅛ teaspoon ground black pepper
- 4 hamburger buns

Directions:
1. Preheat the air fryer to 400°F.
2. In a food processor, add shrimp and pulse four times until broken down.
3. Scoop shrimp into a large bowl and mix with mayonnaise, bread crumbs, Old Bay, salt, and pepper until well combined.
4. Separate mixture into four portions and form into patties. They will feel wet but should be able to hold their shape.
5. Place in the air fryer basket and cook 10 minutes, turning halfway through cooking time, until burgers are brown and internal temperature reaches at least 145°F. Serve warm on buns.

Lobster Tails

Servings:4
Cooking Time: 10 Minutes
Ingredients:
- 4 lobster tails
- 2 tablespoons salted butter, melted
- 1 tablespoon finely minced garlic
- ¼ teaspoon salt
- ¼ teaspoon ground black pepper
- 2 tablespoons lemon juice

Directions:
1. Preheat the air fryer to 400°F.
2. Carefully cut open lobster tails with kitchen scissors and pull back the shell a little to expose the meat. Drizzle butter over each tail, then sprinkle with garlic, salt, and pepper.
3. Place tails in the air fryer basket and cook 10 minutes until lobster is firm and opaque and internal temperature reaches at least 145°F.
4. Drizzle lemon juice over lobster meat. Serve warm.

Buttery Lobster Tails

Servings:4
Cooking Time: 6 Minutes
Ingredients:
- 4 6- to 8-ounce shell-on raw lobster tails
- 2 tablespoons Butter, melted and cooled
- 1 teaspoon Lemon juice
- ½ teaspoon Finely grated lemon zest
- ½ teaspoon Garlic powder
- ½ teaspoon Table salt
- ½ teaspoon Ground black pepper

Directions:
1. Preheat the air fryer to 375°F .
2. To give the tails that restaurant look, you need to butterfly the meat. To do so, place a tail on a cutting board so that the shell is convex. Use kitchen shears to cut a line down the middle of the shell from the larger end to the smaller, cutting only the shell and not the meat below, and stopping before the back fins. Pry open the shell, leaving it intact. Use your clean fingers to separate the meat from the shell's sides and bottom, keeping it attached to the shell at the back near the fins. Pull the meat up and out of the shell through the cut line, laying the meat on top of the shell and closing the shell under the meat. Make two equidistant cuts down the meat from the larger end to near the smaller end, each about ¼ inch deep, for the classic restaurant look on the plate. Repeat this procedure with the remaining tail(s).
3. Stir the butter, lemon juice, zest, garlic powder, salt, and pepper in a small bowl until well combined. Brush this mixture over the lobster meat set atop the shells.
4. When the machine is at temperature, place the tails shell side down in the basket with as much air space between them as possible. Air-fry undisturbed for 6 minutes, or until the lobster meat has pink streaks over it and is firm.

5. Use kitchen tongs to transfer the tails to a wire rack. Cool for only a minute or two before serving.

Catalan Sardines With Romesco Sauce

Servings:2
Cooking Time: 15 Minutes
Ingredients:
- 2 cans skinless, boneless sardines in oil, drained
- ½ cup warmed romesco sauce
- ½ cup bread crumbs

Directions:
1. Preheat air fryer to 350ºF. In a shallow dish, add bread crumbs. Roll in sardines to coat. Place sardines in the greased frying basket and Air Fry for 6 minutes, turning once. Serve with romesco sauce.

Almond Topped Trout

Servings: 4
Cooking Time: 20 Minutes
Ingredients:
- 4 trout fillets
- 2 tbsp olive oil
- Salt and pepper to taste
- 2 garlic cloves, sliced
- 1 lemon, sliced
- 1 tbsp flaked almonds

Directions:
1. Preheat air fryer to 380°F. Lightly brush each fillet with olive oil on both sides and season with salt and pepper. Put the fillets in a single layer in the frying basket. Put the sliced garlic over the tops of the trout fillets, then top with lemon slices and cook for 12-15 minutes. Serve topped with flaked almonds and enjoy!

Fish-in-chips

Servings:4
Cooking Time: 11 Minutes
Ingredients:
- 1 cup All-purpose flour or potato starch
- 2 Large egg(s), well beaten
- 1½ cups Crushed plain potato chips, preferably thick-cut or ruffled (gluten-free, if a concern)
- 4 4-ounce skinless cod fillets

Directions:
1. Preheat the air fryer to 400°F.
2. Set up and fill three shallow soup plates or small pie plates on your counter: one for the flour, one for the beaten egg(s), and one for the crushed potato chips.
3. Dip a piece of cod in the flour, turning it to coat on all sides, even the ends and sides. Gently shake off any excess flour, then dip it in the beaten egg(s). Gently turn to coat it on all sides, then let any excess egg slip back into the rest. Set the fillet in the crushed potato chips and turn several

times and onto all sides, pressing gently to coat the fish. Dip it back in the egg(s), coating all sides but taking care that the coating doesn't slip off; then dip it back in the potato chips for a thick, even coating. Set it aside and coat more fillets in the same way.

4. When the machine is at temperature, set the fillets in the basket with as much air space between them as possible. Air-fry undisturbed for 11 minutes, until golden brown and firm but not hard.

5. Use kitchen tongs to transfer the fillets to a wire rack. Cool for just a minute or two before serving.

Cod Nuggets

Servings:4
Cooking Time: 12 Minutes
Ingredients:
- 2 boneless, skinless cod fillets
- 1 ½ teaspoons salt, divided
- ¾ teaspoon ground black pepper, divided
- 2 large eggs
- 1 cup plain bread crumbs

Directions:
1. Preheat the air fryer to 350°F.
2. Cut cod fillets into sixteen even-sized pieces. In a large bowl, add cod nuggets and sprinkle with 1 teaspoon salt and ½ teaspoon pepper.
3. In a small bowl, whisk eggs. In another small bowl, mix bread crumbs with remaining ½ teaspoon salt and ¼ teaspoon pepper.
4. One by one, dip nuggets in the eggs, shaking off excess before rolling in the bread crumb mixture. Repeat to make sixteen nuggets.
5. Place nuggets in the air fryer basket and spritz with cooking spray. Cook 12 minutes, turning halfway through cooking time. Nuggets will be done when golden brown and have an internal temperature of at least 145°F. Serve warm.

Lemon Pepper–breaded Tilapia

Servings:4
Cooking Time: 10 Minutes
Ingredients:
- 1 large egg
- ⅓ cup all-purpose flour
- ¼ cup grated Parmesan cheese
- ½ tablespoon lemon pepper seasoning
- 4 boneless, skinless tilapia fillets

Directions:
1. Preheat the air fryer to 375°F.
2. In a medium bowl, whisk egg. On a large plate, mix flour, Parmesan, and lemon pepper seasoning.
3. Pat tilapia dry. Dip each fillet into egg, gently shaking off excess. Press into flour mixture, then spritz both sides with cooking spray.
4. Place in the air fryer basket and cook 10 minutes, turning halfway through cooking, until fillets are golden and

crispy and internal temperature reaches at least 145°F. Serve warm.

Crab Cakes

Servings:4
Cooking Time: 12 Minutes
Ingredients:
- 2 cans lump crabmeat, drained
- ½ cup plain bread crumbs
- ½ cup mayonnaise
- 1 ½ teaspoons Old Bay Seasoning
- Zest and juice of ½ medium lemon
- ½ teaspoon salt
- ½ teaspoon ground black pepper
- Cooking spray

Directions:
1. Preheat the air fryer to 375°F.
2. In a large bowl, mix all ingredients.
3. Scoop ¼ cup mixture and form into a 4" patty. Repeat to make eight crab cakes. Spritz cakes with cooking spray.
4. Place in the air fryer basket and cook 12 minutes, turning halfway through cooking time, until edges are brown and center is firm. Serve warm.

Lemon Butter Scallops

Servings: 1
Cooking Time: 30 Minutes
Ingredients:
- 1 lemon
- 1 lb. scallops
- ½ cup butter
- ¼ cup parsley, chopped

Directions:
1. Juice the lemon into a Ziploc bag.
2. Wash your scallops, dry them, and season to taste. Put them in the bag with the lemon juice. Refrigerate for an hour.
3. Remove the bag from the refrigerator and leave for about twenty minutes until it returns to room temperature. Transfer the scallops into a foil pan that is small enough to be placed inside the fryer.
4. Pre-heat the fryer at 400°F and put the rack inside.
5. Place the foil pan on the rack and cook for five minutes.
6. In the meantime, melt the butter in a saucepan over a medium heat. Zest the lemon over the saucepan, then add in the chopped parsley. Mix well.
7. Take care when removing the pan from the fryer. Transfer the contents to a plate and drizzle with the lemon-butter mixture. Serve hot.

Zesty Mahi Mahi

Servings:3
Cooking Time:8 Minutes
Ingredients:
- 1½ pounds Mahi Mahi fillets
- 1 lemon, cut into slices
- 1 tablespoon fresh dill, chopped
- ½ teaspoon red chili powder
- Salt and ground black pepper, as required

Directions:
1. Preheat the Air fryer to 375°F and grease an Air fryer basket.
2. Season the Mahi Mahi fillets evenly with chili powder, salt, and black pepper.
3. Arrange the Mahi Mahi fillets into the Air fryer basket and top with the lemon slices.
4. Cook for about 8 minutes and dish out
5. Place the lemon slices over the salmon the salmon fillets in the serving plates.
6. Garnish with fresh dill and serve warm.

Maple Butter Salmon

Servings:4
Cooking Time: 12 Minutes
Ingredients:
- 2 tablespoons salted butter, melted
- 1 teaspoon low-carb maple syrup
- 1 teaspoon yellow mustard
- 4 boneless, skinless salmon fillets
- ½ teaspoon salt

Directions:
1. In a small bowl, whisk together butter, syrup, and mustard. Brush ½ mixture over each fillet on both sides. Sprinkle fillets with salt on both sides.
2. Place salmon into ungreased air fryer basket. Adjust the temperature to 400°F and set the timer for 12 minutes. Halfway through cooking, brush fillets on both sides with remaining syrup mixture. Salmon will easily flake and have

an internal temperature of at least 145°F when done. Serve warm.

Southern-style Catfish

Servings:4
Cooking Time: 12 Minutes
Ingredients:
- 4 catfish fillets
- ⅓ cup heavy whipping cream
- 1 tablespoon lemon juice
- 1 cup blanched finely ground almond flour
- 2 teaspoons Old Bay Seasoning
- ½ teaspoon salt
- ¼ teaspoon ground black pepper

Directions:
1. Place catfish fillets into a large bowl with cream and pour in lemon juice. Stir to coat.
2. In a separate large bowl, mix flour and Old Bay Seasoning.
3. Remove each fillet and gently shake off excess cream. Sprinkle with salt and pepper. Press each fillet gently into flour mixture on both sides to coat.
4. Place fillets into ungreased air fryer basket. Adjust the temperature to 400°F and set the timer for 12 minutes, turning fillets halfway through cooking. Catfish will be golden brown and have an internal temperature of at least 145°F when done. Serve warm.

Simple Sesame Squid On The Grill

Servings:3
Cooking Time: 10 Minutes
Ingredients:
- 1 ½ pounds squid, cleaned
- 2 tablespoon toasted sesame oil
- Salt and pepper to taste

Directions:
1. Preheat the air fryer at 390°F.
2. Place the grill pan accessory in the air fryer.
3. Season the squid with sesame oil, salt and pepper.
4. Grill the squid for 10 minutes.

Chapter 7. Vegetable Side Dishes Recipes

Grits Again

Servings: 2
Cooking Time: 10 Minutes
Ingredients:
- cooked grits
- plain breadcrumbs
- oil for misting or cooking spray
- honey or maple syrup for serving (optional)

Directions:
1. While grits are still warm, spread them into a square or rectangular baking pan, about ½-inch thick. If your grits are thicker than that, scoop some out into another pan.
2. Chill several hours or overnight, until grits are cold and firm.
3. When ready to cook, pour off any water that has collected in pan and cut grits into 2- to 3-inch squares.
4. Dip grits squares in breadcrumbs and place in air fryer basket in single layer, close but not touching.
5. Cook at 390°F for 10 minutes, until heated through and crispy brown on the outside.
6. Serve while hot either plain or with a drizzle of honey or maple syrup.

French Fries

Servings: 4
Cooking Time: 25 Minutes
Ingredients:
- 2 cups fresh potatoes
- 2 teaspoons oil
- ½ teaspoon salt

Directions:
1. Cut potatoes into ½-inch-wide slices, then lay slices flat and cut into ½-inch sticks.
2. Rinse potato sticks and blot dry with a clean towel.
3. In a bowl or sealable plastic bag, mix the potatoes, oil, and salt together.
4. Pour into air fryer basket.
5. Cook at 390°F for 10minutes. Shake basket to redistribute fries and continue cooking for approximately 15minutes, until fries are golden brown.

Dijon Roast Cabbage

Servings:4
Cooking Time: 10 Minutes
Ingredients:
- 1 small head cabbage, cored and sliced into 1"-thick slices
- 2 tablespoons olive oil, divided
- ½ teaspoon salt
- 1 tablespoon Dijon mustard
- 1 teaspoon apple cider vinegar
- 1 teaspoon granular erythritol

Directions:
1. Drizzle each cabbage slice with 1 tablespoon olive oil, then sprinkle with salt. Place slices into ungreased air fryer basket, working in batches if needed. Adjust the temperature to 350°F and set the timer for 10 minutes. Cabbage will be tender and edges will begin to brown when done.
2. In a small bowl, whisk remaining olive oil with mustard, vinegar, and erythritol. Drizzle over cabbage in a large serving dish. Serve warm.

Buttery Mushrooms

Servings:4
Cooking Time: 10 Minutes
Ingredients:
- 8 ounces cremini mushrooms, halved
- 2 tablespoons salted butter, melted
- ¼ teaspoon salt
- ¼ teaspoon ground black pepper

Directions:
1. In a medium bowl, toss mushrooms with butter, then sprinkle with salt and pepper. Place into ungreased air fryer basket. Adjust the temperature to 400°F and set the timer for 10 minutes, shaking the basket halfway through cooking. Mushrooms will be tender when done. Serve warm.

Roasted Garlic And Thyme Tomatoes

Servings: 2
Cooking Time: 15 Minutes
Ingredients:
- 4 Roma tomatoes
- 1 tablespoon olive oil
- salt and freshly ground black pepper
- 1 clove garlic, minced
- ½ teaspoon dried thyme

Directions:
1. Preheat the air fryer to 390°F.
2. Cut the tomatoes in half and scoop out the seeds and any pithy parts with your fingers. Place the tomatoes in a bowl and toss with the olive oil, salt, pepper, garlic and thyme.
3. Transfer the tomatoes to the air fryer, cut side up. Air-fry for 15 minutes. The edges should just start to brown. Let the tomatoes cool to an edible temperature for a few minutes and then use in pastas, on top of crostini, or as an accompaniment to any poultry, meat or fish.

Simple Baked Potatoes With Dill Yogurt

Servings: 4
Cooking Time: 45 Minutes
Ingredients:
- 4 Yukon gold potatoes
- Salt and black pepper
- ½ cup Greek yogurt
- ¼ cup minced dill
- Cooking spray

Directions:
1. Pierce the potatoes with a fork. Lightly coat them with sprays of cooking oil, then season with salt. Preheat air fryer to 400°F. Air Fry the potatoes in the greased frying basket for 30-35 minutes, flipping once halfway through cooking until completely cooked and slightly crispy. A knife will cut into the center of the potato with ease. Remove them to a serving dish. Add toppings of yogurt, dill, salt, and pepper to taste.

Perfect French Fries

Servings: 3
Cooking Time: 37 Minutes
Ingredients:
- 1 pound Large russet potato(es)
- Vegetable oil or olive oil spray
- ½ teaspoon Table salt

Directions:
1. Cut each potato lengthwise into ¼-inch-thick slices. Cut each of these lengthwise into ¼-inch-thick matchsticks.
2. Set the potato matchsticks in a big bowl of cool water and soak for 5 minutes. Drain in a colander set in the sink, then spread the matchsticks out on paper towels and dry them very well.
3. Preheat the air fryer to 225°F.
4. When the machine is at temperature, arrange the matchsticks in an even layer in the basket. Air-fry for 20 minutes, tossing and rearranging the fries twice.
5. Pour the contents of the basket into a big bowl. Increase the air fryer's temperature to 325°F.
6. Generously coat the fries with vegetable or olive oil spray. Toss well, then coat them again to make sure they're covered on all sides, tossing a couple of times to make sure.
7. When the machine is at temperature, pour the fries into the basket and air-fry for 12 minutes, tossing and rearranging the fries at least twice.
8. Increase the machine's temperature to 375°F. Air-fry for 5 minutes more, tossing and rearranging the fries at least twice to keep them from burning and to make sure they all get an even measure of the heat, until brown and crisp.
9. Pour the contents of the basket into a serving bowl. Toss the fries with the salt and serve hot.

Salt And Pepper Baked Potatoes

Servings: 4
Cooking Time: 40 Minutes
Ingredients:
- 1 to 2 tablespoons olive oil
- 4 medium russet potatoes
- salt and coarsely ground black pepper
- butter, sour cream, chopped fresh chives, scallions or bacon bits (optional)

Directions:
1. Preheat the air fryer to 400°F.
2. Rub the olive oil all over the potatoes and season them generously with salt and coarsely ground black pepper. Pierce all sides of the potatoes several times with the tines of a fork.
3. Air-fry for 40 minutes, turning the potatoes over halfway through the cooking time.
4. Serve the potatoes, split open with butter, sour cream, fresh chives, scallions or bacon bits.

Perfect Asparagus

Servings: 3
Cooking Time: 10 Minutes
Ingredients:
- 1 pound Very thin asparagus spears
- 2 tablespoons Olive oil
- 1 teaspoon Coarse sea salt or kosher salt
- ¾ teaspoon Finely grated lemon zest

Directions:
1. Preheat the air fryer to 400°F.
2. Trim just enough off the bottom of the asparagus spears so they'll fit in the basket. Put the spears on a large plate and drizzle them with some of the olive oil. Turn them over and drizzle more olive oil, working to get all the spears coated.
3. When the machine is at temperature, place the spears in one direction in the basket. They may be touching. Air-fry for 10 minutes, tossing and rearranging the spears twice, until tender.
4. Dump the contents of the basket on a serving platter. Spread out the spears. Sprinkle them with the salt and lemon zest while still warm. Serve at once.

Simple Peppared Carrot Chips

Servings: 4
Cooking Time: 15 Minutes
Ingredients:
- 3 carrots, cut into coins
- 1 tbsp sesame oil
- Salt and pepper to taste

Directions:
1. Preheat air fryer at 375ºF. Combine all ingredients in a bowl. Place carrots in the frying basket and Roast for 10 minutes, tossing once. Serve right away.

Macaroni And Cheese

Servings: 4
Cooking Time: 25 Minutes
Ingredients:
- 1 ½ cups dry elbow macaroni
- 1 cup chicken broth
- ½ cup whole milk
- 2 tablespoons salted butter, melted
- 8 ounces sharp Cheddar cheese, shredded, divided
- ½ teaspoon ground black pepper

Directions:
1. Preheat the air fryer to 350°F.
2. In a 6" baking dish, combine macaroni, broth, milk, butter, half the Cheddar, and pepper. Stir to combine.
3. Place in the air fryer basket and cook 12 minutes.
4. Stir in remaining Cheddar, then return the basket to the air fryer and cook 13 additional minutes.
5. Stir macaroni and cheese until creamy. Let cool 10 minutes before serving.

Brussels Sprouts

Servings: 3
Cooking Time: 5 Minutes
Ingredients:
- 1 10-ounce package frozen brussels sprouts, thawed and halved
- 2 teaspoons olive oil
- salt and pepper

Directions:
1. Toss the brussels sprouts and olive oil together.
2. Place them in the air fryer basket and season to taste with salt and pepper.
3. Cook at 360°F for approximately 5minutes, until the edges begin to brown.

Roman Artichokes

Servings: 4
Cooking Time: 12 Minutes
Ingredients:
- 2 9-ounce box(es) frozen artichoke heart quarters, thawed
- 1½ tablespoons Olive oil
- 2 teaspoons Minced garlic
- 1 teaspoon Table salt
- Up to ½ teaspoon Red pepper flakes

Directions:
1. Preheat the air fryer to 400°F.
2. Gently toss the artichoke heart quarters, oil, garlic, salt, and red pepper flakes in a bowl until the quarters are well coated.
3. When the machine is at temperature, scrape the contents of the bowl into the basket. Spread the artichoke heart quarters out into as close to one layer as possible. Air-fry undisturbed for 8 minutes. Gently toss and rearrange the quarters so that any covered or touching parts are now exposed to the air currents, then air-fry undisturbed for 4 minutes more, until very crisp.
4. Gently pour the contents of the basket onto a wire rack. Cool for a few minutes before serving.

Fried Mashed Potato Balls

Servings:4
Cooking Time: 10 Minutes
Ingredients:
- 2 cups mashed potatoes
- ¾ cup sour cream, divided
- 1 teaspoon salt
- ½ teaspoon ground black pepper
- 1 cup shredded sharp Cheddar cheese
- 4 slices bacon, cooked and crumbled
- 1 cup panko bread crumbs
- Cooking spray

Directions:
1. Preheat the air fryer to 400°F. Cut parchment paper to fit the air fryer basket.
2. In a large bowl, mix mashed potatoes, ½ cup sour cream, salt, pepper, Cheddar, and bacon. Form twelve balls using 2 tablespoons of the potato mixture per ball.
3. Divide remaining ¼ cup sour cream evenly among mashed potato balls, coating each before rolling in bread crumbs.
4. Place balls on parchment in the air fryer basket and spritz with cooking spray. Cook 10 minutes until brown. Serve warm.

Roasted Asparagus

Servings:4
Cooking Time: 12 Minutes
Ingredients:
- 1 tablespoon olive oil
- 1 pound asparagus spears, ends trimmed
- ¼ teaspoon salt
- ¼ teaspoon ground black pepper
- 1 tablespoon salted butter, melted

Directions:
1. In a large bowl, drizzle olive oil over asparagus spears and sprinkle with salt and pepper.
2. Place spears into ungreased air fryer basket. Adjust the temperature to 375°F and set the timer for 12 minutes, shaking the basket halfway through cooking. Asparagus will be lightly browned and tender when done.
3. Transfer to a large dish and drizzle with butter. Serve warm.

Corn On The Cob

Servings: 4
Cooking Time: 12 Minutes
Ingredients:
- 2 large ears fresh corn
- olive oil for misting
- salt (optional)

Directions:
1. Shuck corn, remove silks, and wash.
2. Cut or break each ear in half crosswise.
3. Spray corn with olive oil.
4. Cook at 390°F for 12 minutes or until browned as much as you like.
5. Serve plain or with coarsely ground salt.

Fried Pearl Onions With Balsamic Vinegar And Basil

Servings: 2
Cooking Time: 10 Minutes
Ingredients:
- 1 pound fresh pearl onions
- 1 tablespoon olive oil
- salt and freshly ground black pepper
- 1 teaspoon high quality aged balsamic vinegar
- 1 tablespoon chopped fresh basil leaves (or mint)

Directions:
1. Preheat the air fryer to 400°F.
2. Decide whether you want to peel the onions before or after they cook. Peeling them ahead of time is a little more laborious. Peeling after they cook is easier, but a little messier since the onions are hot and you may discard more of the onion than you'd like to. If you opt to peel them first, trim the tiny root of the onions off and pinch off any loose papery skins. Toss the pearl onions with the olive oil, salt and freshly ground black pepper.
3. Air-fry for 10 minutes, shaking the basket a couple of times during the cooking process.
4. Let the onions cool slightly and then slip off any remaining skins.
5. Toss the onions with the balsamic vinegar and basil and serve.

Crispy Herbed Potatoes

Servings: 6
Cooking Time: 20 Minutes
Ingredients:
- 3 medium baking potatoes, washed and cubed
- ½ teaspoon dried thyme
- 1 teaspoon minced dried rosemary
- ½ teaspoon garlic powder
- 1 teaspoon sea salt
- ½ teaspoon black pepper
- 2 tablespoons extra-virgin olive oil

- ¼ cup chopped parsley

Directions:
1. Preheat the air fryer to 390°F.
2. Pat the potatoes dry. In a large bowl, mix together the cubed potatoes, thyme, rosemary, garlic powder, sea salt, and pepper. Drizzle and toss with olive oil.
3. Pour the herbed potatoes into the air fryer basket. Cook for 20 minutes, stirring every 5 minutes.
4. Toss the cooked potatoes with chopped parsley and serve immediately.
5. VARY IT! Potatoes are versatile — add any spice or seasoning mixture you prefer and create your own favorite side dish.

Cheesy Loaded Broccoli

Servings:2
Cooking Time: 10 Minutes
Ingredients:
- 3 cups fresh broccoli florets
- 1 tablespoon coconut oil
- ¼ teaspoon salt
- ½ cup shredded sharp Cheddar cheese
- ¼ cup sour cream
- 4 slices cooked sugar-free bacon, crumbled
- 1 medium scallion, trimmed and sliced on the bias

Directions:
1. Place broccoli into ungreased air fryer basket, drizzle with coconut oil, and sprinkle with salt. Adjust the temperature to 350°F and set the timer for 8 minutes. Shake basket three times during cooking to avoid burned spots.
2. When timer beeps, sprinkle broccoli with Cheddar and set the timer for 2 additional minutes. When done, cheese will be melted and broccoli will be tender.
3. Serve warm in a large serving dish, topped with sour cream, crumbled bacon, and scallion slices.

Simple Zucchini Ribbons

Servings:4
Cooking Time: 15 Minutes
Ingredients:
- 2 zucchini
- 2 tsp butter, melted
- ¼ tsp garlic powder
- ¼ tsp chili flakes
- 8 cherry tomatoes, halved
- Salt and pepper to taste

Directions:
1. Preheat air fryer to 275ºF. Cut the zucchini into ribbons with a vegetable peeler. Mix them with butter, garlic, chili flakes, salt, and pepper in a bowl. Transfer to the frying basket and Air Fry for 2 minutes. Toss and add the cherry tomatoes. Cook for another 2 minutes. Serve.

Basic Corn On The Cob

Servings: 4
Cooking Time: 15 Minutes
Ingredients:
- 3 ears of corn, shucked and halved
- 2 tbsp butter, melted
- Salt and pepper to taste
- 1 tsp minced garlic
- 1 tsp paprika

Directions:
1. Preheat air fryer at 400ºF. Toss all ingredients in a bowl. Place corn in the frying basket and Bake for 7 minutes, turning once. Serve immediately.

Pancetta Mushroom & Onion Sautée

Servings:4
Cooking Time: 20 Minutes
Ingredients:
- 16 oz white button mushrooms, stems trimmed, halved
- 1 onion, cut into half-moons
- 4 pancetta slices, diced
- 1 clove garlic, minced

Directions:
1. Preheat air fryer to 350ºF. Add all ingredients, except for the garlic, to the frying basket and Air Fry for 8 minutes, tossing once. Stir in the garlic and cook for 1 more minute. Serve right away.

Roasted Fennel Salad

Servings: 3
Cooking Time: 20 Minutes
Ingredients:
- 3 cups (about ¾ pound) Trimmed fennel, roughly chopped
- 1½ tablespoons Olive oil
- ¼ teaspoon Table salt
- ¼ teaspoon Ground black pepper
- 1½ tablespoons White balsamic vinegar

Directions:
1. Preheat the air fryer to 400°F.
2. Toss the fennel, olive oil, salt, and pepper in a large bowl until the fennel is well coated in the oil.
3. When the machine is at temperature, pour the fennel into the basket, spreading it out into as close to one layer as possible. Air-fry for 20 minutes, tossing and rearranging the fennel pieces twice so that any covered or touching parts get exposed to the air currents, until golden at the edges and softened.
4. Pour the fennel into a serving bowl. Add the vinegar while hot. Toss well, then cool a couple of minutes before serving. Or serve at room temperature.

Sweet Roasted Pumpkin Rounds

Servings: 4

Cooking Time: 35 Minutes
Ingredients:
- 1 pumpkin
- 1 tbsp honey
- 1 tbsp melted butter
- ¼ tsp cardamom
- ¼ tsp sea salt

Directions:
1. Preheat the air fryer to 370°F. Cut the pumpkin in half lengthwise and remove the seeds. Slice each half crosswise into 1-inch-wide half-circles, then cut each half-circle in half again to make quarter rounds. Combine the honey, butter, cardamom, and salt in a bowl and mix well. Toss the pumpkin in the mixture until coated, then put into the frying basket. Bake for 15-20 minutes, shaking once during cooking until the edges start to brown and the squash is tender.

Roasted Broccoli

Servings:4
Cooking Time: 8 Minutes
Ingredients:
- 12 ounces broccoli florets
- 2 tablespoons olive oil
- ½ teaspoon salt
- ¼ teaspoon ground black pepper

Directions:
1. Preheat the air fryer to 360°F.
2. In a medium bowl, place broccoli and drizzle with oil. Sprinkle with salt and pepper.
3. Place in the air fryer basket and cook 8 minutes, shaking the basket twice during cooking, until the edges are brown and the center is tender. Serve warm.

Chipotle Chickpea Tacos

Servings: 4
Cooking Time: 10 Minutes
Ingredients:
- 2 cans chickpeas, drained and rinsed
- ¼ cup adobo sauce
- ¾ teaspoon salt
- ¼ teaspoon ground black pepper
- 8 medium flour tortillas, warmed
- 1 ½ cups chopped avocado
- ½ cup chopped fresh cilantro

Directions:
1. Preheat the air fryer to 375°F.
2. In a large bowl, toss chickpeas, adobo, salt, and pepper to fully coat.
3. Using a slotted spoon, place chickpeas in the air fryer basket and cook 10 minutes, shaking the basket twice during cooking, until tender.

4. To assemble, scoop ¼ cup chickpeas into a tortilla, then top with avocado and cilantro. Repeat with remaining tortillas and filling. Serve warm.

Corn Muffins

Servings: 12
Cooking Time: 10 Minutes
Ingredients:
- ½ cup all-purpose flour
- ½ cup cornmeal
- ¼ cup granulated sugar
- ½ teaspoon baking powder
- ¼ cup salted butter, melted
- ½ cup buttermilk
- 1 large egg

Directions:
1. Preheat the air fryer to 350°F.
2. In a large bowl, whisk together flour, cornmeal, sugar, and baking powder.
3. Add butter, buttermilk, and egg to dry mixture. Stir until well combined.
4. Divide batter evenly among twelve silicone or aluminum muffin cups, filling cups about halfway. Working in batches as needed, place in the air fryer and cook 10 minutes until golden brown. Let cool 5 minutes before serving.

Sweet Butternut Squash

Servings:8
Cooking Time: 15 Minutes
Ingredients:
- 1 medium butternut squash, peeled and cubed
- 2 tablespoons salted butter, melted
- ½ teaspoon salt
- 1 ½ tablespoons brown sugar
- ½ teaspoon ground cinnamon

Directions:
1. Preheat the air fryer to 400°F.
2. In a large bowl, place squash and add butter. Toss to coat. Sprinkle salt, brown sugar, and cinnamon over squash and toss to fully coat.
3. Place squash in the air fryer basket and cook 15 minutes, shaking the basket three times during cooking, until the edges are golden and the center is fork-tender. Serve warm.

Green Beans

Servings: 4
Cooking Time: 12 Minutes
Ingredients:
- 1 pound fresh green beans
- 2 tablespoons Italian salad dressing
- salt and pepper

Directions:
1. Wash beans and snap off stem ends.

2. In a large bowl, toss beans with Italian dressing.
3. Cook at 330°F for 5minutes. Shake basket or stir and cook 5minutes longer. Shake basket again and, if needed, continue cooking for 2 minutes, until as tender as you like. Beans should shrivel slightly and brown in places.
4. Sprinkle with salt and pepper to taste.

Pop Corn Broccoli

Servings: 1
Cooking Time: 10 Minutes
Ingredients:
- 4 egg yolks
- ¼ cup butter, melted
- 2 cups coconut flower
- Salt and pepper
- 2 cups broccoli florets

Directions:
1. In a bowl, whisk the egg yolks and melted butter together. Throw in the coconut flour, salt and pepper, then stir again to combine well.
2. Pre-heat the fryer at 400°F.
3. Dip each broccoli floret into the mixture and place in the fryer. Cook for six minutes, in multiple batches if necessary. Take care when removing them from the fryer and enjoy!

Cheesy Baked Asparagus

Servings:4
Cooking Time: 18 Minutes
Ingredients:
- ½ cup heavy whipping cream
- ½ cup grated Parmesan cheese
- 2 ounces cream cheese, softened
- 1 pound asparagus, ends trimmed, chopped into 1" pieces
- ¼ teaspoon salt
- ¼ teaspoon ground black pepper

Directions:
1. In a medium bowl, whisk together heavy cream, Parmesan, and cream cheese until combined.
2. Place asparagus into an ungreased 6" round nonstick baking dish. Pour cheese mixture over top and sprinkle with salt and pepper.
3. Place dish into air fryer basket. Adjust the temperature to 350°F and set the timer for 18 minutes. Asparagus will be tender when done. Serve warm.

Polenta

Servings: 4
Cooking Time: 15 Minutes
Ingredients:
- 1 pound polenta
- ¼ cup flour
- oil for misting or cooking spray

Directions:
1. Cut polenta into ½-inch slices.

2. Dip slices in flour to coat well. Spray both sides with oil or cooking spray.
3. Cook at 390°F for 5minutes. Turn polenta and spray both sides again with oil.
4. Cook 10 more minutes or until brown and crispy.

Spicy Fried Green Beans

Servings: 2
Cooking Time: 8 Minutes
Ingredients:
- 12 ounces green beans, trimmed
- 2 small dried hot red chili peppers (like árbol)
- ¼ cup panko breadcrumbs
- 1 tablespoon olive oil
- ½ teaspoon salt
- ⅛ teaspoon crushed red pepper flakes
- 2 scallions, thinly sliced

Directions:
1. Preheat the air fryer to 400°F.
2. Toss the green beans, chili peppers and panko breadcrumbs with the olive oil, salt and crushed red pepper flakes.
3. Air-fry for 8 minutes, shaking the basket once during the cooking process. The crumbs will fall into the bottom drawer – don't worry.
4. Transfer the green beans to a serving dish, sprinkle the scallions and the toasted crumbs from the air fryer drawer on top and serve. The dried peppers are not to be eaten, but they do look nice with the green beans. You can leave them in, or take them out as you please.

Cheesy Texas Toast

Servings: 2
Cooking Time: 4 Minutes
Ingredients:
- 2 1-inch-thick slice(s) Italian bread
- 4 teaspoons Softened butter
- 2 teaspoons Minced garlic
- ¼ cup (about ¾ ounce) Finely grated Parmesan cheese

Directions:
1. Preheat the air fryer to 400°F.
2. Spread one side of a slice of bread with 2 teaspoons butter. Sprinkle with 1 teaspoon minced garlic, followed by 2 tablespoons grated cheese. Repeat this process if you're making one or more additional toasts.
3. When the machine is at temperature, put the bread slice(s) cheese side up in the basket (with as much air space between them as possible if you're making more than one). Air-fry undisturbed for 4 minutes, or until browned and crunchy.
4. Use a nonstick-safe spatula to transfer the toasts cheese side up to a wire rack. Cool for 5 minutes before serving.

Acorn Squash Halves With Maple Butter Glaze

Servings: 2
Cooking Time: 33 Minutes
Ingredients:
- 1 medium Acorn squash
- Vegetable oil spray
- ¼ teaspoon Table salt
- 1½ tablespoons Butter, melted
- 1½ tablespoons Maple syrup

Directions:
1. Preheat the air fryer to 325°F.
2. Cut a squash in half through the stem end. Use a flatware spoon to scrape out and discard the seeds and membranes in each half. Use a paring knife to make a crisscross pattern of cuts about ½ inch apart and ¼ inch deep across the "meat" of the squash. If working with a second squash, repeat this step for that one.
3. Generously coat the cut side of the squash halves with vegetable oil spray. Sprinkle the halves with the salt. Set them in the basket cut side up with at least ¼ inch between them. Air-fry undisturbed for 30 minutes.
4. Increase the machine's temperature to 400°F. Mix the melted butter and syrup in a small bowl until uniform. Brush this mixture over the cut sides of the squash(es), letting it pool in the center. Air-fry undisturbed for 3 minutes, or until the glaze is bubbling.
5. Use a nonstick-safe spatula and kitchen tongs to transfer the squash halves cut side up to a wire rack. Cool for 5 to 10 minutes before serving.

Taco Okra

Servings: 3
Cooking Time: 10 Minutes
Ingredients:
- 9 oz okra, chopped
- 1 teaspoon taco seasoning
- 1 teaspoon sunflower oil

Directions:
1. In the mixing bowl mix up chopped okra, taco seasoning, and sunflower oil. Then preheat the air fryer to 385°F. Put the okra mixture in the air fryer and cook it for 5 minutes. Then shake the vegetables well and cook them for 5 minutes more.

Spiced Pumpkin Wedges

Servings: 4
Cooking Time: 35 Minutes
Ingredients:
- 2 ½ cups pumpkin, cubed
- 2 tbsp olive oil
- Salt and pepper to taste
- ¼ tsp pumpkin pie spice
- 1 tbsp thyme

- ¼ cup grated Parmesan

Directions:

1. Preheat air fryer to 360°F. Put the cubed pumpkin with olive oil, salt, pumpkin pie spice, black pepper, and thyme in a bowl and stir until the pumpkin is well coated. Pour this mixture into the frying basket and Roast for 18-20 minutes, stirring once. Sprinkle the pumpkin with grated Parmesan. Serve and enjoy!

Foil Packet Lemon Butter Asparagus

Servings: 4
Cooking Time: 15 Minutes

Ingredients:

- 1 pound asparagus, ends trimmed
- ¼ cup salted butter, cubed
- Zest and juice of ½ medium lemon
- ½ teaspoon salt
- ¼ teaspoon ground black pepper

Directions:

1. Preheat the air fryer to 375°F. Cut a 6" × 6" square of foil.
2. Place asparagus on foil square.
3. Dot asparagus with butter. Sprinkle lemon zest, salt, and pepper on top of asparagus. Drizzle lemon juice over asparagus.
4. Fold foil over asparagus and seal the edges closed to form a packet.
5. Place in the air fryer basket and cook 15 minutes until tender. Serve warm.

Parmesan Garlic Fries

Servings: 4
Cooking Time: 20 Minutes

Ingredients:

- 2 medium Yukon gold potatoes, washed
- 1 tablespoon extra-virgin olive oil
- 1 garlic clove, minced
- 2 tablespoons finely grated parmesan cheese
- ¼ teaspoon black pepper
- ¼ teaspoon salt
- 1 tablespoon freshly chopped parsley

Directions:

1. Preheat the air fryer to 400°F.
2. Slice the potatoes into long strips about ¼-inch thick. In a large bowl, toss the potatoes with the olive oil, garlic, cheese, pepper, and salt.
3. Place the fries into the air fryer basket and cook for 4 minutes; shake the basket and cook another 4 minutes.
4. Remove and serve warm.

Tasty Herb Tomatoes

Servings: 4
Cooking Time: 15 Minutes

Ingredients:

- 2 large tomatoes, halved

- 1 tbsp olive oil
- 1/2 tsp thyme, chopped
- 2 garlic cloves, minced
- Pepper
- Salt

Directions:

1. Add all ingredients into the bowl and toss well.
2. Transfer tomatoes into the air fryer basket and cook at 390°F for 15 minutes.
3. Serve and enjoy.

Cinnamon Roasted Pumpkin

Servings: 2
Cooking Time: 25 Minutes

Ingredients:

- 1 lb pumpkin, halved crosswise and seeded
- 1 tsp coconut oil
- 1 tsp sugar
- ½ tsp ground nutmeg
- 1 tsp ground cinnamon

Directions:

1. Prepare the pumpkin by rubbing coconut oil on the cut sides. In a small bowl, combine sugar, nutmeg and cinnamon. Sprinkle over the pumpkin. Preheat air fryer to 325°F. Put the pumpkin in the greased frying basket, cut sides up. Bake until the squash is soft in the center, 15 minutes. Test with a knife to ensure softness. Serve.

Rosemary Roasted Potatoes With Lemon

Servings: 4
Cooking Time: 12 Minutes

Ingredients:

- 1 pound small red-skinned potatoes, halved or cut into bite-sized chunks
- 1 tablespoon olive oil
- 1 teaspoon finely chopped fresh rosemary
- ¼ teaspoon salt
- freshly ground black pepper
- 1 tablespoon lemon zest

Directions:

1. Preheat the air fryer to 400°F.
2. Toss the potatoes with the olive oil, rosemary, salt and freshly ground black pepper.
3. Air-fry for 12 minutes, tossing the potatoes a few times throughout the cooking process.
4. As soon as the potatoes are tender to a knifepoint, toss them with the lemon zest and more salt if desired.

Roasted Brussels Sprouts

Servings:6
Cooking Time: 10 Minutes
Ingredients:
- 1 pound fresh Brussels sprouts, trimmed and halved
- 2 tablespoons coconut oil
- ½ teaspoon salt
- ¼ teaspoon ground black pepper
- ½ teaspoon garlic powder
- 1 tablespoon salted butter, melted

Directions:
1. Place Brussels sprouts into a large bowl. Drizzle with coconut oil and sprinkle with salt, pepper, and garlic powder.
2. Place Brussels sprouts into ungreased air fryer basket. Adjust the temperature to 350°F and set the timer for 10 minutes, shaking the basket three times during cooking. Brussels sprouts will be dark golden and tender when done.
3. Place cooked sprouts in a large serving dish and drizzle with butter. Serve warm.

Charred Radicchio Salad

Servings: 4
Cooking Time: 5 Minutes
Ingredients:
- 2 Small 5- to 6-ounce radicchio head(s)
- 3 tablespoons Olive oil
- ½ teaspoon Table salt
- 2 tablespoons Balsamic vinegar
- Up to ¼ teaspoon Red pepper flakes

Directions:
1. Preheat the air fryer to 375°F.
2. Cut the radicchio head(s) into quarters through the stem end. Brush the oil over the heads, particularly getting it between the leaves along the cut sides. Sprinkle the radicchio quarters with the salt.
3. When the machine is at temperature, set the quarters cut sides up in the basket with as much air space between them as possible. They should not touch. Air-fry undisturbed for 5 minutes, watching carefully because they burn quickly, until blackened in bits and soft.
4. Use a nonstick-safe spatula to transfer the quarters to a cutting board. Cool for a minute or two, then cut out the thick stems inside the heads. Discard these tough bits and chop the remaining heads into bite-size bits. Scrape them into a bowl. Add the vinegar and red pepper flakes. Toss well and serve warm.

Wilted Brussels Sprout Slaw

Servings: 4
Cooking Time: 18 Minutes
Ingredients:
- 2 Thick-cut bacon strip(s), halved widthwise (gluten-free, if a concern)
- 4½ cups Bagged shredded Brussels sprouts
- ¼ teaspoon Table salt
- 2 tablespoons White balsamic vinegar
- 2 teaspoons Worcestershire sauce (gluten-free, if a concern)
- 1 teaspoon Dijon mustard (gluten-free, if a concern)
- ¼ teaspoon Ground black pepper

Directions:
1. Preheat the air fryer to 375°F .
2. When the machine is at temperature, lay the bacon strip halves in the basket in one layer and air-fry for 10 minutes, or until crisp.
3. Use kitchen tongs to transfer the bacon pieces to a wire rack. Put the shredded Brussels sprouts in a large bowl. Drain any fat from the basket or the tray under the basket onto the Brussels sprouts. Add the salt and toss well to coat.
4. Put the Brussels sprout shreds in the basket, spreading them out into as close to an even layer as you can. Air-fry for 8 minutes, tossing the basket's contents at least three times, until wilted and lightly browned.
5. Pour the contents of the basket into a serving bowl. Chop the bacon and add it to the Brussels sprouts. Add the vinegar, Worcestershire sauce, mustard, and pepper. Toss well to blend the dressing and coat the Brussels sprout shreds. Serve warm.

Mini Hasselback Potatoes

Servings: 4
Cooking Time: 25 Minutes
Ingredients:
- 1½ pounds baby Yukon Gold potatoes
- 5 tablespoons butter, cut into very thin slices
- salt and freshly ground black pepper
- 1 tablespoon vegetable oil
- ¼ cup grated Parmesan cheese (optional)
- chopped fresh parsley or chives

Directions:
1. Preheat the air fryer to 400°F.
2. Make six to eight deep vertical slits across the top of each potato about three quarters of the way down. Make sure the slits are deep enough to allow the slices to spread apart a little, but don't cut all the way through the potato. Place a thin slice of butter between each of the slices and season generously with salt and pepper.
3. Transfer the potatoes to the air fryer basket. Pack them in next to each other. It's alright if some of the potatoes sit on top or rest on another potato. Air-fry for 20 minutes.
4. Spray or brush the potatoes with a little vegetable oil and sprinkle the Parmesan cheese on top. Air-fry for an additional 5 minutes. Garnish with chopped parsley or chives and serve hot.

Mushrooms, Sautéed

Servings: 4
Cooking Time: 4 Minutes
Ingredients:

- 8 ounces sliced white mushrooms, rinsed and well drained
- ¼ teaspoon garlic powder
- 1 tablespoon Worcestershire sauce

Directions:

1. Place mushrooms in a large bowl and sprinkle with garlic powder and Worcestershire. Stir well to distribute seasonings evenly.
2. Place in air fryer basket and cook at 390°F for 4 minutes, until tender.

Smashed Fried Baby Potatoes

Servings: 3
Cooking Time: 18 Minutes
Ingredients:

- 1½ pounds baby red or baby Yukon gold potatoes
- ¼ cup butter, melted
- 1 teaspoon olive oil
- ½ teaspoon paprika
- 1 teaspoon dried parsley
- salt and freshly ground black pepper
- 2 scallions, finely chopped

Directions:

1. Bring a large pot of salted water to a boil. Add the potatoes and boil for 18 minutes or until the potatoes are fork-tender.
2. Drain the potatoes and transfer them to a cutting board to cool slightly. Spray or brush the bottom of a drinking glass with a little oil. Smash or flatten the potatoes by pressing the glass down on each potato slowly. Try not to completely flatten the potato or smash it so hard that it breaks apart.
3. Combine the melted butter, olive oil, paprika, and parsley together.
4. Preheat the air fryer to 400°F.
5. Spray the bottom of the air fryer basket with oil and transfer one layer of the smashed potatoes into the basket. Brush with some of the butter mixture and season generously with salt and freshly ground black pepper.
6. Air-fry at 400°F for 10 minutes. Carefully flip the potatoes over and air-fry for an additional 8 minutes until crispy and lightly browned.
7. Keep the potatoes warm in a 170°F oven or tent with aluminum foil while you cook the second batch. Sprinkle minced scallions over the potatoes and serve warm.

Zucchini Bites

Servings: 4
Cooking Time: 15 Minutes
Ingredients:

- 4 zucchinis
- 1 egg
- ½ cup parmesan cheese, grated
- 1 tbsp. Italian herbs
- 1 cup coconut, grated

Directions:

1. Thinly grate the zucchini and dry with a cheesecloth, ensuring to remove all of the moisture.
2. In a bowl, combine the zucchini with the egg, parmesan, Italian herbs, and grated coconut, mixing well to incorporate everything. Using your hands, mold the mixture into balls.
3. Pre-heat the fryer at 400°F and place a rack inside. Lay the zucchini balls on the rack and cook for ten minutes. Serve hot.

Cheesy Garlic Bread

Servings: 6
Cooking Time: 12 Minutes
Ingredients:

- 1 cup self-rising flour
- 1 cup plain full-fat Greek yogurt
- ¼ cup salted butter, softened
- 1 tablespoon minced garlic
- 1 cup shredded mozzarella cheese

Directions:

1. Preheat the air fryer to 320°F. Cut parchment paper to fit the air fryer basket.
2. In a large bowl, mix flour and yogurt until a sticky, soft dough forms. Let sit 5 minutes.
3. Turn dough onto a lightly floured surface. Knead dough 1 minute, then transfer to prepared parchment. Press out into an 8" round.
4. In a small bowl, mix butter and garlic. Brush over dough. Sprinkle with mozzarella.
5. Place in the air fryer and cook 12 minutes until edges are golden and cheese is brown. Serve warm.

Mashed Potato Pancakes

Servings: 6
Cooking Time: 10 Minutes
Ingredients:

- 2 cups leftover mashed potatoes
- ½ cup grated cheddar cheese
- ¼ cup thinly sliced green onions
- ½ teaspoon salt
- ¼ teaspoon black pepper
- 1 cup breadcrumbs

Directions:

1. Preheat the air fryer to 380°F.
2. In a large bowl, mix together the potatoes, cheese, and onions. Using a ¼ cup measuring cup, measure out 6 patties. Form the potatoes into ½-inch thick patties. Season the patties with salt and pepper on both sides.

3. In a small bowl, place the breadcrumbs. Gently press the potato pancakes into the breadcrumbs.

4. Place the potato pancakes into the air fryer basket and spray with cooking spray. Cook for 5 minutes, turn the pancakes over, and cook another 3 to 5 minutes or until golden brown on the outside and cooked through on the inside.

Bacon-jalapeño Cheesy "breadsticks"

Servings:8
Cooking Time: 15 Minutes
Ingredients:
- 2 cups shredded mozzarella cheese
- ¼ cup grated Parmesan cheese
- ¼ cup chopped pickled jalapeños
- 2 large eggs, whisked
- 4 slices cooked sugar-free bacon, chopped

Directions:
1. Mix all ingredients together in a large bowl. Cut a piece of parchment paper to fit inside air fryer basket.

2. Dampen your hands with a bit of water and press out mixture into a circle to fit on ungreased parchment. You may need to separate into two smaller circles, depending on the size of air fryer.

3. Place parchment with cheese mixture into air fryer basket. Adjust the temperature to 320°F and set the timer for 15 minutes. Carefully flip when 5 minutes remain on timer. The top will be golden brown when done. Slice into eight sticks. Serve warm.

Simple Roasted Sweet Potatoes

Servings: 2
Cooking Time: 45 Minutes
Ingredients:
- 2 10- to 12-ounce sweet potato(es)

Directions:
1. Preheat the air fryer to 350°F.

2. Prick the sweet potato(es) in four or five different places with the tines of a flatware fork.

3. When the machine is at temperature, set the sweet potato(es) in the basket with as much air space between them as possible. Air-fry undisturbed for 45 minutes, or until soft when pricked with a fork.

4. Use kitchen tongs to transfer the sweet potato(es) to a wire rack. Cool for 5 minutes before serving.

Yeast Rolls

Servings:16
Cooking Time: 1 Hour 10 Minutes
Ingredients:
- 4 tablespoons salted butter
- ¼ cup granulated sugar
- 1 cup hot water
- 1 tablespoon quick-rise yeast
- 1 large egg
- 1 teaspoon salt
- 2 ½ cups all-purpose flour, divided
- Cooking spray

Directions:
1. In a microwave-safe bowl, microwave butter 30 seconds until melted. Pour 2 tablespoons of butter into a large bowl. Add sugar, hot water, and yeast. Mix until yeast is dissolved.

2. Using a rubber spatula, mix in egg, salt, and 2 ¼ cups flour. Dough will be very sticky.

3. Cover bowl with plastic wrap and let rise in a warm place 1 hour.

4. Sprinkle remaining ¼ cup flour on dough and turn onto a lightly floured surface. Knead 2 minutes, then cut into sixteen even pieces.

5. Preheat the air fryer to 350°F. Spray a 6" round cake pan with cooking spray.

6. Sprinkle each roll with flour and arrange in pan. Brush with remaining melted butter. Place pan in the air fryer basket and cook 10 minutes until fluffy and golden on top. Serve warm.

Spicy Kale

Servings: 4
Cooking Time: 10 Minutes
Ingredients:
- 1 pound kale, torn
- 1 tablespoon olive oil
- 1 teaspoon hot paprika
- A pinch of salt and black pepper
- 2 tablespoons oregano, chopped

Directions:
1. In a pan that fits the air fryer, combine all the ingredients and toss. Put the pan in the air fryer and cook at 380ºF for 10 minutes. Divide between plates and serve.

Burger Bun For One

Servings:1
Cooking Time: 5 Minutes
Ingredients:
- 2 tablespoons salted butter, melted
- ¼ cup blanched finely ground almond flour
- ¼ teaspoon baking powder
- ⅛ teaspoon apple cider vinegar
- 1 large egg, whisked

Directions:
1. Pour butter into an ungreased 4" ramekin. Add flour, baking powder, and vinegar to ramekin and stir until combined. Add egg and stir until batter is mostly smooth.

2. Place ramekin into air fryer basket. Adjust the temperature to 350°F and set the timer for 5 minutes. When done, the center will be firm and the top slightly browned.

Let cool, about 5 minutes, then remove from ramekin and slice in half. Serve.

Cheesy Cauliflower Tots

Servings:4
Cooking Time: 12 Minutes Per Batch
Ingredients:
- 1 steamer bag riced cauliflower
- ⅓ cup Italian bread crumbs
- ¼ cup all-purpose flour
- 1 large egg
- ¾ cup shredded sharp Cheddar cheese
- ½ teaspoon salt
- ¼ teaspoon ground black pepper

Directions:
1. Cook cauliflower according to the package directions. Let cool, then squeeze in a cheesecloth or kitchen towel to drain excess water.
2. Preheat the air fryer to 400°F. Cut parchment paper to fit the air fryer basket.
3. In a large bowl, mix drained cauliflower, bread crumbs, flour, egg, and Cheddar. Sprinkle in salt and pepper, then mix until well combined.
4. Roll 2 tablespoons of mixture into a tot shape. Repeat to use all of the mixture.
5. Place tots on parchment in the air fryer basket, working in batches as necessary. Spritz with cooking spray. Cook 12 minutes, turning tots halfway through cooking time, until golden brown. Serve warm.

Okra

Servings: 4
Cooking Time: 12 Minutes
Ingredients:
- 7–8 ounces fresh okra
- 1 egg
- 1 cup milk
- 1 cup breadcrumbs
- ½ teaspoon salt
- oil for misting or cooking spray

Directions:
1. Remove stem ends from okra and cut in ½-inch slices.
2. In a medium bowl, beat together egg and milk. Add okra slices and stir to coat.
3. In a sealable plastic bag or container with lid, mix together the breadcrumbs and salt.
4. Remove okra from egg mixture, letting excess drip off, and transfer into bag with breadcrumbs.
5. Shake okra in crumbs to coat well.
6. Place all of the coated okra into the air fryer basket and mist with oil or cooking spray. Okra doesn't need to cook in a single layer, nor is it necessary to spray all sides at this point. A good spritz on top will do.
7. Cook at 390°F for 5minutes. Shake basket to redistribute and give it another spritz as you shake.

8. Cook 5 more minutes. Shake and spray again. Cook for 2 minutes longer or until golden brown and crispy.

Spicy Roasted Potatoes

Servings: 2
Cooking Time: 15 Minutes
Ingredients:
- 4 potatoes, peeled and cut into wedges
- 2 tablespoons olive oil
- Sea salt and ground black pepper, to taste
- 1 teaspoon cayenne pepper
- 1/2 teaspoon ancho chili powder

Directions:
1. Toss all ingredients in a mixing bowl until the potatoes are well covered.
2. Transfer them to the Air Fryer basket and cook at 400ºF for 6 minutes; shake the basket and cook for a further 6 minutes.
3. Serve warm with your favorite sauce for dipping. Bon appétit!

Roasted Cauliflower With Garlic And Capers

Servings: 3
Cooking Time: 10 Minutes
Ingredients:
- 3 cups 1-inch cauliflower florets
- 2 tablespoons Olive oil
- 1½ tablespoons Drained and rinsed capers, chopped
- 2 teaspoons Minced garlic
- ¼ teaspoon Table salt
- Up to ¼ teaspoon Red pepper flakes

Directions:
1. Preheat the air fryer to 375°F .
2. Stir the cauliflower florets, olive oil, capers, garlic, salt, and red pepper flakes in a large bowl until the florets are evenly coated.
3. When the machine is at temperature, put the florets in the basket, spreading them out to as close to one layer as you can. Air-fry for 10 minutes, tossing once to get any covered pieces exposed to the air currents, until tender and lightly browned.
4. Dump the contents of the basket into a serving bowl or onto a serving platter. Cool for a minute or two before serving.

Lemon Tempeh

Servings: 4
Cooking Time: 12 Minutes
Ingredients:
- 1 teaspoon lemon juice
- 1 tablespoon sunflower oil
- ¼ teaspoon ground coriander
- 6 oz tempeh, chopped

Directions:

1. Sprinkle the tempeh with lemon juice, sunflower oil, and ground coriander. Massage the tempeh gently with the help of the fingertips. After this, preheat the air fryer to 325ºF. Put the tempeh in the air fryer and cook it for 12 minutes. Flip the tempeh every 2 minutes during cooking.

Perfect Broccoli

Servings: 4

Cooking Time: 12 Minutes

Ingredients:

- 5 cups 1- to 1½-inch fresh broccoli florets (not frozen)
- Olive oil spray
- ¾ teaspoon Table salt

Directions:

1. Preheat the air fryer to 375°F .
2. Put the broccoli florets in a big bowl, coat them generously with olive oil spray, then toss to coat all surfaces, even down into the crannies, spraying them in a couple of times more. Sprinkle the salt on top and toss again.
3. When the machine is at temperature, pour the florets into the basket. Air-fry for 10 minutes, tossing and rearranging the pieces twice so that all the covered or touching bits are eventually exposed to the air currents, until lightly browned but still crunchy.
4. Pour the florets into a serving bowl. Cool for a minute or two, then serve hot.

Chapter 8. Vegetarians Recipes

Parmesan Artichokes

Servings: 4

Cooking Time: 35 Minutes

Ingredients:

- 2 medium artichokes, trimmed and quartered, with the centers removed
- 2 tbsp. coconut oil, melted
- 1 egg, beaten
- ½ cup parmesan cheese, grated
- ¼ cup blanched, finely ground flour

Directions:

1. Place the artichokes in a bowl with the coconut oil and toss to coat, then dip the artichokes into a bowl of beaten egg.
2. In a separate bowl, mix together the parmesan cheese and the flour. Combine with the pieces of artichoke, making sure to coat each piece well. Transfer the artichoke to the fryer.
3. Cook at 400°F for ten minutes, shaking occasionally throughout the cooking time. Serve hot.

Spicy Celery Sticks

Servings: 4

Cooking Time: 20 Minutes

Ingredients:

- 1 pound celery, cut into matchsticks
- 2 tablespoons peanut oil
- 1 jalapeño, seeded and minced
- 1/4 teaspoon dill
- 1/2 teaspoon basil
- Salt and white pepper to taste

Directions:

1. Start by preheating your Air Fryer to 380°F.
2. Toss all ingredients together and place them in the Air Fryer basket.
3. Cook for 15 minutes, shaking the basket halfway through the cooking time. Transfer to a serving platter and enjoy!

Pizza Dough

Servings:4

Cooking Time: 1 Hour 10 Minutes, Plus 10 Minutes For Additional Batches

Ingredients:

- 2 cups all-purpose flour
- 1 tablespoon granulated sugar
- 1 tablespoon quick-rise yeast
- 4 tablespoons olive oil, divided
- ¾ cup warm water

Directions:

1. In a large bowl, mix flour, sugar, and yeast until combined. Add 2 tablespoons oil and warm water and mix until dough becomes smooth.
2. On a lightly floured surface, knead dough 10 minutes, then form into a smooth ball. Drizzle with remaining 2 tablespoons oil, then cover with plastic. Let dough rise 1 hour until doubled in size.
3. Preheat the air fryer to 320°F.
4. Separate dough into four pieces and press each into a 6" pan or air fryer pizza tray that has been spritzed with cooking oil.

5. Add any desired toppings. Place in the air fryer basket, working in batches as necessary, and cook 10 minutes until crust is brown at the edges and toppings are heated through. Serve warm.

Colorful Vegetable Medley

Servings: 4
Cooking Time: 20 Minutes
Ingredients:
- 1 lb green beans, chopped
- 2 carrots, cubed
- Salt and pepper to taste
- 1 zucchini, cut into chunks
- 1 red bell pepper, sliced
- Cooking spray

Directions:
1. Preheat air fryer to 390°F. Combine green beans, carrots, salt and pepper in a large bowl. Spray with cooking oil and transfer to the frying basket. Roast for 6 minutes.
2. Combine zucchini and red pepper in a bowl. Season to taste and spray with cooking oil; set aside. When the cooking time is up, add the zucchini and red pepper to the basket. Cook for another 6 minutes. Serve and enjoy.

Stuffed Mushrooms

Servings:4
Cooking Time: 10 Minutes
Ingredients:
- 12 baby bella mushrooms, stems removed
- 4 ounces full-fat cream cheese, softened
- ¼ cup grated vegetarian Parmesan cheese
- ¼ cup Italian bread crumbs
- 1 teaspoon crushed red pepper flakes

Directions:
1. Preheat the air fryer to 400°F.
2. Use a spoon to hollow out mushroom caps.
3. In a medium bowl, combine cream cheese, Parmesan, bread crumbs, and red pepper flakes. Scoop approximately 1 tablespoon mixture into each mushroom cap.
4. Place stuffed mushrooms in the air fryer basket and cook 10 minutes until stuffing is brown. Let cool 5 minutes before serving.

Crustless Spinach And Cheese Frittata

Servings:4
Cooking Time: 20 Minutes
Ingredients:
- 6 large eggs
- ½ cup heavy whipping cream
- 1 cup frozen chopped spinach, drained
- 1 cup shredded sharp Cheddar cheese
- ¼ cup peeled and diced yellow onion
- ½ teaspoon salt
- ¼ teaspoon ground black pepper

Directions:
1. In a large bowl, whisk eggs and cream together. Whisk in spinach, Cheddar, onion, salt, and pepper.
2. Pour mixture into an ungreased 6" round nonstick baking dish. Place dish into air fryer basket. Adjust the temperature to 320°F and set the timer for 20 minutes. Eggs will be firm and slightly browned when done. Serve immediately.

Avocado Rolls

Servings:5
Cooking Time: 15 Minutes
Ingredients:
- 10 egg roll wrappers
- 1 tomato, diced
- ¼ tsp pepper
- ½ tsp salt

Directions:
1. Place all filling ingredients in a bowl; mash with a fork until somewhat smooth. There should be chunks left. Divide the feeling between the egg wrappers. Wet your finger and brush along the edges, so the wrappers can seal well. Roll and seal the wrappers.
2. Arrange them on a baking sheet lined dish, and place in the air fryer. Cook at 350°F for 5 minutes. Serve with sweet chili dipping and enjoy.

Turmeric Crispy Chickpeas

Servings:4
Cooking Time: 22 Minutes
Ingredients:
- 1 tbsp butter, melted
- ½ tsp dried rosemary
- ¼ tsp turmeric
- Salt to taste

Directions:
1. Preheat the Air fryer to 380°F.
2. In a bowl, combine together chickpeas, butter, rosemary, turmeric, and salt; toss to coat. Place the prepared chickpeas in your Air Fryer's cooking basket and cook for 6 minutes. Slide out the basket and shake; cook for another 6 minutes until crispy.

Bell Peppers Cups

Servings:4
Cooking Time:8 Minutes
Ingredients:
- 8 mini red bell peppers, tops and seeds removed
- 1 teaspoon fresh parsley, chopped
- ¾ cup feta cheese, crumbled
- ½ tablespoon olive oil
- Freshly ground black pepper, to taste

Directions:

1. Preheat the Air fryer to 390°F and grease an Air fryer basket.
2. Mix feta cheese, parsley, olive oil and black pepper in a bowl.
3. Stuff the bell peppers with feta cheese mixture and arrange in the Air fryer basket.
4. Cook for about 8 minutes and dish out to serve hot.

Broccoli With Cauliflower

Servings:4
Cooking Time:20 Minutes
Ingredients:
- 1½ cups broccoli, cut into 1-inch pieces
- 1½ cups cauliflower, cut into 1-inch pieces
- 1 tablespoon olive oil
- Salt, as required

Directions:
1. Preheat the Air fryer to 375°F and grease an Air fryer basket.
2. Mix the vegetables, olive oil, and salt in a bowl and toss to coat well.
3. Arrange the veggie mixture in the Air fryer basket and cook for about 20 minutes, tossing once in between.
4. Dish out in a bowl and serve hot.

Twice-baked Broccoli-cheddar Potatoes

Servings:4
Cooking Time: 35 Minutes
Ingredients:
- 4 large russet potatoes
- 2 tablespoons plus 2 teaspoons ranch dressing
- 1 teaspoon salt
- ½ teaspoon ground black pepper
- ¼ cup chopped cooked broccoli florets
- 1 cup shredded sharp Cheddar cheese

Directions:
1. Preheat the air fryer to 400°F.
2. Using a fork, poke several holes in potatoes. Place in the air fryer basket and cook 30 minutes until fork-tender.
3. Once potatoes are cool enough to handle, slice lengthwise and scoop out the cooked potato into a large bowl, being careful to maintain the structural integrity of potato skins. Add ranch dressing, salt, pepper, broccoli, and Cheddar to potato flesh and stir until well combined.
4. Scoop potato mixture back into potato skins and return to the air fryer basket. Cook an additional 5 minutes until cheese is melted. Serve warm.

Effortless Mac `n´ Cheese

Servings: 4
Cooking Time: 15 Minutes
Ingredients:
- 1 cup heavy cream

- 1 cup milk
- ½ cup mozzarella cheese
- 2 tsp grated Parmesan cheese
- 16 oz cooked elbow macaroni

Directions:
1. Preheat air fryer to 400°F. Whisk the heavy cream, milk, mozzarella cheese, and Parmesan cheese until smooth in a bowl. Stir in the macaroni and pour into a baking dish. Cover with foil and Bake in the air fryer for 6 minutes. Remove foil and Bake until cooked through and bubbly, 3-5 minutes. Serve warm.

Roasted Spaghetti Squash

Servings:6
Cooking Time: 45 Minutes
Ingredients:
- 1 spaghetti squash, halved and seeded
- 2 tablespoons coconut oil
- 4 tablespoons salted butter, melted
- 1 teaspoon garlic powder
- 2 teaspoons dried parsley

Directions:
1. Brush shell of spaghetti squash with coconut oil. Brush inside with butter. Sprinkle inside with garlic powder and parsley.
2. Place squash skin side down into ungreased air fryer basket, working in batches if needed. Adjust the temperature to 350°F and set the timer for 30 minutes. When the timer beeps, flip squash and cook an additional 15 minutes until fork-tender.
3. Use a fork to remove spaghetti strands from shell and serve warm.

Easy Baked Root Veggies

Servings:4
Cooking Time: 45 Minutes
Ingredients:
- ¼ cup olive oil
- 1 head broccoli, cut into florets
- 1 tablespoon dry onion powder
- 2 sweet potatoes, peeled and cubed
- 4 carrots, cut into chunks
- 4 zucchinis, sliced thickly
- salt and pepper to taste

Directions:
1. Preheat the air fryer to 400°F.
2. In a baking dish that can fit inside the air fryer, mix all the ingredients and bake for 45 minutes or until the vegetables are tender and the sides have browned.

Roasted Vegetable Pita Pizza

Servings: 4
Cooking Time: 20 Minutes
Ingredients:

- 1 medium red bell pepper, seeded and cut into quarters
- 1 teaspoon extra-virgin olive oil
- ⅛ teaspoon black pepper
- ⅛ teaspoon salt
- Two 6-inch whole-grain pita breads
- 6 tablespoons pesto sauce
- ¼ small red onion, thinly sliced
- ½ cup shredded part-skim mozzarella cheese

Directions:
1. Preheat the air fryer to 400°F.
2. In a small bowl, toss the bell peppers with the olive oil, pepper, and salt.
3. Place the bell peppers in the air fryer and cook for 15 minutes, shaking every 5 minutes to prevent burning.
4. Remove the peppers and set aside. Turn the air fryer temperature down to 350°F.
5. Lay the pita bread on a flat surface. Cover each with half the pesto sauce; then top with even portions of the red bell peppers and onions. Sprinkle cheese over the top. Spray the air fryer basket with olive oil mist.
6. Carefully lift the pita bread into the air fryer basket with a spatula.
7. Cook for 5 to 8 minutes, or until the outer edges begin to brown and the cheese is melted.
8. Serve warm with desired sides.

Sautéed Spinach

Servings:2
Cooking Time:9 Minutes
Ingredients:

- 1 small onion, chopped
- 6 ounces fresh spinach
- 2 tablespoons olive oil
- 1 teaspoon ginger, minced
- Salt and black pepper, to taste

Directions:
1. Preheat the Air fryer to 360°F and grease an Air fryer pan.
2. Put olive oil, onions and ginger in the Air fryer pan and place in the Air fryer basket.
3. Cook for about 4 minutes and add spinach, salt, and black pepper.
4. Cook for about 4 more minutes and dish out in a bowl to serve.

Stuffed Portobellos

Servings:4
Cooking Time: 8 Minutes
Ingredients:

- 3 ounces cream cheese, softened
- ½ medium zucchini, trimmed and chopped
- ¼ cup seeded and chopped red bell pepper
- 1½ cups chopped fresh spinach leaves
- 4 large portobello mushrooms, stems removed
- 2 tablespoons coconut oil, melted
- ½ teaspoon salt

Directions:
1. In a medium bowl, mix cream cheese, zucchini, pepper, and spinach.
2. Drizzle mushrooms with coconut oil and sprinkle with salt. Scoop ¼ zucchini mixture into each mushroom.
3. Place mushrooms into ungreased air fryer basket. Adjust the temperature to 400°F and set the timer for 8 minutes. Portobellos will be tender and tops will be browned when done. Serve warm.

Almond Asparagus

Servings:3
Cooking Time:6 Minutes
Ingredients:

- 1 pound asparagus
- 1/3 cup almonds, sliced
- 2 tablespoons olive oil
- 2 tablespoons balsamic vinegar
- Salt and black pepper, to taste

Directions:
1. Preheat the Air fryer to 400°F and grease an Air fryer basket.
2. Mix asparagus, oil, vinegar, salt, and black pepper in a bowl and toss to coat well.
3. Arrange asparagus into the Air fryer basket and sprinkle with the almond slices.
4. Cook for about 6 minutes and dish out to serve hot.

Crispy Eggplant Rounds

Servings:4
Cooking Time: 10 Minutes
Ingredients:

- 1 large eggplant, ends trimmed, cut into ½" slices
- ½ teaspoon salt
- 2 ounces Parmesan 100% cheese crisps, finely ground
- ½ teaspoon paprika
- ¼ teaspoon garlic powder
- 1 large egg

Directions:
1. Sprinkle eggplant rounds with salt. Place rounds on a kitchen towel for 30 minutes to draw out excess water. Pat rounds dry.
2. In a medium bowl, mix cheese crisps, paprika, and garlic powder. In a separate medium bowl, whisk egg. Dip each eggplant round in egg, then gently press into cheese crisps to coat both sides.
3. Place eggplant rounds into ungreased air fryer basket. Adjust the temperature to 400°F and set the timer for 10

minutes, turning rounds halfway through cooking. Eggplant will be golden and crispy when done. Serve warm.

Breadcrumbs Stuffed Mushrooms

Servings:4
Cooking Time:10 Minutes
Ingredients:
- 1½ spelt bread slices
- 1 tablespoon flat-leaf parsley, finely chopped
- 16 small button mushrooms, stemmed and gills removed
- 1½ tablespoons olive oil
- 1 garlic clove, crushed
- Salt and black pepper, to taste

Directions:
1. Preheat the Air fryer to 390°F and grease an Air fryer basket.
2. Put the bread slices in a food processor and pulse until fine crumbs form.
3. Transfer the crumbs into a bowl and stir in the olive oil, garlic, parsley, salt, and black pepper.
4. Stuff the breadcrumbs mixture in each mushroom cap and arrange the mushrooms in the Air fryer basket.
5. Cook for about 10 minutes and dish out in a bowl to serve warm.

Sweet And Spicy Barbecue Tofu

Servings:4
Cooking Time: 1 Hour 15 Minutes
Ingredients:
- 1 package extra-firm tofu, drained
- ½ cup barbecue sauce
- ½ cup brown sugar
- 1 teaspoon liquid smoke
- 1 teaspoon crushed red pepper flakes
- ½ teaspoon salt
- Cooking spray

Directions:
1. Press tofu block to remove excess moisture. If you don't have a tofu press, line a baking sheet with paper towels and set tofu on top. Set a second baking sheet on top of tofu and weight it with a heavy item such as a skillet. Let tofu sit at least 30 minutes, changing paper towels if necessary.
2. Cut pressed tofu into twenty-four equal pieces. Set aside.
3. In a large bowl, combine barbecue sauce, brown sugar, liquid smoke, red pepper flakes, and salt. Mix well and add tofu, coating completely. Cover and let marinate at least 30 minutes on the counter.
4. Preheat the air fryer to 400°F.
5. Spray the air fryer basket with cooking spray and add marinated tofu. Cook 15 minutes, shaking the basket twice during cooking.
6. Let cool 10 minutes before serving warm.

Two-cheese Grilled Sandwiches

Servings: 2

Cooking Time: 30 Minutes
Ingredients:
- 4 sourdough bread slices
- 2 cheddar cheese slices
- 2 Swiss cheese slices
- 1 tbsp butter
- 2 dill pickles, sliced

Directions:
1. Preheat air fryer to 360°F. Smear both sides of the sourdough bread with butter and place them in the frying basket. Toast the bread for 6 minutes, flipping once.
2. Divide the cheddar cheese between 2 of the bread slices. Cover the remaining 2 bread slices with Swiss cheese slices. Bake for 10 more minutes until the cheeses have melted and lightly bubbled and the bread has golden brown. Set the cheddar-covered bread slices on a serving plate, cover with pickles, and top each with the Swiss-covered slices. Serve and enjoy!

Tortilla Pizza Margherita

Servings: 1
Cooking Time: 15 Minutes
Ingredients:
- 1 flour tortilla
- ¼ cup tomato sauce
- 1/3 cup grated mozzarella
- 3 basil leaves

Directions:
1. Preheat air fryer to 350°F. Put the tortilla in the greased basket and pour the sauce in the center. Spread across the whole tortilla. Sprinkle with cheese and Bake for 8-10 minutes or until crisp. Remove carefully and top with basil leaves. Serve hot.

Cheesy Brussel Sprouts

Servings:3
Cooking Time:10 Minutes
Ingredients:
- 1 pound Brussels sprouts, trimmed and halved
- ¼ cup whole wheat breadcrumbs
- ¼ cup Parmesan cheese, shredded
- 1 tablespoon balsamic vinegar
- 1 tablespoon extra-virgin olive oil
- Salt and black pepper, to taste

Directions:
1. Preheat the Air fryer to 400°F and grease an Air fryer basket.
2. Mix Brussel sprouts, vinegar, oil, salt, and black pepper in a bowl and toss to coat well.
3. Arrange the Brussel sprouts in the Air fryer basket and cook for about 5 minutes.
4. Sprinkle with breadcrumbs and cheese and cook for about 5 more minutes.
5. Dish out and serve hot.

Curried Eggplant

Servings:2
Cooking Time:10 Minutes
Ingredients:
- 1 large eggplant, cut into ½-inch thick slices
- 1 garlic clove, minced
- ½ fresh red chili, chopped
- 1 tablespoon vegetable oil
- ¼ teaspoon curry powder
- Salt, to taste

Directions:
1. Preheat the Air fryer to 300°F and grease an Air fryer basket.
2. Mix all the ingredients in a bowl and toss to coat well.
3. Arrange the eggplant slices in the Air fryer basket and cook for about 10 minutes, tossing once in between.
4. Dish out onto serving plates and serve hot.

Zucchini Gratin

Servings: 2
Cooking Time: 15 Minutes
Ingredients:
- 5 oz. parmesan cheese, shredded
- 1 tbsp. coconut flour
- 1 tbsp. dried parsley
- 2 zucchinis
- 1 tsp. butter, melted

Directions:
1. Mix the parmesan and coconut flour together in a bowl, seasoning with parsley to taste.
2. Cut the zucchini in half lengthwise and chop the halves into four slices.
3. Pre-heat the fryer at 400°F.
4. Pour the melted butter over the zucchini and then dip the zucchini into the parmesan-flour mixture, coating it all over. Cook the zucchini in the fryer for thirteen minutes.

Spinach Pesto Flatbread

Servings:4
Cooking Time: 8 Minutes Per Batch
Ingredients:
- 1 cup basil pesto
- 4 round flatbreads
- ½ cup chopped frozen spinach, thawed and drained
- 8 ounces fresh mozzarella cheese, sliced
- 1 teaspoon crushed red pepper flakes

Directions:
1. Preheat the air fryer to 350°F.
2. For each flatbread, spread ¼ cup pesto across flatbread, then scatter 2 tablespoons spinach over pesto. Top with 2 ounces mozzarella slices and ¼ teaspoon red pepper flakes. Repeat with remaining flatbread and toppings.

3. Place in the air fryer basket, working in batches as necessary, and cook 8 minutes until cheese is brown and bubbling. Serve warm.

Falafels

Servings: 12
Cooking Time: 10 Minutes
Ingredients:
- 1 pouch falafel mix
- 2–3 tablespoons plain breadcrumbs
- oil for misting or cooking spray

Directions:
1. Prepare falafel mix according to package directions.
2. Preheat air fryer to 390°F.
3. Place breadcrumbs in shallow dish or on wax paper.
4. Shape falafel mixture into 12 balls and flatten slightly. Roll in breadcrumbs to coat all sides and mist with oil or cooking spray.
5. Place falafels in air fryer basket in single layer and cook for 5 minutes. Shake basket, and continue cooking for 5 minutes, until they brown and are crispy.

Savory Herb Cloud Eggs

Servings:2
Cooking Time: 8 Minutes
Ingredients:
- 2 large eggs, whites and yolks separated
- ¼ teaspoon salt
- ¼ teaspoon dried oregano
- 2 tablespoons chopped fresh chives
- 2 teaspoons salted butter, melted

Directions:
1. In a large bowl, whip egg whites until stiff peaks form, about 3 minutes. Place egg whites evenly into two ungreased 4" ramekins. Sprinkle evenly with salt, oregano, and chives. Place 1 whole egg yolk in center of each ramekin and drizzle with butter.
2. Place ramekins into air fryer basket. Adjust the temperature to 350°F and set the timer for 8 minutes. Egg whites will be fluffy and browned when done. Serve warm.

White Cheddar And Mushroom Soufflés

Servings:4
Cooking Time: 12 Minutes
Ingredients:
- 3 large eggs, whites and yolks separated
- ½ cup sharp white Cheddar cheese
- 3 ounces cream cheese, softened
- ¼ teaspoon cream of tartar
- ¼ teaspoon salt
- ¼ teaspoon ground black pepper
- ½ cup cremini mushrooms, sliced

Directions:

1. In a large bowl, whip egg whites until stiff peaks form, about 2 minutes. In a separate large bowl, beat Cheddar, egg yolks, cream cheese, cream of tartar, salt, and pepper together until combined.

2. Fold egg whites into cheese mixture, being careful not to stir. Fold in mushrooms, then pour mixture evenly into four ungreased 4" ramekins.

3. Place ramekins into air fryer basket. Adjust the temperature to 350°F and set the timer for 12 minutes. Eggs will be browned on the top and firm in the center when done. Serve warm.

Cheesy Cauliflower Crust Pizza

Servings:2

Cooking Time: 12 Minutes Per Batch

Ingredients:

- 2 steamer bags cauliflower florets
- 1 large egg
- 1 cup grated vegetarian Parmesan cheese
- 3 cups shredded mozzarella cheese, divided
- 1 cup pizza sauce

Directions:

1. Preheat the air fryer to 375°F. Cut two pieces of parchment paper to fit the air fryer basket, one for each crust.

2. Cook cauliflower in the microwave according to package instructions, then drain in a colander. Run under cold water until cool to the touch. Use a cheesecloth to squeeze the excess water from cauliflower, removing as much as possible.

3. In a food processor, combine cauliflower, egg, Parmesan, and 1 cup mozzarella. Process on low about 15 seconds until a sticky ball forms.

4. Separate dough into two pieces. Working with damp hands to prevent dough from sticking, press each dough ball into a 6" round.

5. Place crust on parchment in the air fryer basket, working in batches as necessary. Cook 6 minutes, then flip over with a spatula and top the crust with ½ cup pizza sauce and 1 cup mozzarella. Cook an additional 6 minutes until edges are dark brown and cheese is brown and bubbling. Let cool at least 5 minutes before serving. The crust firms up as it cools.

Italian Seasoned Easy Pasta Chips

Servings:2

Cooking Time:10 Minutes

Ingredients:

- ½ teaspoon salt
- 1 ½ teaspoon Italian seasoning blend
- 1 tablespoon nutritional yeast
- 1 tablespoon olive oil
- 2 cups whole wheat bowtie pasta

Directions:

1. Place the baking dish accessory in the air fryer.

2. Give a good stir.

3. Close the air fryer and cook for 10 minutes at 390°F.

Portobello Mini Pizzas

Servings:4

Cooking Time: 10 Minutes

Ingredients:

- 4 large portobello mushrooms, stems removed
- 2 cups shredded mozzarella cheese, divided
- ½ cup full-fat ricotta cheese
- 1 teaspoon salt, divided
- ½ teaspoon ground black pepper
- 1 teaspoon Italian seasoning
- 1 cup pizza sauce

Directions:

1. Preheat the air fryer to 350°F.

2. Use a spoon to hollow out mushroom caps. Spritz mushrooms with cooking spray. Place ¼ cup mozzarella into each mushroom cap.

3. In a small bowl, mix ricotta, ½ teaspoon salt, pepper, and Italian seasoning. Divide mixture evenly and spoon into mushroom caps.

4. Pour ¼ cup pizza sauce into each mushroom cap, then top each with ¼ cup mozzarella. Sprinkle tops of pizzas with remaining salt.

5. Place mushrooms in the air fryer basket and cook 10 minutes until cheese is brown and bubbling. Serve warm.

Healthy Apple-licious Chips

Servings:1

Cooking Time: 6 Minutes

Ingredients:

- ½ teaspoon ground cumin
- 1 apple, cored and sliced thinly
- 1 tablespoon sugar
- A pinch of salt

Directions:

1. Place all ingredients in a bowl and toss to coat everything.

2. Put the grill pan accessory in the air fryer and place the sliced apples on the grill pan.

3. Close the air fryer and cook for 6 minutes at 390°F.

Broccoli With Olives

Servings:4

Cooking Time:19 Minutes

Ingredients:

- 2 pounds broccoli, stemmed and cut into 1-inch florets
- 1/3 cup Kalamata olives, halved and pitted
- ¼ cup Parmesan cheese, grated
- 2 tablespoons olive oil
- Salt and ground black pepper, as required
- 2 teaspoons fresh lemon zest, grated

Directions:

1. Preheat the Air fryer to 400°F and grease an Air fryer basket.
2. Boil the broccoli for about 4 minutes and drain well.
3. Mix broccoli, oil, salt, and black pepper in a bowl and toss to coat well.
4. Arrange broccoli into the Air fryer basket and cook for about 15 minutes.
5. Stir in the olives, lemon zest and cheese and dish out to serve.

Home-style Cinnamon Rolls

Servings: 4
Cooking Time: 40 Minutes
Ingredients:
- ½ pizza dough
- 1/3 cup dark brown sugar
- ¼ cup butter, softened
- ½ tsp ground cinnamon

Directions:
1. Preheat air fryer to 360°F. Roll out the dough into a rectangle. Using a knife, spread the brown sugar and butter, covering all the edges, and sprinkle with cinnamon. Fold the long side of the dough into a log, then cut it into 8 equal pieces, avoiding compression. Place the rolls, spiral-side up, onto a parchment-lined sheet. Let rise for 20 minutes. Grease the rolls with cooking spray and Bake for 8 minutes until golden brown. Serve right away.

Cauliflower Steak With Thick Sauce

Servings:2
Cooking Time: 15 Minutes
Ingredients:
- ¼ cup almond milk
- ¼ teaspoon vegetable stock powder
- 1 cauliflower, sliced into two
- 1 tablespoon olive oil
- 2 tablespoons onion, chopped
- salt and pepper to taste

Directions:
1. Soak the cauliflower in salted water or brine for at least 2 hours.
2. Preheat the air fryer to 400°F.
3. Rinse the cauliflower and place inside the air fryer and cook for 15 minutes.
4. Meanwhile, heat oil in a skillet over medium flame. Sauté the onions and stir until translucent. Add the vegetable stock powder and milk.
5. Bring to boil and adjust the heat to low.
6. Allow the sauce to reduce and season with salt and pepper.
7. Place cauliflower steak on a plate and pour over sauce.

Pepper-pineapple With Butter-sugar Glaze

Servings:2
Cooking Time: 10 Minutes
Ingredients:
- 1 medium-sized pineapple, peeled and sliced
- 1 red bell pepper, seeded and julienned
- 1 teaspoon brown sugar
- 2 teaspoons melted butter
- Salt to taste

Directions:
1. Preheat the air fryer to 390°F.
2. Place the grill pan accessory in the air fryer.
3. Mix all ingredients in a Ziploc bag and give a good shake.
4. Dump onto the grill pan and cook for 10 minutes making sure that you flip the pineapples every 5 minutes.

Eggplant Parmesan

Servings:4
Cooking Time: 17 Minutes
Ingredients:
- 1 medium eggplant, ends trimmed, sliced into ½" rounds
- ¼ teaspoon salt
- 2 tablespoons coconut oil
- ½ cup grated Parmesan cheese
- 1 ounce 100% cheese crisps, finely crushed
- ½ cup low-carb marinara sauce
- ½ cup shredded mozzarella cheese

Directions:
1. Sprinkle eggplant rounds with salt on both sides and wrap in a kitchen towel for 30 minutes. Press to remove excess water, then drizzle rounds with coconut oil on both sides.
2. In a medium bowl, mix Parmesan and cheese crisps. Press each eggplant slice into mixture to coat both sides.
3. Place rounds into ungreased air fryer basket. Adjust the temperature to 350°F and set the timer for 15 minutes, turning rounds halfway through cooking. They will be crispy around the edges when done.
4. When timer beeps, spoon marinara over rounds and sprinkle with mozzarella. Continue cooking an additional 2 minutes at 350°F until cheese is melted. Serve warm.

Buttered Broccoli

Servings:4
Cooking Time:7 Minutes
Ingredients:
- 4 cups fresh broccoli florets
- 2 tablespoons butter, melted
- ¼ cup water
- Salt and black pepper, to taste

Directions:

1. Preheat the Air fryer to 400°F and grease an Air fryer basket.
2. Mix broccoli, butter, salt, and black pepper in a bowl and toss to coat well.
3. Place water at the bottom of Air fryer pan and arrange the broccoli florets into the Air fryer basket.
4. Cook for about 7 minutes and dish out in a bowl to serve hot.

Roasted Cauliflower

Servings: 2
Cooking Time: 20 Minutes
Ingredients:
- medium head cauliflower
- 2 tbsp. salted butter, melted
- 1 medium lemon
- 1 tsp. dried parsley
- ½ tsp. garlic powder

Directions:
1. Having removed the leaves from the cauliflower head, brush it with the melted butter. Grate the rind of the lemon over it and then drizzle some juice. Finally add the parsley and garlic powder on top.
2. Transfer the cauliflower to the basket of the fryer.
3. Cook for fifteen minutes at 350°F, checking regularly to ensure it doesn't overcook. The cauliflower is ready when it is hot and fork tender.
4. Take care when removing it from the fryer, cut up and serve.

Black Bean And Rice Burrito Filling

Servings:4
Cooking Time: 20 Minutes
Ingredients:
- 1 cup uncooked instant long-grain white rice
- 1 cup salsa
- ½ cup vegetable broth
- 1 cup black beans
- ½ cup corn

Directions:
1. Preheat the air fryer to 400°F.
2. Mix all ingredients in a 3-quart baking dish until well combined.
3. Cover with foil, being sure to tuck foil under the bottom of the pan to ensure the air fryer fan does not blow it off.
4. Cook 20 minutes, stirring twice during cooking. Serve warm.

Spicy Roasted Cashew Nuts

Servings: 4
Cooking Time: 20 Minutes
Ingredients:
- 1 cup whole cashews
- 1 teaspoon olive oil
- Salt and ground black pepper, to taste

- 1/2 teaspoon smoked paprika
- 1/2 teaspoon ancho chili powder

Directions:
1. Toss all ingredients in the mixing bowl.
2. Line the Air Fryer basket with baking parchment. Spread out the spiced cashews in a single layer in the basket.
3. Roast at 350°F for 6 to 8 minutes, shaking the basket once or twice. Work in batches. Enjoy!

Layered Ravioli Bake

Servings:4
Cooking Time: 20 Minutes
Ingredients:
- 2 cups marinara sauce, divided
- 2 packages fresh cheese ravioli
- 12 slices provolone cheese
- ½ cup Italian bread crumbs
- ½ cup grated vegetarian Parmesan cheese

Directions:
1. Preheat the air fryer to 350°F.
2. In the bottom of a 3-quart baking pan, spread ⅓ cup marinara. Place 6 ravioli on top of the sauce, then add 3 slices provolone on top, then another layer of ⅓ cup marinara. Repeat these layers three times to use up remaining ravioli, provolone, and sauce.
3. In a small bowl, mix bread crumbs and Parmesan. Sprinkle over the top of dish.
4. Cover pan with foil, being sure to tuck foil under the bottom of the pan to ensure the air fryer fan does not blow it off. Place pan in the air fryer basket and cook 15 minutes.
5. Remove foil and cook an additional 5 minutes until the top is brown and bubbling. Serve warm.

Broccoli Salad

Servings: 2
Cooking Time: 15 Minutes
Ingredients:
- 3 cups fresh broccoli florets
- 2 tbsp. coconut oil, melted
- ¼ cup sliced s
- ½ medium lemon, juiced

Directions:
1. Take a six-inch baking dish and fill with the broccoli florets. Pour the melted coconut oil over the broccoli and add in the sliced s. Toss together. Put the dish in the air fryer.
2. Cook at 380°F for seven minutes, stirring at the halfway point.
3. Place the broccoli in a bowl and drizzle the lemon juice over it.

Crispy Cabbage Steaks

Servings:4
Cooking Time: 10 Minutes
Ingredients:

- 1 small head green cabbage, cored and cut into ½"-thick slices
- ¼ teaspoon salt
- ¼ teaspoon ground black pepper
- 2 tablespoons olive oil
- 1 clove garlic, peeled and finely minced
- ½ teaspoon dried thyme
- ½ teaspoon dried parsley

Directions:

1. Sprinkle each side of cabbage with salt and pepper, then place into ungreased air fryer basket, working in batches if needed.
2. Drizzle each side of cabbage with olive oil, then sprinkle with remaining ingredients on both sides. Adjust the temperature to 350°F and set the timer for 10 minutes, turning "steaks" halfway through cooking. Cabbage will be browned at the edges and tender when done. Serve warm.

Garden Fresh Green Beans

Servings:4
Cooking Time:12 Minutes
Ingredients:

- 1 pound green beans, washed and trimmed
- 1 teaspoon butter, melted
- 1 tablespoon fresh lemon juice
- ¼ teaspoon garlic powder
- Salt and freshly ground pepper, to taste

Directions:

1. Preheat the Air fryer to 400°F and grease an Air fryer basket.
2. Put all the ingredients in a large bowl and transfer into the Air fryer basket.
3. Cook for about 8 minutes and dish out in a bowl to serve warm.

Alfredo Eggplant Stacks

Servings:6
Cooking Time: 12 Minutes
Ingredients:

- 1 large eggplant, ends trimmed, cut into ¼" slices
- 1 medium beefsteak tomato, cored and cut into ¼" slices
- 1 cup Alfredo sauce
- 8 ounces fresh mozzarella cheese, cut into 18 slices
- 2 tablespoons fresh parsley leaves

Directions:

1. Place 6 slices eggplant in bottom of an ungreased 6" round nonstick baking dish. Place 1 slice tomato on top of each eggplant round, followed by 1 tablespoon Alfredo and 1 slice mozzarella. Repeat with remaining ingredients, about three repetitions.

2. Cover dish with aluminum foil and place dish into air fryer basket. Adjust the temperature to 350°F and set the timer for 12 minutes. Eggplant will be tender when done.
3. Sprinkle parsley evenly over each stack. Serve warm.

Pesto Spinach Flatbread

Servings:4
Cooking Time: 8 Minutes
Ingredients:

- 1 cup blanched finely ground almond flour
- 2 ounces cream cheese
- 2 cups shredded mozzarella cheese
- 1 cup chopped fresh spinach leaves
- 2 tablespoons basil pesto

Directions:

1. Place flour, cream cheese, and mozzarella in a large microwave-safe bowl and microwave on high 45 seconds, then stir.
2. Fold in spinach and microwave an additional 15 seconds. Stir until a soft dough ball forms.
3. Cut two pieces of parchment paper to fit air fryer basket. Separate dough into two sections and press each out on ungreased parchment to create 6" rounds.
4. Spread 1 tablespoon pesto over each flatbread and place rounds on parchment into ungreased air fryer basket. Adjust the temperature to 350°F and set the timer for 8 minutes, turning crusts halfway through cooking. Flatbread will be golden when done.
5. Let cool 5 minutes before slicing and serving.

Basil Tomatoes

Servings:2
Cooking Time:10 Minutes
Ingredients:

- 2 tomatoes, halved
- 1 tablespoon fresh basil, chopped
- Olive oil cooking spray
- Salt and black pepper, as required

Directions:

1. Preheat the Air fryer to 320°F and grease an Air fryer basket.
2. Spray the tomato halves evenly with olive oil cooking spray and season with salt, black pepper and basil.
3. Arrange the tomato halves into the Air fryer basket, cut sides up.
4. Cook for about 10 minutes and dish out onto serving plates.

Vegetable Burgers

Servings:4
Cooking Time: 12 Minutes
Ingredients:
- 8 ounces cremini mushrooms
- 2 large egg yolks
- ½ medium zucchini, trimmed and chopped
- ¼ cup peeled and chopped yellow onion
- 1 clove garlic, peeled and finely minced
- ½ teaspoon salt
- ¼ teaspoon ground black pepper

Directions:
1. Place all ingredients into a food processor and pulse twenty times until finely chopped and combined.
2. Separate mixture into four equal sections and press each into a burger shape. Place burgers into ungreased air fryer basket. Adjust the temperature to 375°F and set the timer for 12 minutes, turning burgers halfway through cooking. Burgers will be browned and firm when done.
3. Place burgers on a large plate and let cool 5 minutes before serving.

Cauliflower Pizza Crust

Servings:2
Cooking Time: 7 Minutes
Ingredients:
- 1 steamer bag cauliflower, cooked according to package instructions
- ½ cup shredded sharp Cheddar cheese
- 1 large egg
- 2 tablespoons blanched finely ground almond flour
- 1 teaspoon Italian seasoning

Directions:
1. Let cooked cauliflower cool for 10 minutes. Using a kitchen towel, wring out excess moisture from cauliflower and place into food processor.
2. Add Cheddar, egg, flour, and Italian seasoning to processor and pulse ten times until cauliflower is smooth and all ingredients are combined.
3. Cut two pieces of parchment paper to fit air fryer basket. Divide cauliflower mixture into two equal portions and press each into a 6" round on ungreased parchment.
4. Place crusts on parchment into air fryer basket. Adjust the temperature to 360°F and set the timer for 7 minutes, gently turning crusts halfway through cooking.
5. Store crusts in refrigerator in an airtight container up to 4 days or freeze between sheets of parchment in a sealable storage bag for up to 2 months.

Cheesy Broccoli Sticks

Servings:2
Cooking Time: 16 Minutes
Ingredients:
- 1 steamer bag broccoli florets, cooked according to package instructions
- 1 large egg
- 1 ounce Parmesan 100% cheese crisps, finely ground
- ½ cup shredded sharp Cheddar cheese
- ½ teaspoon salt
- ½ cup ranch dressing

Directions:
1. Let cooked broccoli cool 5 minutes, then place into a food processor with egg, cheese crisps, Cheddar, and salt. Process on low for 30 seconds until all ingredients are combined and begin to stick together.
2. Cut a sheet of parchment paper to fit air fryer basket. Take one scoop of mixture, about 3 tablespoons, and roll into a 4" stick shape, pressing down gently to flatten the top. Place stick on ungreased parchment into air fryer basket. Repeat with remaining mixture to form eight sticks.
3. Adjust the temperature to 350°F and set the timer for 16 minutes, turning sticks halfway through cooking. Sticks will be golden brown when done.
4. Serve warm with ranch dressing on the side for dipping.

Easy Glazed Carrots

Servings:4
Cooking Time:12 Minutes
Ingredients:
- 3 cups carrots, peeled and cut into large chunks
- 1 tablespoon olive oil
- 1 tablespoon honey
- Salt and black pepper, to taste

Directions:
1. Preheat the Air fryer to 390°F and grease an Air fryer basket.
2. Mix all the ingredients in a bowl and toss to coat well.
3. Transfer into the Air fryer basket and cook for about 12 minutes.
4. Dish out and serve hot.

Green Bean Sautée

Servings: 4
Cooking Time: 25 Minutes
Ingredients:
- 1 ½ lb green beans, trimmed
- 1 tbsp olive oil
- ½ tsp garlic powder
- Salt and pepper to taste
- 4 garlic cloves, thinly sliced
- 1 tbsp fresh basil, chopped

Directions:
1. Preheat the air fryer to 375°F. Toss the beans with the olive oil, garlic powder, salt, and pepper in a bowl, then add to the frying basket. Air Fry for 6 minutes, shaking the basket halfway through the cooking time. Add garlic to the air fryer and cook for 3-6 minutes or until the green beans

are tender and the garlic slices start to brown. Sprinkle with basil and serve warm.

Caribbean-style Fried Plantains

Servings: 2
Cooking Time: 20 Minutes
Ingredients:
- 2 plantains, peeled and cut into slices
- 2 tablespoons avocado oil
- 2 teaspoons Caribbean Sorrel Rum Spice Mix

Directions:
1. Toss the plantains with the avocado oil and spice mix.
2. Cook in the preheated Air Fryer at 400°F for 10 minutes, shaking the cooking basket halfway through the cooking time.
3. Adjust the seasonings to taste and enjoy!

Brussels Sprouts With Balsamic Oil

Servings:4
Cooking Time: 15 Minutes
Ingredients:
- ¼ teaspoon salt
- 1 tablespoon balsamic vinegar
- 2 cups Brussels sprouts, halved
- 2 tablespoons olive oil

Directions:
1. Preheat the air fryer for 5 minutes.
2. Mix all ingredients in a bowl until the zucchini fries are well coated.
3. Place in the air fryer basket.
4. Close and cook for 15 minutes for 350°F.

Crispy Shawarma Broccoli

Servings: 4
Cooking Time: 25 Minutes
Ingredients:
- 1 pound broccoli, steamed and drained
- 2 tablespoons canola oil
- 1 teaspoon cayenne pepper
- 1 teaspoon sea salt
- 1 tablespoon Shawarma spice blend

Directions:
1. Toss all ingredients in a mixing bowl.
2. Roast in the preheated Air Fryer at 380°F for 10 minutes, shaking the basket halfway through the cooking time.
3. Work in batches. Bon appétit!

Cheese And Bean Enchiladas

Servings:4
Cooking Time: 9 Minutes
Ingredients:
- 1 can pinto beans, drained and rinsed
- 1 ½ tablespoons taco seasoning
- 1 cup red enchilada sauce, divided
- 1 ½ cups shredded Mexican-blend cheese, divided
- 4 fajita-size flour tortillas

Directions:
1. Preheat the air fryer to 320°F.
2. In a large microwave-safe bowl, microwave beans for 1 minute. Mash half the beans and fold into whole beans. Mix in taco seasoning, ¼ cup enchilada sauce, and 1 cup cheese until well combined.
3. Place ¼ cup bean mixture onto each tortilla. Fold up one end about 1", then roll to close.
4. Place enchiladas into a 3-quart baking pan, pushing together as needed to make them fit. Pour remaining ¾ cup enchilada sauce over enchiladas and top with remaining ½ cup cheese.
5. Place pan in the air fryer basket and cook 8 minutes until cheese is brown and bubbling and the edges of tortillas are brown. Serve warm.

Cottage And Mayonnaise Stuffed Peppers

Servings: 2
Cooking Time: 20 Minutes
Ingredients:
- 1 red bell pepper, top and seeds removed
- 1 yellow bell pepper, top and seeds removed
- Salt and pepper, to taste
- 1 cup Cottage cheese
- 4 tablespoons mayonnaise
- 2 pickles, chopped

Directions:
1. Arrange the peppers in the lightly greased cooking basket. Cook in the preheated Air Fryer at 400°F for 15 minutes, turning them over halfway through the cooking time.
2. Season with salt and pepper.
3. Then, in a mixing bowl, combine the cream cheese with the mayonnaise and chopped pickles. Stuff the pepper with the cream cheese mixture and serve. Enjoy!

Spinach And Artichoke–stuffed Peppers

Servings:4
Cooking Time: 15 Minutes
Ingredients:
- 2 ounces cream cheese, softened
- ½ cup shredded mozzarella cheese
- ½ cup chopped fresh spinach leaves
- ¼ cup chopped canned artichoke hearts
- 2 medium green bell peppers, halved and seeded

Directions:
1. In a medium bowl, mix cream cheese, mozzarella, spinach, and artichokes. Spoon ¼ cheese mixture into each pepper half.

2. Place peppers into ungreased air fryer basket. Adjust the temperature to 320°F and set the timer for 15 minutes. Peppers will be tender and cheese will be bubbling and brown when done. Serve warm.

Garlic Okra Chips

Servings: 4
Cooking Time: 20 Minutes
Ingredients:
- 2 cups okra, cut into rounds
- 1 ½ tbsp. melted butter
- 1 garlic clove, minced
- 1 tsp powdered paprika
- Salt and pepper to taste

Directions:
1. Preheat air fryer to 350°F. Toss okra, melted butter, paprika, garlic, salt and pepper in a medium bowl until okra is coated. Place okra in the frying basket and Air Fry for 5 minutes. Shake the basket and Air Fry for another 5 minutes. Shake one more time and Air Fry for 2 minutes until crispy. Serve warm and enjoy.

Chapter 9. Desserts And Sweets

Cinnamon Apple Chips

Servings: 6
Cooking Time: 8 Minutes
Ingredients:
- 3 Granny Smith apples, wash, core and thinly slice
- 1 tsp ground cinnamon
- Pinch of salt

Directions:
1. Rub apple slices with cinnamon and salt and place into the air fryer basket.
2. Cook at 390°F for 8 minutes. Turn halfway through.
3. Serve and enjoy.

Fiesta Pastries

Servings:8
Cooking Time:20 Minutes
Ingredients:
- ½ of apple, peeled, cored and chopped
- 1 teaspoon fresh orange zest, grated finely
- 7.05-ounce prepared frozen puff pastry, cut into 16 squares
- ½ tablespoon white sugar
- ½ teaspoon ground cinnamon

Directions:
1. Preheat the Air fryer to 390°F and grease an Air fryer basket.
2. Mix all ingredients in a bowl except puff pastry.
3. Arrange about 1 teaspoon of this mixture in the center of each square.
4. Fold each square into a triangle and slightly press the edges with a fork.
5. Arrange the pastries in the Air fryer basket and cook for about 10 minutes.
6. Dish out and serve immediately.

Fried Cannoli Wontons

Servings: 10
Cooking Time: 8 Minutes
Ingredients:
- 8 ounces Neufchâtel cream cheese
- ¼ cup powdered sugar
- 1 teaspoon vanilla extract
- ¼ teaspoon salt
- ¼ cup mini chocolate chips
- 2 tablespoons chopped pecans (optional)
- 20 wonton wrappers
- ¼ cup filtered water

Directions:
1. Preheat the air fryer to 370°F.
2. In a large bowl, use a hand mixer to combine the cream cheese with the powdered sugar, vanilla, and salt. Fold in the chocolate chips and pecans. Set aside.
3. Lay the wonton wrappers out on a flat, smooth surface and place a bowl with the filtered water next to them.
4. Use a teaspoon to evenly divide the cream cheese mixture among the 20 wonton wrappers, placing the batter in the center of the wontons.
5. Wet the tip of your index finger, and gently moisten the outer edges of the wrapper. Then fold each wrapper until it creates a secure pocket.
6. Liberally spray the air fryer basket with olive oil mist.
7. Place the wontons into the basket, and cook for 5 to 8 minutes. When the outer edges begin to brown, remove the wontons from the air fryer basket. Repeat cooking with remaining wontons.
8. Serve warm.

Apple Pie

Servings: 7
Cooking Time: 25 Minutes
Ingredients:
- 2 large apples
- ½ cup flour
- 2 tbsp. unsalted butter
- 1 tbsp. sugar
- ½ tsp. cinnamon

Directions:
1. Pre-heat the Air Fryer to 360°F
2. In a large bowl, combine the flour and butter. Pour in the sugar, continuing to mix.
3. Add in a few tablespoons of water and combine everything to create a smooth dough.
4. Grease the insides of a few small pastry tins with butter. Divide the dough between each tin and lay each portion flat inside.
5. Peel, core and dice up the apples. Put the diced apples on top of the pastry and top with a sprinkling of sugar and cinnamon.
6. Place the pastry tins in your Air Fryer and cook for 15 - 17 minutes.
7. Serve.

Grilled Banana Boats

Servings: 3
Cooking Time: 15 Minutes
Ingredients:
- 3 large bananas
- 1 tablespoon ginger snaps
- 2 tablespoons mini chocolate chips
- 3 tablespoons mini marshmallows
- 3 tablespoons crushed vanilla wafers

Directions:
1. In the peel, slice your banana lengthwise; make sure not to slice all the way through the banana. Divide the remaining ingredients between the banana pockets.
2. Place in the Air Fryer grill pan. Cook at 395°F for 7 minutes.
3. Let the banana boats cool for 5 to 6 minutes, and then eat with a spoon. Bon appétit!

Apple Pie Crumble

Servings:4
Cooking Time:25 Minutes
Ingredients:
- 1 can apple pie
- ¼ cup butter, softened
- 9 tablespoons self-rising flour
- 7 tablespoons caster sugar
- Pinch of salt

Directions:
1. Preheat the Air fryer to 320°F and grease a baking dish.

2. Mix all the ingredients in a bowl until a crumbly mixture is formed.
3. Arrange the apple pie in the baking dish and top with the mixture.
4. Transfer the baking dish into the Air fryer basket and cook for about 25 minutes.
5. Dish out in a platter and serve.

Peanut Butter Cookies

Servings:9
Cooking Time: 27 Minutes
Ingredients:
- 2 tablespoons salted butter, melted
- 2 tablespoons all-natural, no-sugar-added peanut butter
- ⅓ cup granular brown erythritol
- 1 large egg
- ½ teaspoon vanilla extract
- 1 cup blanched finely ground almond flour
- ½ teaspoon baking powder

Directions:
1. In a large bowl, whisk together butter, peanut butter, erythritol, egg, and vanilla. Add flour and baking powder, and stir until combined.
2. Separate dough into nine equal pieces and roll each into a ball, about 2 tablespoons each.
3. Cut three pieces of parchment to fit your air fryer basket and place three cookies on each ungreased piece.
4. Place one piece of parchment with cookies into air fryer basket. Adjust the temperature to 300°F and set the timer for 9 minutes. Edges of cookies will be browned when done. Repeat with remaining cookies. Serve warm.

Orange Marmalade

Servings: 4
Cooking Time: 20 Minutes
Ingredients:
- 4 oranges, peeled and chopped
- 3 cups sugar
- 1½ cups water

Directions:
1. In a pan that fits your air fryer, mix the oranges with the sugar and the water; stir.
2. Place the pan in the fryer and cook at 340°F for 20 minutes.
3. Stir well, divide into cups, refrigerate, and serve cold.

Tortilla Fried Pies

Servings: 12
Cooking Time: 5 Minutes
Ingredients:
- 12 small flour tortillas
- ½ cup fig preserves
- ¼ cup sliced almonds
- 2 tablespoons shredded, unsweetened coconut

- oil for misting or cooking spray

Directions:

1. Wrap refrigerated tortillas in damp paper towels and heat in microwave 30 seconds to warm.
2. Working with one tortilla at a time, place 2 teaspoons fig preserves, 1 teaspoon sliced almonds, and ½ teaspoon coconut in the center of each.
3. Moisten outer edges of tortilla all around.
4. Fold one side of tortilla over filling to make a half-moon shape and press down lightly on center. Using the tines of a fork, press down firmly on edges of tortilla to seal in filling.
5. Mist both sides with oil or cooking spray.
6. Place hand pies in air fryer basket close but not overlapping. It's fine to lean some against the sides and corners of the basket. You may need to cook in 2 batches.
7. Cook at 390°F for 5 minutes or until lightly browned. Serve hot.
8. Refrigerate any leftover pies in a closed container. To serve later, toss them back in the air fryer basket and cook for 2 or 3 minutes to reheat.

Nutella And Banana Pastries

Servings:4

Cooking Time:12 Minutes

Ingredients:

- 1 puff pastry sheet, cut into 4 equal squares
- ½ cup Nutella
- 2 bananas, sliced
- 2 tablespoons icing sugar

Directions:

1. Preheat the Air fryer to 375°F and grease an Air fryer basket.
2. Spread Nutella on each pastry square and top with banana slices and icing sugar.
3. Fold each square into a triangle and slightly press the edges with a fork.
4. Arrange the pastries in the Air fryer basket and cook for about 12 minutes.
5. Dish out and serve immediately.

Chocolate Chip Cookie Cake

Servings:8

Cooking Time: 15 Minutes

Ingredients:

- 4 tablespoons salted butter, melted
- ⅓ cup granular brown erythritol
- 1 large egg
- ½ teaspoon vanilla extract
- 1 cup blanched finely ground almond flour
- ½ teaspoon baking powder
- ¼ cup low-carb chocolate chips

Directions:

1. In a large bowl, whisk together butter, erythritol, egg, and vanilla. Add flour and baking powder, and stir until combined.

2. Fold in chocolate chips, then spoon batter into an ungreased 6" round nonstick baking dish.
3. Place dish into air fryer basket. Adjust the temperature to 300°F and set the timer for 15 minutes. When edges are browned, cookie cake will be done.
4. Slice and serve warm.

Strawberry Shortcake

Servings:6

Cooking Time: 25 Minutes

Ingredients:

- 2 tablespoons coconut oil
- 1 cup blanched finely ground almond flour
- 2 large eggs, whisked
- ½ cup granular erythritol
- 1 teaspoon baking powder
- 1 teaspoon vanilla extract
- 2 cups sugar-free whipped cream
- 6 medium fresh strawberries, hulled and sliced

Directions:

1. In a large bowl, combine coconut oil, flour, eggs, erythritol, baking powder, and vanilla. Pour batter into an ungreased 6" round nonstick baking dish.
2. Place dish into air fryer basket. Adjust the temperature to 300°F and set the timer for 25 minutes. When done, shortcake should be golden and a toothpick inserted in the middle will come out clean.
3. Remove dish from fryer and let cool 1 hour.
4. Once cooled, top cake with whipped cream and strawberries to serve.

Hot Coconut 'n Cocoa Buns

Servings:8

Cooking Time: 15 Minutes

Ingredients:

- ¼ cup cacao nibs
- 1 cup coconut milk
- 1/3 cup coconut flour
- 3 tablespoons cacao powder
- 4 eggs, beaten

Directions:

1. Preheat the air fryer for 5 minutes.
2. Combine all ingredients in a mixing bowl.
3. Form buns using your hands and place in a baking dish that will fit in the air fryer.
4. Bake for 15 minutes for 375°F.
5. Once air fryer turns off, leave the buns in the air fryer until it cools completely.

Pumpkin Cake

Servings:8
Cooking Time: 25 Minutes
Ingredients:
- 4 tablespoons salted butter, melted
- ½ cup granular brown erythritol
- ¼ cup pure pumpkin puree
- 1 cup blanched finely ground almond flour
- ½ teaspoon baking powder
- ⅛ teaspoon salt
- 1 teaspoon pumpkin pie spice

Directions:
1. Mix all ingredients in a large bowl. Pour batter into an ungreased 6" round nonstick baking dish.
2. Place dish into air fryer basket. Adjust the temperature to 300°F and set the timer for 25 minutes. The top will be dark brown, and a toothpick inserted in the center should come out clean when done. Let cool 30 minutes before serving.

Glazed Donuts

Servings: 2 – 4
Cooking Time: 25 Minutes
Ingredients:
- 1 can [8 oz.] refrigerated croissant dough
- Cooking spray
- 1 can [16 oz.] vanilla frosting

Directions:
1. Cut the croissant dough into 1-inch-round slices. Make a hole in the center of each one to create a donut.
2. Put the donuts in the Air Fryer basket, taking care not to overlap any, and spritz with cooking spray. You may need to cook everything in multiple batches.
3. Cook at 400°F for 2 minutes. Turn the donuts over and cook for another 3 minutes.
4. Place the rolls on a paper plate.
5. Microwave a half-cup of frosting for 30 seconds and pour a drizzling of the frosting over the donuts before serving.

Grape Stew

Servings: 4
Cooking Time: 14 Minutes
Ingredients:
- 1 pound red grapes
- Juice and zest of 1 lemon
- 26 ounces grape juice

Directions:
1. In a pan that fits your air fryer, add all ingredients and toss.
2. Place the pan in the fryer and cook at 320°F for 14 minutes.
3. Divide into cups, refrigerate, and serve cold.

Merengues

Servings: 6
Cooking Time: 65 Minutes
Ingredients:
- 2 egg whites
- 1 teaspoon lime zest, grated
- 1 teaspoon lime juice
- 4 tablespoons Erythritol

Directions:
1. Whisk the egg whites until soft peaks. Then add Erythritol and lime juice and whisk the egg whites until you get strong peaks. After this, add lime zest and carefully stir the egg white mixture. Preheat the air fryer to 275°F. Line the air fryer basket with baking paper. With the help of the spoon make the small merengues and put them in the air fryer in one layer. Cook the dessert for 65 minutes.

Peanut Butter S'mores

Servings:10
Cooking Time: 1 Minute
Ingredients:
- 10 Graham crackers (full, double-square cookies as they come out of the package)
- 5 tablespoons Natural-style creamy or crunchy peanut butter
- ½ cup Milk chocolate chips
- 10 Standard-size marshmallows (not minis and not jumbo campfire ones)

Directions:
1. Preheat the air fryer to 350°F .
2. Break the graham crackers in half widthwise at the marked place, so the rectangle is now in two squares. Set half of the squares flat side up on your work surface. Spread each with about 1½ teaspoons peanut butter, then set 10 to 12 chocolate chips point side up into the peanut butter on each, pressing gently so the chips stick.
3. Flatten a marshmallow between your clean, dry hands and set it atop the chips. Do the same with the remaining marshmallows on the other coated graham crackers. Do not set the other half of the graham crackers on top of these coated graham crackers.
4. When the machine is at temperature, set the treats graham cracker side down in a single layer in the basket. They may touch, but even a fraction of an inch between them will provide better air flow. Air-fry undisturbed for 45 seconds.
5. Use a nonstick-safe spatula to transfer the topped graham crackers to a wire rack. Set the other graham cracker squares flat side down over the marshmallows. Cool for a couple of minutes before serving.

Chocolate Soufflés

Servings:2
Cooking Time: 15 Minutes
Ingredients:
- 2 large eggs, whites and yolks separated
- 1 teaspoon vanilla extract
- 2 ounces low-carb chocolate chips
- 2 teaspoons coconut oil, melted

Directions:
1. In a medium bowl, beat egg whites until stiff peaks form, about 2 minutes. Set aside. In a separate medium bowl, whisk egg yolks and vanilla together. Set aside.
2. In a separate medium microwave-safe bowl, place chocolate chips and drizzle with coconut oil. Microwave on high 20 seconds, then stir and continue cooking in 10-second increments until melted, being careful not to overheat chocolate. Let cool 1 minute.
3. Slowly pour melted chocolate into egg yolks and whisk until smooth. Then, slowly begin adding egg white mixture to chocolate mixture, about ¼ cup at a time, folding in gently.
4. Pour mixture into two 4" ramekins greased with cooking spray. Place ramekins into air fryer basket. Adjust the temperature to 400°F and set the timer for 15 minutes. Soufflés will puff up while cooking and deflate a little once cooled. The center will be set when done. Let cool 10 minutes, then serve warm.

Nutty Fudge Muffins

Servings:10
Cooking Time:10 Minutes
Ingredients:
- 1 package fudge brownie mix
- 1 egg
- 2 teaspoons water
- ¼ cup walnuts, chopped
- 1/3 cup vegetable oil

Directions:
1. Preheat the Air fryer to 300°F and grease 10 muffin tins lightly.
2. Mix brownie mix, egg, oil and water in a bowl.
3. Fold in the walnuts and pour the mixture in the muffin cups.
4. Transfer the muffin tins in the Air fryer basket and cook for about 10 minutes.
5. Dish out and serve immediately.

Fruit Turnovers

Servings: 6
Cooking Time: 25 Minutes
Ingredients:
- 1 sheet puff pastry dough
- 6 tsp peach preserves
- 3 kiwi, sliced
- 1 large egg, beaten
- 1 tbsp icing sugar

Directions:
1. Prepare puff pastry by cutting it into 6 rectangles. Roll out the pastry with a rolling pin into 5-inch squares. On your workspace, position one square so that it looks like a diamond with points to the top and bottom. Spoon 1 tsp of the preserves on the bottom half and spread it, leaving a ½-inch border from the edge. Place half of one kiwi on top of the preserves. Brush the clean edges with the egg, then fold the top corner over the filling to make a triangle. Crimp with a fork to seal the pastry. Brush the top of the pastry with egg. Preheat air fryer to 350°F. Put the pastries in the greased frying basket. Air Fry for 10 minutes, flipping once until golden and puffy. Remove from the fryer, let cool and dush with icing sugar. Serve.

Custard

Servings: 4
Cooking Time: 45 Minutes
Ingredients:
- 2 cups whole milk
- 2 eggs
- ¼ cup sugar
- ⅛ teaspoon salt
- ¼ teaspoon vanilla
- cooking spray
- ⅛ teaspoon nutmeg

Directions:
1. In a blender, process milk, egg, sugar, salt, and vanilla until smooth.
2. Spray a 6 x 6-inch baking pan with nonstick spray and pour the custard into it.
3. Cook at 300°F for 45 minutes. Custard is done when the center sets.
4. Sprinkle top with the nutmeg.
5. Allow custard to cool slightly.
6. Serve it warm, at room temperature, or chilled.

Lemon Iced Donut Balls

Servings: 6
Cooking Time: 25 Minutes
Ingredients:
- 1 can jumbo biscuit dough
- 2 tsp lemon juice
- ½ cup icing sugar, sifted

Directions:
1. Preheat air fryer to 360°F. Divide the biscuit dough into 16 equal portions. Roll the dough into balls of 1½ inches thickness. Place the donut holes in the greased frying basket and Air Fry for 8 minutes, flipping once. Mix the icing sugar and lemon juice until smooth. Spread the icing over the top of the donuts. Leave to set a bit. Serve.

Cream Cheese Shortbread Cookies

Servings:12
Cooking Time: 20 Minutes
Ingredients:
- ¼ cup coconut oil, melted
- 2 ounces cream cheese, softened
- ½ cup granular erythritol
- 1 large egg, whisked
- 2 cups blanched finely ground almond flour
- 1 teaspoon almond extract

Directions:
1. Combine all ingredients in a large bowl to form a firm ball.
2. Place dough on a sheet of plastic wrap and roll into a 12"-long log shape. Roll log in plastic wrap and place in refrigerator 30 minutes to chill.
3. Remove log from plastic and slice into twelve equal cookies. Cut two sheets of parchment paper to fit air fryer basket. Place six cookies on each ungreased sheet. Place one sheet with cookies into air fryer basket. Adjust the temperature to 320°F and set the timer for 10 minutes, turning cookies halfway through cooking. They will be lightly golden when done. Repeat with remaining cookies.
4. Let cool 15 minutes before serving to avoid crumbling.

Roasted Pumpkin Seeds & Cinnamon

Servings: 2
Cooking Time: 35 Minutes
Ingredients:
- 1 cup pumpkin raw seeds
- 1 tbsp. ground cinnamon
- 2 tbsp. sugar
- 1 cup water
- 1 tbsp. olive oil

Directions:
1. In a frying pan, combine the pumpkin seeds, cinnamon and water.
2. Boil the mixture over a high heat for 2 - 3 minutes.
3. Pour out the water and place the seeds on a clean kitchen towel, allowing them to dry for 20 - 30 minutes.
4. In a bowl, mix together the sugar, dried seeds, a pinch of cinnamon and one tablespoon of olive oil.
5. Pre-heat the Air Fryer to 340°F.
6. Place the seed mixture in the fryer basket and allow to cook for 15 minutes, shaking the basket periodically throughout.

Monkey Bread

Servings:6
Cooking Time: 20 Minutes
Ingredients:
- 1 can refrigerated biscuit dough
- ½ cup granulated sugar
- 1 tablespoon ground cinnamon
- ¼ cup salted butter, melted
- ¼ cup brown sugar
- Cooking spray

Directions:
1. Preheat the air fryer to 325°F. Spray a 6" round cake pan with cooking spray. Separate biscuits and cut each into four pieces.
2. In a large bowl, stir granulated sugar with cinnamon. Toss biscuit pieces in the cinnamon and sugar mixture until well coated. Place each biscuit piece in prepared pan.
3. In a medium bowl, stir together butter and brown sugar. Pour mixture evenly over the biscuit pieces.
4. Place pan in the air fryer basket and cook 20 minutes until brown. Let cool 10 minutes before flipping bread out of the pan and serving.

Lime Bars

Servings:12
Cooking Time: 33 Minutes
Ingredients:
- 1½ cups blanched finely ground almond flour, divided
- ¾ cup confectioners' erythritol, divided
- 4 tablespoons salted butter, melted
- ½ cup fresh lime juice
- 2 large eggs, whisked

Directions:
1. In a medium bowl, mix together 1 cup flour, ¼ cup erythritol, and butter. Press mixture into bottom of an ungreased 6" round nonstick cake pan.
2. Place pan into air fryer basket. Adjust the temperature to 300°F and set the timer for 13 minutes. Crust will be brown and set in the middle when done.
3. Allow to cool in pan 10 minutes.
4. In a medium bowl, combine remaining flour, remaining erythritol, lime juice, and eggs. Pour mixture over cooled crust and return to air fryer for 20 minutes at 300°F. Top will be browned and firm when done.
5. Let cool completely in pan, about 30 minutes, then chill covered in the refrigerator 1 hour. Serve chilled.

Chilled Strawberry Pie

Servings:6
Cooking Time: 10 Minutes
Ingredients:
- 1½ cups whole shelled pecans
- 1 tablespoon unsalted butter, softened
- 1 cup heavy whipping cream
- 12 medium fresh strawberries, hulled
- 2 tablespoons sour cream

Directions:
1. Place pecans and butter into a food processor and pulse ten times until a dough forms. Press dough into the bottom of an ungreased 6" round nonstick baking dish.

2. Place dish into air fryer basket. Adjust the temperature to 320°F and set the timer for 10 minutes. Crust will be firm and golden when done. Let cool 20 minutes.

3. In a large bowl, whisk cream until fluffy and doubled in size, about 2 minutes.

4. In a separate large bowl, mash strawberries until mostly liquid. Fold strawberries and sour cream into whipped cream.

5. Spoon mixture into cooled crust, cover, and place into refrigerator for at least 30 minutes to set. Serve chilled.

Ricotta Lemon Cake

Servings: 8
Cooking Time: 40 Minutes
Ingredients:
- 1 lb ricotta
- 4 eggs
- 1 lemon juice
- 1 lemon zest
- ¼ cup erythritol

Directions:
1. Preheat the air fryer to 325°F.
2. Spray air fryer baking dish with cooking spray.
3. In a bowl, beat ricotta cheese until smooth.
4. Whisk in the eggs one by one.
5. Whisk in lemon juice and zest.
6. Pour batter into the prepared baking dish and place into the air fryer.
7. Cook for 40 minutes.
8. Allow to cool completely then slice and serve.

Fried Twinkies

Servings:6
Cooking Time: 5 Minutes
Ingredients:
- 2 Large egg white(s)
- 2 tablespoons Water
- 1½ cups Ground gingersnap cookie crumbs
- 6 Twinkies
- Vegetable oil spray

Directions:
1. Preheat the air fryer to 400°F.
2. Set up and fill two shallow soup plates or small pie plates on your counter: one for the egg white(s), whisked with the water until foamy; and one for the gingersnap crumbs.
3. Dip a Twinkie in the egg white(s), turning it to coat on all sides, even the ends. Let the excess egg white mixture slip back into the rest, then set the Twinkie in the crumbs. Roll it to coat on all sides, even the ends, pressing gently to get an even coating. Then repeat this process: egg white(s), followed by crumbs. Lightly coat the prepared Twinkie on all sides with vegetable oil spray. Set aside and coat each of the remaining Twinkies with the same double-dipping technique, followed by spraying.

4. Set the Twinkies flat side up in the basket with as much air space between them as possible. Air-fry for 5 minutes, or until browned and crunchy.

5. Use a nonstick-safe spatula to gently transfer the Twinkies to a wire rack. Cool for at least 10 minutes before serving.

Raspberry Empanada

Servings: 6
Cooking Time: 35 Minutes
Ingredients:
- 1 can raspberry pie filling
- 1 puff pastry dough
- 1 egg white, beaten
- Cooking spray

Directions:
1. Preheat air fryer to 370°F. Unroll the two sheets of dough and cut into 4 squares each, or 8 squares total. Scoop ½ to 1 tbsp of the raspberry pie filling in the center of each square. Brush the edges with egg white. Fold diagonally to form a triangle and close the turnover. Press the edges with the back of a fork to seal. Arrange the turnovers in a single layer in the greased basket. Spray the empanadas with cooking oil and Bake for 8 minutes. Let them sit in the air fryer for 3-4 minutes to cool before removing. Repeat for the other batch. Serve and enjoy!

Almond Shortbread Cookies

Servings:8
Cooking Time: 1 Hour 10 Minutes
Ingredients:
- ½ cup salted butter, softened
- ¼ cup granulated sugar
- 1 teaspoon almond extract
- 1 teaspoon vanilla extract
- 2 cups all-purpose flour

Directions:
1. In a large bowl, cream butter, sugar, and extracts. Gradually add flour, mixing until well combined.
2. Roll dough into a 12" x 2" log and wrap in plastic. Chill in refrigerator at least 1 hour.
3. Preheat the air fryer to 300°F.
4. Slice dough into ¼"-thick cookies. Place in the air fryer basket 2" apart, working in batches as needed, and cook 10 minutes until the edges start to brown. Let cool completely before serving.

Easy Mug Brownie

Servings: 1
Cooking Time: 10 Minutes
Ingredients:
- 1 scoop chocolate protein powder
- 1 tbsp cocoa powder
- 1/2 tsp baking powder
- 1/4 cup unsweetened almond milk

Directions:
1. Add baking powder, protein powder, and cocoa powder in a mug and mix well.
2. Add milk in a mug and stir well.
3. Place the mug in the air fryer and cook at 390°F for 10 minutes.
4. Serve and enjoy.

Honey-roasted Mixed Nuts

Servings: 8
Cooking Time: 15 Minutes
Ingredients:
- ½ cup raw, shelled pistachios
- ½ cup raw almonds
- 1 cup raw walnuts
- 2 tablespoons filtered water
- 2 tablespoons honey
- 1 tablespoon vegetable oil
- 2 tablespoons sugar
- ½ teaspoon salt

Directions:
1. Preheat the air fryer to 300°F.
2. Lightly spray an air-fryer-safe pan with olive oil; then place the pistachios, almonds, and walnuts inside the pan and place the pan inside the air fryer basket.
3. Cook for 15 minutes, shaking the basket every 5 minutes to rotate the nuts.
4. While the nuts are roasting, boil the water in a small pan and stir in the honey and oil. Continue to stir while cooking until the water begins to evaporate and a thick sauce is formed. Note: The sauce should stick to the back of a wooden spoon when mixed. Turn off the heat.
5. Remove the nuts from the air fryer and spoon the nuts into the stovetop pan. Use a spatula to coat the nuts with the honey syrup.
6. Line a baking sheet with parchment paper and spoon the nuts onto the sheet. Lightly sprinkle the sugar and salt over the nuts and let cool in the refrigerator for at least 2 hours.
7. When the honey and sugar have hardened, store the nuts in an airtight container in the refrigerator.

S'mores Pockets

Servings: 6
Cooking Time: 5 Minutes
Ingredients:
- 12 sheets phyllo dough, thawed

- 1½ cups butter, melted
- ¾ cup graham cracker crumbs
- 1 Giant Hershey's milk chocolate bar
- 12 marshmallows, cut in half

Directions:
1. Place one sheet of the phyllo on a large cutting board. Keep the rest of the phyllo sheets covered with a slightly damp, clean kitchen towel. Brush the phyllo sheet generously with some melted butter. Place a second phyllo sheet on top of the first and brush it with more butter. Repeat with one more phyllo sheet until you have a stack of 3 phyllo sheets with butter brushed between the layers. Cover the phyllo sheets with one quarter of the graham cracker crumbs leaving a 1-inch border on one of the short ends of the rectangle. Cut the phyllo sheets lengthwise into 3 strips.
2. Take 2 of the strips and crisscross them to form a cross with the empty borders at the top and to the left. Place 2 of the chocolate rectangles in the center of the cross. Place 4 of the marshmallow halves on top of the chocolate. Now fold the pocket together by folding the bottom phyllo strip up over the chocolate and marshmallows. Then fold the right side over, then the top strip down and finally the left side over. Brush all the edges generously with melted butter to seal shut. Repeat with the next three sheets of phyllo, until all the sheets have been used. You will be able to make 2 pockets with every second batch because you will have an extra graham cracker crumb strip from the previous set of sheets.
3. Preheat the air fryer to 350°F.
4. Transfer 3 pockets at a time to the air fryer basket. Air-fry at 350°F for 4 to 5 minutes, until the phyllo dough is light brown in color. Flip the pockets over halfway through the cooking process. Repeat with the remaining 3 pockets.
5. Serve warm.

Sweet Potato Pie Rolls

Servings: 3
Cooking Time: 8 Minutes
Ingredients:
- 6 Spring roll wrappers
- 1½ cups Canned yams in syrup, drained
- 2 tablespoons Light brown sugar
- ¼ teaspoon Ground cinnamon
- 1 Large egg(s), well beaten
- Vegetable oil spray

Directions:
1. Preheat the air fryer to 400°F.
2. Set a spring roll wrapper on a clean, dry work surface. Scoop up ¼ cup of the pulpy yams and set along one edge of the wrapper, leaving 2 inches on each side of the yams. Top the yams with about 1 teaspoon brown sugar and a pinch of ground cinnamon. Fold the sides of the wrapper perpendicular to the yam filling up and over the filling, partially covering it. Brush beaten egg(s) over the side of the wrapper farthest from the yam. Starting with the yam end,

roll the wrapper closed, ending at the part with the beaten egg that you can press gently to seal. Lightly coat the roll on all sides with vegetable oil spray. Set it aside seam side down and continue filling, rolling, and spraying the remaining wrappers in the same way.

3. Set the rolls seam side down in the basket with as much air space between them as possible. Air-fry undisturbed for 8 minutes, or until crisp and golden brown.

4. Use a nonstick-safe spatula and perhaps kitchen tongs for balance to gently transfer the rolls to a wire rack. Cool for at least 5 minutes or up to 30 minutes before serving.

Sage Cream

Servings: 4
Cooking Time: 30 Minutes
Ingredients:
- 7 cups red currants
- 1 cup swerve
- 1 cup water
- 6 sage leaves

Directions:
1. In a pan that fits your air fryer, mix all the ingredients, toss, put the pan in the fryer and cook at 330°F for 30 minutes. Discard sage leaves, divide into cups and serve cold.

Brownies

Servings: 8
Cooking Time: 20 Minutes
Ingredients:
- ½ cup all-purpose flour
- 1 cup granulated sugar
- ¼ cup cocoa powder
- ½ teaspoon baking powder
- 6 tablespoons salted butter, melted
- 1 large egg
- ½ cup semisweet chocolate chips

Directions:
1. Preheat the air fryer to 350°F. Generously grease two 6" round cake pans.
2. In a large bowl, combine flour, sugar, cocoa powder, and baking powder.
3. Add butter, egg, and chocolate chips to dry ingredients. Stir until well combined.
4. Divide batter between prepared pans. Place in the air fryer basket and cook 20 minutes until a toothpick inserted into the center comes out clean. Cool 5 minutes before serving.

Fried Banana S'mores

Servings: 4
Cooking Time: 6 Minutes
Ingredients:
- 4 bananas
- 3 tablespoons mini semi-sweet chocolate chips
- 3 tablespoons mini peanut butter chips
- 3 tablespoons mini marshmallows
- 3 tablespoons graham cracker cereal

Directions:
1. Preheat the air fryer to 400°F.
2. Slice into the un-peeled bananas lengthwise along the inside of the curve, but do not slice through the bottom of the peel. Open the banana slightly to form a pocket.
3. Fill each pocket with chocolate chips, peanut butter chips and marshmallows. Poke the graham cracker cereal into the filling.
4. Place the bananas in the air fryer basket, resting them on the side of the basket and each other to keep them upright with the filling facing up. Air-fry for 6 minutes, or until the bananas are soft to the touch, the peels have blackened and the chocolate and marshmallows have melted and toasted.
5. Let them cool for a couple of minutes and then simply serve with a spoon to scoop out the filling.

Peanut Cookies

Servings: 4
Cooking Time: 5 Minutes
Ingredients:
- 4 tablespoons peanut butter
- 4 teaspoons Erythritol
- 1 egg, beaten
- ¼ teaspoon vanilla extract

Directions:
1. In the mixing bowl mix up peanut butter, Erythritol, egg, and vanilla extract. Stir the mixture with the help of the fork. Then make 4 cookies. Preheat the air fryer to 355°F. Place the cookies in the air fryer and cook them for 5 minutes.

Chocolate-covered Maple Bacon

Servings: 4
Cooking Time: 25 Minutes
Ingredients:
- 8 slices sugar-free bacon
- 1 tbsp. granular erythritol
- 1/3 cup low-carb sugar-free chocolate chips
- 1 tsp. coconut oil
- ½ tsp. maple extract

Directions:
1. Place the bacon in the fryer's basket and add the erythritol on top. Cook for six minutes at 350°F and turn the bacon over. Leave to cook another six minutes or until the bacon is sufficiently crispy.
2. Take the bacon out of the fryer and leave it to cool.
3. Microwave the chocolate chips and coconut oil together for half a minute. Remove from the microwave and mix together before stirring in the maple extract.
4. Set the bacon flat on a piece of parchment paper and pour the mixture over. Allow to harden in the refrigerator for roughly five minutes before serving.

Cinnamon Canned Biscuit Donuts

Servings: 4

Cooking Time: 25 Minutes

Ingredients:

- 1 can jumbo biscuits
- 1 cup cinnamon sugar

Directions:

1. Preheat air fryer to 360°F. Divide biscuit dough into 8 biscuits and place on a flat work surface. Cut a small circle in the center of the biscuit with a small cookie cutter. Place a batch of 4 donuts in the air fryer. Spray with oil and Bake for 8 minutes, flipping once. Drizzle the cinnamon sugar over the donuts and serve.

Pecan Snowball Cookies

Servings: 12

Cooking Time: 24 Minutes

Ingredients:

- 1 cup chopped pecans
- ½ cup salted butter, melted
- ½ cup coconut flour
- ¾ cup confectioners' erythritol, divided
- 1 teaspoon vanilla extract

Directions:

1. In a food processor, blend together pecans, butter, flour, ½ cup erythritol, and vanilla 1 minute until a dough forms.
2. Form dough into twelve individual cookie balls, about 1 tablespoon each.
3. Cut three pieces of parchment to fit air fryer basket. Place four cookies on each ungreased parchment and place one piece parchment with cookies into air fryer basket. Adjust air fryer temperature to 325°F and set the timer for 8 minutes. Repeat cooking with remaining batches.
4. When the timer goes off, allow cookies to cool 5 minutes on a large serving plate until cool enough to handle. While still warm, dust cookies with remaining erythritol. Allow to cool completely, about 15 minutes, before serving.

Kiwi Pastry Bites

Servings: 6

Cooking Time: 45 Minutes

Ingredients:

- 3 kiwi fruits, cut into 12 pieces
- 12 wonton wrappers
- ½ cup peanut butter

Directions:

1. Lay out wonton wrappers on a flat, clean surface. Place a kiwi piece on each wrapper, then with 1 tsp of peanut butter. Fold each wrapper from one corner to another to create a triangle. Bring the 2 bottom corners together, but do not seal. Gently press out any air, then press the open edges to seal. Preheat air fryer to 370°F. Bake the wontons in the greased frying basket for 15-18 minutes, flipping once

halfway through cooking, until golden and crisp. Let cool for a few minutes.

Molten Lava Cakes

Servings: 3

Cooking Time: 10 Minutes

Ingredients:

- 2 large eggs
- 1 teaspoon vanilla extract
- ¼ teaspoon salt
- 3 tablespoons unsalted butter
- ¾ cup milk chocolate chips
- ¼ cup all-purpose flour
- Cooking spray

Directions:

1. Preheat the air fryer to 350°F. Spray three 4" ramekins with cooking spray.
2. In a medium bowl, whisk eggs, vanilla, and salt until well combined.
3. In a large microwave-safe bowl, microwave butter and chocolate chips in 20-second intervals, stirring after each interval, until mixture is fully melted, smooth, and pourable.
4. Whisk chocolate and slowly add egg mixture. Whisk until fully combined.
5. Sprinkle flour into bowl and whisk into chocolate mixture. It should be easily pourable.
6. Divide batter evenly among prepared ramekins. Place in the air fryer basket and cook 5 minutes until the edges and top are set.
7. Let cool 5 minutes and use a butter knife to loosen the edges from ramekins.
8. To serve, place a small dessert plate upside down on top of each ramekin. Quickly flip ramekin and plate upside down so lava cake drops to the plate. Let cool 5 minutes. Serve.

Apple Dumplings

Servings: 4

Cooking Time: 10 Minutes

Ingredients:

- 4 Small tart apples, preferably McIntosh, peeled and cored
- ¼ cup Granulated white sugar
- 1½ tablespoons Ground cinnamon
- 1 sheet, thawed and cut into four quarters A 17.25-ounce box frozen puff pastry (vegetarian, if a concern)

Directions:

1. Set the apples stem side up on a microwave-safe plate, preferably a glass pie plate. Microwave on high for 3 minutes, or until somewhat tender when poked with the point of a knife. Cool to room temperature, about 30 minutes.
2. Preheat the air fryer to 400°F.
3. Combine the sugar and cinnamon in a small bowl. Roll the apples in this mixture, coating them completely on their

outsides. Also sprinkle this cinnamon sugar into each hole where the core was.

4. Roll the puff pastry squares into 6 x 6-inch squares. Slice the corners off each rolled square so that it's sort of like a circle. Place an apple in the center of one of these squares and fold it up and all around the apple, sealing it at the top by pressing the pastry together. The apple must be completely sealed in the pastry. Repeat for the remaining apples.

5. Set the pastry-covered apples in the basket with at least ½ inch between them. Air-fry undisturbed for 10 minutes, or until puffed and golden brown.

6. Use a nonstick-safe spatula, and maybe a flatware tablespoon for balance, to transfer the apples to a wire rack. Cool for at least 5 minutes or up to 15 minutes before serving warm.

Creamy Pudding

Servings: 6
Cooking Time: 25 Minutes
Ingredients:
- 2 cups fresh cream
- 6 egg yolks, whisked
- 6 tablespoons white sugar
- Zest of 1 orange

Directions:
1. Combine all ingredients in a bowl and whisk well.
2. Divide the mixture between 6 small ramekins.
3. Place the ramekins in your air fryer and cook at 340°F for 25 minutes.
4. Place in the fridge for 1 hour before serving.

Cinnamon Pretzels

Servings:6
Cooking Time: 10 Minutes
Ingredients:
- 1½ cups shredded mozzarella cheese
- 1 cup blanched finely ground almond flour
- 2 tablespoons salted butter, melted, divided
- ¼ cup granular erythritol, divided
- 1 teaspoon ground cinnamon

Directions:
1. Place mozzarella, flour, 1 tablespoon butter, and 2 tablespoons erythritol in a large microwave-safe bowl. Microwave on high 45 seconds, then stir with a fork until a smooth dough ball forms.
2. Separate dough into six equal sections. Gently roll each section into a 12" rope, then fold into a pretzel shape.
3. Place pretzels into ungreased air fryer basket. Adjust the temperature to 370°F and set the timer for 8 minutes, turning pretzels halfway through cooking.
4. In a small bowl, combine remaining butter, remaining erythritol, and cinnamon. Brush ½ mixture on both sides of pretzels.

5. Place pretzels back into air fryer and cook an additional 2 minutes at 370°F.
6. Transfer pretzels to a large plate. Brush on both sides with remaining butter mixture, then let cool 5 minutes before serving.

Marshmallow Pastries

Servings:8
Cooking Time:5 Minutes
Ingredients:
- 4-ounce butter, melted
- 8 phyllo pastry sheets, thawed
- ½ cup chunky peanut butter
- 8 teaspoons marshmallow fluff
- Pinch of salt

Directions:
1. Preheat the Air fryer to 360°F and grease an Air fryer basket.
2. Brush butter over 1 filo pastry sheet and top with a second filo sheet.
3. Brush butter over second filo pastry sheet and repeat with all the remaining sheets.
4. Cut the phyllo layers in 8 strips and put 1 tablespoon of peanut butter and 1 teaspoon of marshmallow fluff on the underside of a filo strip.
5. Fold the tip of the sheet over the filling to form a triangle and fold repeatedly in a zigzag manner.
6. Arrange the pastries into the Air fryer basket and cook for about 5 minutes.
7. Season with a pinch of salt and serve warm.

Baked Apple

Servings: 6
Cooking Time: 20 Minutes
Ingredients:
- 3 small Honey Crisp or other baking apples
- 3 tablespoons maple syrup
- 3 tablespoons chopped pecans
- 1 tablespoon firm butter, cut into 6 pieces

Directions:
1. Put ½ cup water in the drawer of the air fryer.
2. Wash apples well and dry them.
3. Split apples in half. Remove core and a little of the flesh to make a cavity for the pecans.
4. Place apple halves in air fryer basket, cut side up.
5. Spoon 1½ teaspoons pecans into each cavity.
6. Spoon ½ tablespoon maple syrup over pecans in each apple.
7. Top each apple with ½ teaspoon butter.
8. Cook at 360°F for 20 minutes, until apples are tender.

Chocolate Doughnut Holes

Servings: 20
Cooking Time: 6 Minutes
Ingredients:
- 1 cup blanched finely ground almond flour
- ½ cup low-carb vanilla protein powder
- ½ cup granular erythritol
- ¼ cup unsweetened cocoa powder
- ½ teaspoon baking powder
- 2 large eggs, whisked
- ½ teaspoon vanilla extract

Directions:
1. Mix all ingredients in a large bowl until a soft dough forms. Separate and roll dough into twenty balls, about 2 tablespoons each.
2. Cut a piece of parchment to fit your air fryer basket. Working in batches if needed, place doughnut holes into air fryer basket on ungreased parchment. Adjust the temperature to 380°F and set the timer for 6 minutes, flipping doughnut holes halfway through cooking. Doughnut holes will be golden and firm when done. Let cool completely before serving, about 10 minutes.

Brown Sugar Cookies

Servings: 9
Cooking Time: 27 Minutes
Ingredients:
- 4 tablespoons salted butter, melted
- ⅓ cup granular brown erythritol
- 1 large egg
- ½ teaspoon vanilla extract
- 1 cup blanched finely ground almond flour
- ½ teaspoon baking powder

Directions:
1. In a large bowl, whisk together butter, erythritol, egg, and vanilla. Add flour and baking powder, and stir until combined.
2. Separate dough into nine pieces and roll into balls, about 2 tablespoons each.
3. Cut three pieces of parchment paper to fit your air fryer basket and place three cookies on each ungreased piece. Place one piece of parchment into air fryer basket. Adjust the temperature to 300°F and set the timer for 9 minutes. Edges of cookies will be browned when done. Repeat with remaining cookies. Serve warm.

Banana Chips With Chocolate Glaze

Servings: 2
Cooking Time: 20 Minutes
Ingredients:
- 2 banana, cut into slices
- 1/4 teaspoon lemon zest
- 1 tablespoon agave syrup
- 1 tablespoon cocoa powder
- 1 tablespoon coconut oil, melted

Directions:
1. Toss the bananas with the lemon zest and agave syrup. Transfer your bananas to the parchment-lined cooking basket.
2. Bake in the preheated Air Fryer at 370°F for 12 minutes, turning them over halfway through the cooking time.
3. In the meantime, melt the coconut oil in your microwave; add the cocoa powder and whisk to combine well.
4. Serve the baked banana chips. Enjoy!

Coconut Rice Cake

Servings: 8
Cooking Time: 30 Minutes
Ingredients:
- 1 cup all-natural coconut water
- 1 cup unsweetened coconut milk
- 1 teaspoon almond extract
- ¼ teaspoon salt
- 4 tablespoons honey
- cooking spray
- ¾ cup raw jasmine rice
- 2 cups sliced or cubed fruit

Directions:
1. In a medium bowl, mix together the coconut water, coconut milk, almond extract, salt, and honey.
2. Spray air fryer baking pan with cooking spray and add the rice.
3. Pour liquid mixture over rice.
4. Cook at 360°F for 15minutes. Stir and cook for 15 minutes longer or until rice grains are tender.
5. Allow cake to cool slightly. Run a dull knife around edge of cake, inside the pan. Turn the cake out onto a platter and garnish with fruit.

Pumpkin Pie–spiced Pork Rinds

Servings: 4
Cooking Time: 5 Minutes
Ingredients:
- 3 ounces plain pork rinds
- 2 tablespoons salted butter, melted
- 1 teaspoon pumpkin pie spice
- ¼ cup confectioners' erythritol

Directions:
1. In a large bowl, toss pork rinds in butter. Sprinkle with pumpkin pie spice, then toss to evenly coat.
2. Place pork rinds into ungreased air fryer basket. Adjust the temperature to 400°F and set the timer for 5 minutes. Pork rinds will be golden when done.
3. Transfer rinds to a medium serving bowl and sprinkle with erythritol. Serve immediately.

Cranberry Jam

Servings: 8
Cooking Time: 20 Minutes
Ingredients:
- 2 pounds cranberries
- 4 ounces black currant
- 2 pounds sugar
- Zest of 1 lime
- 3 tablespoons water

Directions:
1. In a pan that fits your air fryer, add all the ingredients and stir.
2. Place the pan in the fryer and cook at 360°F for 20 minutes.
3. Stir the jam well, divide into cups, refrigerate, and serve cold.

Easy Keto Danish

Servings:6
Cooking Time: 12 Minutes
Ingredients:
- 1½ cups shredded mozzarella cheese
- ½ cup blanched finely ground almond flour
- 3 ounces cream cheese, divided
- ¼ cup confectioners' erythritol
- 1 tablespoon lemon juice

Directions:
1. Place mozzarella, flour, and 1 ounce cream cheese in a large microwave-safe bowl. Microwave on high 45 seconds, then stir with a fork until a soft dough forms.
2. Separate dough into six equal sections and press each in a single layer into an ungreased 4" × 4" square nonstick baking dish to form six even squares that touch.
3. In a small bowl, mix remaining cream cheese, erythritol, and lemon juice. Place 1 tablespoon mixture in center of each piece of dough in baking dish. Fold all four corners of each dough piece halfway to center to reach cream cheese mixture.
4. Place dish into air fryer. Adjust the temperature to 320°F and set the timer for 12 minutes. The center and edges will be browned when done. Let cool 10 minutes before serving.

Hearty Banana Pastry

Servings:2
Cooking Time: 15 Minutes
Ingredients:
- 3 tbsp honey
- 2 puff pastry sheets, cut into thin strips
- fresh berries to serve

Directions:
1. Preheat your air fryer up to 340°F.

2. Place the banana slices into the cooking basket. Cover with the pastry strips and top with honey. Cook for 10 minutes. Serve with fresh berries.

Cinnamon-sugar Pretzel Bites

Servings:4
Cooking Time: 1 Hour 10 Minutes
Ingredients:
- 1 cup all-purpose flour
- 1 teaspoon quick-rise yeast
- 2 tablespoons granulated sugar, divided
- ¼ teaspoon salt
- 1 tablespoon olive oil
- ⅓ cup warm water
- 2 teaspoons baking soda
- 1 teaspoon ground cinnamon
- Cooking spray

Directions:
1. In a large bowl, mix flour, yeast, 2 teaspoons sugar, and salt until combined.
2. Pour in oil and water and stir until a dough begins to form and pull away from the edges of the bowl. Remove dough from the bowl and transfer to a lightly floured surface. Knead 10 minutes until dough is mostly smooth.
3. Spritz dough with cooking spray and place into a large clean bowl. Cover with plastic wrap and let rise 1 hour.
4. Preheat the air fryer to 400°F.
5. Press dough into a 6" × 4" rectangle. Cut dough into twenty-four even pieces.
6. Fill a medium saucepan over medium-high heat halfway with water and bring to a boil. Add baking soda and let it boil 1 minute, then add pretzel bites. You may need to work in batches. Cook 45 seconds, then remove from water and drain. They will be puffy but should have mostly maintained their shape.
7. Spritz pretzel bites with cooking spray. Place in the air fryer basket and cook 5 minutes until golden brown.
8. In a small bowl, mix remaining sugar and cinnamon. When pretzel bites are done cooking, immediately toss in cinnamon and sugar mixture and serve.

Roasted Pecan Clusters

Servings:8
Cooking Time: 8 Minutes
Ingredients:
- 3 ounces whole shelled pecans
- 1 tablespoon salted butter, melted
- 2 teaspoons confectioners' erythritol
- ½ teaspoon ground cinnamon
- ½ cup low-carb chocolate chips

Directions:
1. In a medium bowl, toss pecans with butter, then sprinkle with erythritol and cinnamon.
2. Place pecans into ungreased air fryer basket. Adjust the temperature to 350°F and set the timer for 8 minutes,

shaking the basket two times during cooking. They will feel soft initially but get crunchy as they cool.

3. Line a large baking sheet with parchment paper.

4. Place chocolate in a medium microwave-safe bowl. Microwave on high, heating in 20-second increments and stirring until melted. Place 1 teaspoon chocolate in a rounded mound on ungreased parchment-lined baking sheet, then press 1 pecan into top, repeating with remaining chocolate and pecans.

5. Place baking sheet into refrigerator to cool at least 30 minutes. Once cooled, store clusters in a large sealed container in refrigerator up to 5 days.

Delicious Spiced Apples

Servings: 6
Cooking Time: 10 Minutes
Ingredients:
- 4 small apples, sliced
- 1 tsp apple pie spice
- 1/2 cup erythritol
- 2 tbsp coconut oil, melted

Directions:

1. Add apple slices in a mixing bowl and sprinkle sweetener, apple pie spice, and coconut oil over apple and toss to coat.

2. Transfer apple slices in air fryer dish. Place dish in air fryer basket and cook at 350°F for 10 minutes.

3. Serve and enjoy.
Cooking Time: 4 Minutes

Fried Snickers Bars

Servings:8
Ingredients:
- ⅓ cup All-purpose flour
- 1 Large egg white(s), beaten until foamy
- 1½ cups Vanilla wafer cookie crumbs
- 8 Fun-size Snickers bars, frozen
- Vegetable oil spray

Directions:

1. Preheat the air fryer to 400°F.

2. Set up and fill three shallow soup plates or small pie plates on your counter: one for the flour, one for the beaten egg white(s), and one for the cookie crumbs.

3. Unwrap the frozen candy bars. Dip one in the flour, turning it to coat on all sides. Gently shake off any excess, then set it in the beaten egg white(s). Turn it to coat all sides, even the ends, then let any excess egg white slip back into the rest. Set the candy bar in the cookie crumbs. Turn to coat on all sides, even the ends. Dip the candy bar back in the egg white(s) a second time, then into the cookie crumbs a second time, making sure you have an even coating all around. Coat the covered candy bar all over with vegetable oil spray. Set aside so you can dip and coat the remaining candy bars.

4. Set the coated candy bars in the basket with as much air space between them as possible. Air-fry undisturbed for 4 minutes, or until golden brown.

5. Remove the basket from the machine and let the candy bars cool in the basket for 10 minutes. Use a nonstick-safe spatula to transfer them to a wire rack and cool for 5 minutes more before chowing down.

INDEX

Printed in Great Britain
by Amazon

11236923R00072